TRANSNATIONAL LEGAL ORDERING AND STATE CHANGE

Law can no longer be viewed through a purely national lens. Transnational legal ordering affects the boundary of the state and the market, the allocation of power among national institutions, the role of professions and their expertise, and associational patterns that provide new normative frames. This book breaks new ground for understanding the impacts of transnational legal ordering within nation-states in today's globalized world. The book addresses the different dimensions of state change at stake and the factors that determine these impacts. It brings together leading scholars from sociology and law who study the effects of transnational legal ordering within different countries. Their case studies illustrate how transnational legal ordering interacts with national law and institutions in different regulatory areas, and cover anti–money laundering, bankruptcy, competition, education, intellectual property, health, and municipal water law and policy in different countries. The book explains the extent and limits of transnational legal ordering in today's world.

Gregory Shaffer is the Melvin C. Steen Professor of Law at the University of Minnesota Law School and Affiliated Professor in the Department of Political Science. His other publications include *Dispute Settlement at the WTO: The Developing Country Experience* (with Ricardo Meléndez-Ortiz, 2010); *When Cooperation Fails: The International Law and Politics of Genetically Modified Foods* (with Mark Pollack, 2009); *Defending Interests: Public-Private Partnerships in WTO Litigation* (2003); *Transatlantic Governance in the Global Economy* (with Mark Pollack, 2001); and more than seventy articles and book chapters.

CAMBRIDGE STUDIES IN LAW AND SOCIETY

Cambridge Studies in Law and Society aims to publish the best scholarly work on legal discourse and practice in its social and institutional contexts, combining theoretical insights and empirical research.

The fields that it covers are studies of law in action; the sociology of law; the anthropology of law; cultural studies of law, including the role of legal discourses in social formations; law and economics; law and politics; and studies of governance. The books consider all forms of legal discourse across societies and are not limited to lawyers' discourses alone.

The series editors come from a range of disciplines: academic law, sociolegal studies, sociology, and anthropology. All have been actively involved in teaching and writing about law in context.

Books in the Series

Diseases of the Will Mariana Valverde

The Politics of Truth and Reconciliation in South Africa: Legitimizing the Post-Apartheid State Richard A. Wilson

Modernism and the Grounds of Law Peter Fitzpatrick

Unemployment and Government: Genealogies of the Social William Walters

Autonomy and Ethnicity: Negotiating Competing Claims in Multi-Ethnic States Yash Ghai

Constituting Democracy: Law, Globalism and South Africa's Political Reconstruction Heinz Klug

The Ritual of Rights in Japan: Law, Society, and Health Policy Eric A. Feldman

The Invention of the Passport: Surveillance, Citizenship and the State John Torpey

Governing Morals: A Social History of Moral Regulation Alan Hunt

(continued after Index)

Transnational Legal Ordering and State Change

Edited by

GREGORY SHAFFER
University of Minnesota Law School

CAMBRIDGE
UNIVERSITY PRESS

CAMBRIDGE UNIVERSITY PRESS
Cambridge, New York, Melbourne, Madrid, Cape Town,
Singapore, São Paulo, Delhi, Mexico City

Cambridge University Press
32 Avenue of the Americas, New York, NY 10013-2473, USA

www.cambridge.org
Information on this title: www.cambridge.org/9781107026117

First published 2013

Printed in the United States of America

A catalog record for this publication is available from the British Library.

Library of Congress Cataloging in Publication Data

Transnational legal ordering and state change / Gregory C. Shaffer.
p. cm. – (Cambridge Studies in Law and Society)
ISBN 978-1-107-02611-7
1. Law and economics devlopment – Congresses. 2. State, The – Congresses. 3. Comparative law – Congresses. 4. Law and Globalization – Congresses. I. Shaffer, Gregory C., 1958–
K3820.A6T73 2013
341.26–dc23 2012029080

ISBN 978-1-107-02611-7 Hardback

I dedicate this book to my wife Michele Goodwin, and our children Brooks and Sage, whose love and sustenance ease life and make it joyful and rewarding.

Contents

Notes on the Contributors

Elizabeth Heger Boyle, Professor of Sociology and Law at the University of Minnesota, studies the role of international laws and policies in children's survival and development around the world. She has written extensively on the impetus for, and impact of, laws related to female genital cutting. Her current research is a cross-national study of abortion policies and teen birth rates. Professor Boyle's research has been supported by the National Science Foundation and the National Institutes of Health and appears in many outlets, including *Law & Society Review*, *Law & Social Inquiry*, and *Social Problems*. Professor Boyle received a J.D. from the University of Iowa in 1987, practiced law for several years, and then received her Ph.D. in sociology from Stanford University in 1996.

Terence C. Halliday is Research Professor, American Bar Foundation; Co-Director, Center on Law and Globalization; Adjunct Professor of Sociology, Northwestern University; and Adjunct Professor, School of Regulation, Justice and Diplomacy, Australian National University. Halliday directs several research programs on law and globalization. The most recent volume in his long-standing research program on the politics of lawyers, *Fates of Political Liberalism in the British Post-Colony: The Politics of the Legal Complex* (Cambridge University Press 2012), includes studies of lawyers' struggles for basic legal rights in South Asia, South East Asia, and Africa. A book-in-progress with Susan Block-Lieb, *Global Legislators*, analyzes global lawmaking for international trade. A collaboration with Sida Liu, University of Wisconsin, is funded by the National Science Foundation and involves wide-ranging fieldwork and media analysis in China on criminal defense lawyers and their struggles to protect basic legal freedoms. Halliday and Gregory Shaffer currently are editing a volume on transnational legal orders.

Minzee Kim is a lecturer in the School of Social Science and a research Fellow in the Institute for Social Science Research at the University School Queensland. Her scholarship lies at the intersection of globalization, law, and women and children.

She is interested in explaining cross-national variations in, and outcomes of, state policies for women and children. Her research appears in *Law & Society Review*, *Law and Social Inquiry*, *Journal of Marriage and Family*, *New Directions for Research on Child and Adolescent Development*, and others. Her dissertation research integrates global and state institutional factors to explain not only levels of women's employment worldwide but also the quality of that employment. Her current research includes an examination of adolescent fertility and abortion in developing countries in relation to the emergence of adolescent reproductive health as a global child rights and women's rights issue.

Heinz Klug is Evjue-Bascom Professor of Law, Associate Dean for Research and Faculty Development, and Director of the Global Legal Studies Center at the University of Wisconsin Law School. He is also an Honorary Senior Research Associate in the School of Law at the University of the Witwatersrand, Johannesburg, South Africa. Growing up in Durban, South Africa, he participated in the antiapartheid struggle, spent 11 years in exile, and returned to South Africa in 1990 as a member of the ANC Land Commission and researcher for Zola Skweyiya, chairperson of the ANC Constitutional Committee. Professor Klug has published numerous articles and books, including *Constituting Democracy* (Cambridge University Press 2000) and *The Constitution of South Africa: A Contextual Analysis* (Hart 2010).

Maíra Rocha Machado is Associate Professor of Law at Getulio Vargas Foundation Law School, Brazil. She teaches courses on Criminal Law, Criminology, and Sociology of Law. She graduated in Law from the University of São Paulo (1997) and obtained her Ph.D. in philosophy and theory of law at the University of São Paulo (2003). Her current research focuses on sentencing, corruption, and transnational organizations. She is the author of *The Internationalization of Criminal Law* (Editora 34 2004) and co-editor of *Money Laundering and Asset Recovery: Brazil, Nigeria, the United Kingdom and Switzerland* (Editora Quartier Latin 2006); *New Directions in the Governance of Justice and Security* (Ministério da Justiça 2006) (all in Portuguese); and *La rationalité pénale moderne: réflexions conceptuelles et explorations empiriques* (Presses de l' Université d'Ottawa 2012).

Bronwen Morgan is Professor of Socio-legal Studies at the University of Bristol, United Kingdom, and take up a Future Fellowship at the University of New South Wales, Australia, in October 2012. Her research focuses on global governance; regulation, especially in relation to sustainable development; and the intersection between regulation and socioeconomic human rights. Her most recent book is *Water on Tap: Rights and Regulation in the Transnational Governance of Urban Water Services* (Cambridge University Press 2011), which explores the patterns of social protest generated by private sector participation in urban water services in six different national contexts. Earlier publications include *Social Citizenship in the Shadow of Competition* (Ashgate 2003), *An Introduction to Law and Regulation* (with

Karen Yeung, Cambridge 2007), and editorship of *The Intersection Between Rights and Regulation: New Directions in Socio-legal Scholarship* (Ashgate 2007).

Gregory Shaffer is Melvin C. Steen Professor of Law at the University of Minnesota Law School and Affiliated Professor of the Department of Political Science at the University of Minnesota. Professor Shaffer's work applies a socio-legal approach to international and transnational law. A recipient of two National Science Foundation awards, he is the author of more than seventy articles and book chapters, as well as the books *When Cooperation Fails: The International Law and Politics of Genetically Modified Foods* (Oxford University Press 2009) and *Defending Interests: Public-Private Partnerships in WTO Litigation* (Brookings Institution Press 2003); he edited the volumes *Dispute Settlement at the WTO: The Developing Country Experience* (Cambridge University Press 2010) and *Transatlantic Governance in the Global Economy* (Rowman & Littlefield 2001).

Acknowledgments

This book was developed through an iterative process. Each of the contributors participated in the Collaborative Research Network of the Law and Society Association entitled Transnational Legal Orders, and they presented earlier drafts of the papers at the annual meetings of the Law and Society Association in Baltimore, Berlin, Montreal, Denver, Chicago, San Francisco, and Honolulu from 2006 to 2012. Terry Halliday, Heinz Klug, and Minzee Kim and Liz Boyle presented revised versions of their papers at a seminar I organized at the University of Minnesota Law School with the same title. Earlier versions of five of the papers appeared as a special symposium issue of *Law and Social Inquiry*. Our thanks go to that journal's fabulous editor Laura Beth Nielsen, its editorial board, and its anonymous reviewers. The manuscript was then revised, extended, and submitted to John Berger at Cambridge University Press and has been produced under his wonderful care. We are extremely grateful to him for publishing the book as part of the Cambridge Studies in Law and Society series. We thank their anonymous reviewers.

Many people commented on the analytic framework set forth in Chapters 1 and 2 of the book, and I am personally extremely grateful to them. They include Bobby Ahdieh; William Alford; Karen Alter; Elizabeth Boyle; Jeffrey Dunoff; Bryant Garth; Tom Ginsburg; Terence Halliday; Minzee Kim; Heinz Klug; Bronwen Morgan; Leigh Payne; Judith Resnik; Brian Tamanaha; Lucie White; five anonymous reviewers; the participants at workshops at Harvard Law School, the Sandra Day O'Connor College of Law at Arizona State University, the University of Minnesota Law School, and the University of Wisconsin Law School; and panels at meetings of the American Political Science Association, the American Society of International Law, the Law and Society Association, the Society for the Advancement of Socio-Economics, and the Society of International Economic Law. I also thank the students of my seminar on Transnational Legal Orders from whom I learned much. All errors, of course, remain mine.

1

Transnational Legal Ordering and State Change

Gregory Shaffer

We live in an age of transnationalism. We always have, but its intensity has increased. The sources of US law, for example, derive in large part from empire. Most remotely, they come from Rome. Closer in time, they come from England and its common law heritage. Most recently, they reflect the intensification of transnational economic and cultural interactions, which have catalyzed a proliferation of international, regional, and bilateral agreements, regulatory networks, and institutions that foment and promote legal and institutional change. We unconsciously experience such transnationalism in our daily lives, and we sometimes embrace it. Yet, we can also be anxious about its effects on our social order and our identities. Our laws and legal systems reflect how we see ourselves and our communities. As the migration of law across borders intensifies, we can become anxious about it, as illustrated by the US clamor over citations to foreign and international law and legal decisions in federal courts.

Legal norms in almost all domains of law circulate around the globe. The norms do not travel by themselves. Actors convey them, whether instrumentally or reflexively. The norms are sometimes codified in international treaties, whether of a binding or nonbinding nature. At other times, they are diffused through informal processes involving bureaucratic networks of public officials; transnational networks of private actors such as business representatives, nongovernmental activists, and professionals; and hybrid combinations. Over time, distinct *transnational legal orders* may emerge that impose or impart legal norms governing particular areas of law. Where the transnational legal norms are relatively clear, coherent, and accepted, the transnational legal order can be viewed in systematic terms. Where they are less so, the transnational legal order is more contingent and fragile. The effects of transnational legal norm conveyance, however, are not homogeneous across states. They vary in light of identifiable factors. *Transnational legal processes*, the processes through which these norms are constructed, carried, and conveyed, always confront national and local processes, which may block, adapt, translate, or appropriate a transnational legal norm, and spur its reassessment – in other words, feeding back into the modification of transnational legal norms.

This book contends that, in vast areas of law today, one cannot understand domestic legal change and legal practice without understanding transnational legal ordering. Counterfactually, take out the transnational story and what one would see across jurisdictions would be quite different. The centrality of transnational legal processes can best be understood through empirical work involving discrete domains of law that address the *interaction* of transnational lawmaking and national legal practice, holding them in tension. To understand transnational legal ordering, one needs to not only assess the development of international and transnational legal norms (the focus of much international law scholarship), but also evaluate their impact on practice in national legal systems. Such studies can be viewed as combining international and comparative legal analysis, and international and comparative political economy, within a single sociolegal frame.[1]

Although the terms transnational law, transnational legal process, and state transformations are increasingly used, we need both clarifying conceptual work and detailed case studies applying it. There have been intensive debates over the concept and operation of "legal transplants" among comparative law and sociolegal scholars (Nelken & Feest 2001). However, as William Twining (2005: 237) writes, "[p]erhaps the most striking aspect of the literature is that it very rarely tells us in any detail about actual impact on the ground." This book aims to provide both clarifying conceptual analysis and empirical grounding. It first sets forth a sociolegal analytic framework for empirically assessing transnational legal processes and their deeper implications and variable impacts within states. It then follows through with five case studies of transnational legal processes' differential effects in six regulatory areas. This introductory chapter clarifies the concepts of transnational law, legal process, and legal ordering in relation to alternative approaches that have been used to study international and transnational law. The case studies then apply the framework, and, at the same time, the framework draws from them. In this way, the book provides an example of what I have elsewhere called "emergent analytics," analytics that oscillate between empirical findings, abstract theorizing, real-world assessment, and back again (Nourse & Shaffer 2009; Shaffer & Ginsburg 2012).

[1] For two leading sociolegal books in a related vein, see Halliday & Carruthers 2009 (focusing on the globalization of insolvency law and its reception in China, Korea, and Indonesia); and Merry 2006a: 29 ("My approach is to focus on a single issue, the movement against gender violence, in five local places in the Asia-Pacific region and in the deterritorialized world of UN conferences, transnational NGO activism, and academic, legal and social service exchanges of ideas and practices").

1. THE CONCEPTS OF TRANSNATIONAL LAW, LEGAL PROCESS, LEGAL ORDERING, AND STATE CHANGE

The term "transnational law" is increasingly used in scholarship, but often without adequate conceptual work regarding what the term covers. This section clarifies how the term transnational law has been used to date, and then shifts orientation from a focus on transnational law (which suggests the existence of a particular body of law), to that of transnational legal ordering and the transnational processes that implicate it. This shift in analytic focus enables us to show that the nation-state and national law remain central to understanding transnational law and legal ordering.

A. *Transnational Law, Legal Process, and Legal Orders*

Since the rise of sovereign states in the seventeenth century associated conventionally with the Treaty of Westphalia, law has been associated with state law and national legal systems. Law, as John Glenn (2003: 839) writes, was "an essential element . . . of national construction." Law helped to provide legitimacy to governing institutions, including by constructing a sense of national identity. Constitution building, following war and civil conflict, helped to consolidate legal order within defined boundaries for a given populace, constituting new imagined communities (Arnold 1983; Bobbitt 2002). Public international law was based on and came into existence with the creation of states, governing their relations and providing for their mutual recognition. The central aim, in the words of Peter Malanczuk (1997: 3) was to provide "the legal regulation of the international intercourse of states." Private international law concurrently provides rules and standards to govern situations in which more than one state asserts jurisdiction over a transaction or event involving nonstate actors. Thus, the concepts of public and private *international law* are both state-centric, addressing relations between nation-states and between national legal systems, as reflected in the term "international."

With the fall of the Berlin Wall and the spread of economic globalization, scholarly work has increasingly applied new concepts of "global" and "transnational law," but often without clear conceptualizations of either. Under each of these two overlapping concepts, law is being denationalized, to varying degrees, because the legal norms may not be formally part of international or national law as conventionally construed. *Global law* posits, by its name, that universal legal norms are being created and diffused globally in different legal domains that may or may not involve agreements between states.[2] For example, in the legal academy, the *global administrative law* project chose the title of "global" administrative law under the intuition

[2] See, e.g., Boyle & Meyer 1998: 213–32 (applying a world polity model); and Braithwaite & Drahos 2000 (examining the relative role of different mechanisms in thirteen areas of global business law).

that regulatory structures are being pressed to respond to common demands "that have a common normative character, specifically an administrative law character. The growing commonality of these administrative law-type principles and practices is building a unity between otherwise disparate areas of governance" (Kingsbury 2009: 3).

The concept of *transnational law* has been developed to address legal norms that do not clearly fall within traditional conceptions of national and international law, but are not necessarily global in nature. In his influential 1956 Storrs Lecture, Judge Philip Jessup turned to the concept of transnational law because he found "the term 'international' misleading since it suggests that one is concerned only with the relations of one nation (or state) to other nations (or states)" (Jessup 1956: 1).[3] The concept of transnational law used in scholarship can be narrow or broad, depending on the user, but it generally is composed of legal norms that apply across borders to parties located in more than one jurisdiction. From a broad conception, transnational law encompasses public and private international law, as well as law governing transnational activities not traditionally included within them (Jessup 1956). From a narrow perspective, transnational law is composed only of rules, "which regulate actions or events that transcend national frontiers . . . which do not wholly fit into such standard categories" of public and private international law.[4]

Let us look at two examples of the transnationalization of law that fall outside traditional conceptions of public and private international law. The first is the formation by private actors of substantive law that applies across borders (e.g., the "new *lex mercatoria*") (Schmitthoff 1961; Teubner 1996). Gralf Peter Calliess and Peer Zumbansen (2010), for example, have assessed the development of transnational private lawmaking in consumer and corporate governance law that involves the interaction of publicly and privately made law. A second example is the rise of common approaches of national judges and regulators to cross-border legal and regulatory issues as a result of transjudicial and transgovernmental regulatory dialogues (Slaughter 2004).[5] As Hanna Buxbaum (2006: 316) contends, "transnational regulatory litigation can, under proper circumstances, enable national courts to participate in implementing effective regulatory strategies for global markets." Robert Wai (2008: 107) likewise views such lawmaking in terms of "a decentralized and

[3] See also Friedmann 1964: 37 (distinguishing international and transnational society, and maintaining that "international society is represented by the traditional system of interstate diplomatic relations, the relations of 'coexistence'"). See also the work on legal pluralism in global and transnational context by von Benda-Beckman (2006), Berman (2007), and Teubner (1996).

[4] The language is carved out from the broader definition of transnational law adopted by Jessup (1956).

[5] See also Scott & Wai 2004 (arguing for a more activist conception of the role of private law courts in a process of *transnational comity* with respect to transnational corporate liability and human rights concerns); Djelic & Andersson 2006; Hepple 2005: 4 (on transnational labor regulation); and Wai (2005).

intermediate form of transnational governance that recognizes and manages the multiplicity of norms generated by plural normative systems in our contemporary world society."

The increasing use of the term "transnational law" can be distilled into two concepts, which can be differentiated by whether they focus on subjects (law addressing transnational activities and situations) or on sources (law, whether international or foreign, that is imported and exported across borders). Most legal studies that use the term transnational law refer to law that targets transnational events and activities – that is, transnational situations that involve more than one national jurisdiction.[6] Specific transnational legal rules and legal doctrine can develop to address these situations. (We call this concept *transnational law applying to transnational situations.*) Many sociolegal studies, in contrast, conceive of transnational law and legal norms in terms of the source of legal change within a national legal system. In this latter conception, transnational law consists of legal norms that are exported and imported across borders, and that involve transnational networks and international and regional institutions that help to construct and convey the legal norm within a field of law. (We call this conception *transnational law as transnational legal ordering.*)[7]

In his famous 1956 Storrs Lecture, Jessup defined "transnational law" in the first "situational" sense as "all law which regulates actions or events that transcend national frontiers." This concept is a functional one, reflecting a professional concern that, because both international and national law are inadequate to address the flow of actions and the impact of events across borders, we need a more accurate and useful concept to govern these situations. As Jessup (1956: 7) wrote, "[t]he more wedded we become to a particular classification or definition, the more our thinking tends to become frozen and thus to have a rigidity which hampers progress toward the ever needed new solutions of problems whether old or new." In their path-breaking casebook *Transnational Legal Problems* (1994), Henry Steiner, Detlev Vagts, and Harold Koh similarly conceptualized transnational

[6] Many legal scholars build from and cite the famous lecture of Jessup 1956. See, e.g., Koh 2004: 53 (citing Jessup's definition of law addressing "events that transcend national frontiers"); Burley 1993 ("I define transnational law to include all municipal law and a subset of intergovernmental agreements that directly regulate transnational activity between individuals and between individuals and state governments," citing Jessup); Slaughter 2000: 245 ("Transnational law has many definitions. I mean to include here simply national law that is designed to reach actors beyond national borders: the assertion of extraterritorial jurisdiction. Extraterritorial jurisdictional provisions are often the first effort a national government is inclined to make to regulate activity outside its borders with substantial effects within its borders," citing Jessup); Hathaway 2005: 473 n.11 ("transnational law includes all law that has cross-border effect, whereas international law refers only to treaties or other law that governs interactions between states," citing Jessup); Dibadj 2008 (classifying the range of sources "applicable to cross-border events" together with the range of actors involved, citing Jessup).

[7] In the Law and Social Inquiry symposium, I called this conception *transnational law as transnational construction and flow of legal norms* (Shaffer 2012). The term *transnational legal ordering* is a more succinct label for this sociolegal conception.

law as the law addressing "transnational problems." The growing use of the concept of transnational law in this sense reflects a practical legal response to increasing economic interconnectedness, sometimes involving new international treaties, sometimes involving the application of national law to events that occur outside a state's borders but have effects within it, and sometimes involving private legal ordering. The concept permits legal academics to assess and advocate (or contest) particular transnational legal rules and legal doctrine applied by courts and other bodies to transnational situations.

In an excellent conceptual analysis, Craig Scott (2009) examines three perspectives of transnational law that lie within this first conception, which he labels traditionalist, decisional, and sociolegal. First, he notes that the concept of transnational law, at a minimum, simply aggregates the *traditionalist* concepts of public and private international law. Public international law addresses relations between states, whereas private international law (in its traditional meaning) addresses conflicts between national jurisdictions asserting authority over the transnational activities of private actors. These private law situations give rise to the development of doctrinal principles and rules regarding choice of law, jurisdiction, and enforcement and recognition of judgments.[8] Second, as national courts and international arbitrators issue an increasing number of decisions to address these situations, they create disaggregated clusters of *decisional* principles and rules that can be extracted, used by advocates, and guide subsequent decisions. As Scott (2009: 871) writes, "this approach to 'law' understands law in disaggregation, not as whole legal orders or systems but rather as discrete norms or normative clusters that are capable of reasoned extraction from the whole and then of being brought to bear on constantly changing particulars." Third, as a pool of legal norms in this area becomes relatively coherent and systematized over time, we may discern the emergence, from a *sociolegal* perspective, of a distinct body of law that is not "statist," but rather is "transnational," one that is developed by the ongoing interaction of public and private actors across states, including national judges, international arbitral bodies, and international private law rule-making institutions.

The concept of *transnational law as transnational legal ordering*, in contrast, focuses on the transnational production of legal norms and institutional forms in particular fields and their migration across borders, regardless of whether they address transnational activities or purely national ones. The concept includes legal norms that are substantive and specific to discrete areas of law, and not just general principles of conflicts of law, or only substantive law applied to cross-border business transactions. This book adopts this sociolegal conception. In doing so, it

[8] In focusing on law applying to foreign transactions, Jessup (1956) particularly addressed issues of jurisdiction and choice of law. The three chapters resulting from the lectures, respectively, were entitled the "The Universality of Human Problems," "The Power to Deal with the Problems" (i.e., jurisdiction), and "The Choice of Law Governing the Problems" (i.e., conflicts of law).

shifts the focus from transnational law as a body of law or legal doctrine to processes of transnational legal ordering. It does so by turning its attention to the transnational construction and migration of *legal norms*, by which we refer, for heuristic purposes, to *formalized norms that lay out behavioral prescriptions issued by an authoritative source, whether or not formally binding or backed by a dispute settlement or other enforcement system.*[9] Transnational legal norms include those purported to be global and those that are more limited in their reach. The source of the transnational legal norm may be an international treaty, international soft law, privately created codes or standards, a foreign legal model promoted by transnational actors, or a combination of them. In other words, they can involve both hard and soft law; can be bilateral, regional, or multilateral in nature; can be constructed by states or nonstate actors; and can be directed at states, corporations, or individuals.

This concept of *transnational legal ordering* is used to assess the construction, flow, and impact of transnational legal norms. The term *transnational legal order* is conceptualized as *a collection of legal norms and associated institutions within a given domain that order behavior across national jurisdictions.*[10] Such ordering, as we will see, is typically discrete and fragmented, involving particular legal subject areas, because the world lacks an overarching global legal system. Where the transnational legal norms in a subject area are relatively clear, coherent, and accepted in practice, the transnational legal ordering is more salient. Where they are less so, the transnational legal ordering is more contingent, and thus less likely to be effective in producing domestic legal and institutional change.

This second, sociolegal concept of transnational legal ordering is methodologically used to evaluate how law is produced transnationally and migrates across borders, whether it is formally enacted by national legislatures, is directly applied by national courts, shapes interpretation of existing domestic law, or otherwise affects private behavior. This concept is not a doctrinal or functional one, but a *methodological* one that is used to assess empirically how transnational-induced legal change occurs and what type of effects it has. The concept, in other words, does not aim to delineate a particular body or field of law or legal doctrine, but cuts across fields of law and provides an analytic means for assessing transnationally induced change in a globalized world.[11] In sum, the two different conceptions of transnational law and legal ordering are adopted because they are useful for different purposes, one for *internal* functional use by legal actors and the other for *external* sociolegal analysis of how law is constructed and operates.

9 This conception of legal norms is captured in the conception of hard and soft law along the dimensions of precision, obligation, and delegation in Abbot & Snidal 2000.

10 See also Halliday & Shaffer 2012 (further developing the study of this concept).

11 For use of the term in a similar "methodological" way, see Zumbansen 2010. See also Calliess & Zumbansen 2010: x, 11 (understanding transnational law "primarily as a *methodological* perspective rather than as a demarcated substantive field of law").

A related concept central to this book is that of *transnational legal process*, conceptualized as *the process through which the transnational construction and conveyance of legal norms take place*. Transnational legal norms do not travel by themselves. They are constructed and conveyed by actors, including by government officials, members of international secretariats, professionals, business representatives, and civil society activists. Actors with agendas often drive these processes. At other times, the legal norms may be carried less consciously as a reflection of intensified cross-border interaction characterizing economic and cultural globalization. For those focused solely on international law – whether they define international law narrowly or broadly – this book's assessment of transnational legal processes, the dimensions of state change implicated by them, and the factors that facilitate and constrain such change are central for understanding international law as well.

Over time, transnational legal processes can constitute transnational legal orders through processes of ongoing articulation and rearticulation of legal norms and their application. The resulting transnational legal orders can be viewed as semi-autonomous, functionally differentiated fields, because transnational legal processes occur differentially in discrete legal areas. Andreas Fischer-Lescano and Gunther Teubner (2004: 1009) thus view transnational legal regimes in terms of the "external reach of their jurisdiction along issue-specific rather than territorial lines."

Transnational legal ordering arises in many areas of law, including human rights, criminal, regulatory, and business law, involving different degrees of consensus and coherence. It may include global, multilateral, regional, and bilateral legal norms. It may encompass associated international and supranational organizations, transgovernmental regulatory networks, and the activities of transnational corporate and civil society actors, whether or not working through formal organizations. Transnational legal ordering may be reflected in treaties, nonbinding standards, model codes, and different forms of monitoring and dispute settlement. These instruments may include amalgams of hard law and soft law varying in their obligatory nature, precision, and institutionalization of monitoring, peer review, and dispute settlement mechanisms (Abbott & Snidal 2000; Shaffer & Pollack 2010).

The two concepts of transnational law have a clear overlap because the cross-border construction and flow of legal norms is often catalyzed by cross-border activities and policy concerns. As Lawrence Friedman (1996: 77) writes, "[t]he global economy is the engine driving convergence, and is what stimulates jurists to draft model laws and to worry about harmonization." Yet, under this book's conception of transnational legal ordering, the legal norms in question address not only transnational activities, but also purely national ones. For example, primary education law and municipal water services regulation, respectively assessed by Bronwen Morgan (in Chapter 6) and by Minzee Kim and Elizabeth Boyle (in Chapter 7), are exclusively national activities, but they can be significantly shaped by the transnational construction and flow of legal norms, whether human rights norms or neoliberal law and development norms. The transnational legal norms in question may be adopted voluntarily in a planned fashion pursuant to harmonization efforts, or adopted without a plan as part of a process of diffusion conveyed through transnational actors and interactions (Simmons, Dobbin, & Garrett 2008). Regardless of the transnational source and nature of the legal norm, it is given particular force and effect when it becomes embedded in a national legal system.

Harold Koh (2006: 745–6) captures this latter conception of transnational law, in part, when he combines the vertical and horizontal dimensions of the transnational flow of legal norms:

> Perhaps the best operational definition of transnational law, using computer-age imagery, is (1) law that is "downloaded" from international to domestic law: for example, an international law concept that is domesticated or internalized into municipal law, such as the international human rights norm against disappearance, now recognized as domestic law in most municipal systems; (2) law that is "uploaded, then downloaded": for example, a rule that originates in a domestic legal system, such as the guarantee of a free trial under the concept of due process of law in Western legal systems, which then becomes part of international law, as in the Universal Declaration of Human Rights and the International Covenant on Civil and Political Rights, and from there becomes internalized into nearly every legal system in the world; and (3) law that is borrowed or "horizontally transplanted" from one national system to another: for example, the "unclean hands" doctrine, which migrated from the British law of equity to many other legal systems.

Koh's metaphors, although helpful in conveying the idea of transnational legal processes, risk reducing their complexity because the processes, in practice, are multifold, simultaneous, and iterative, involving disparate actors, applications, and flows in multiple directions. For some, the third example used by Koh may broaden the analysis too far by including all migrations of legal norms. In practice, however, there likely will be both horizontal and vertical flows that comprise a transnational legal order. Transnational legal orders will build from national models, and national actors will deploy transnational networks and institutions as means to export and diffuse national legal norms. Transnational legal ordering, in other words, involves international and transnational organizations and networks of public and private actors that play a role in constructing and diffusing legal norms. The legal norm is often taken from a national legal model, such as from a powerful state like the United States (Braithwaite & Drahos 2000), but the construction of transnational legal norms also varies, as shown by the empirical chapters in this book.

This book builds from Koh's important conception of transnational legal process, while aiming to improve the tools for empirically assessing its implications for state change. Critically for our purposes, Koh did not provide a framework for assessing the conditions and factors determining the extent, location, and limits of transnationally induced legal change. He likewise did not engage in extensive empirical study of them. Moreover, he did not assess the source of transnational legal norms, and whether transnational legal norms reflect a structural tilt in favor of some interests over others. In contrast, this book aims to assess the transnational sources of legal norms, their reception in countries, and the broader dimensions of state change that are implicated and thus at stake. Although this book focuses primarily on the factors leading to the variable reception of transnational legal norms within countries and the dimensions of state change at stake, the studies also highlight the importance of addressing the source, production, and change of these legal norms over time.

Finally, the concept of transnational legal orders has parallels with that of "global administrative orders" used in the global administrative law project out of New York University School of Law. Both projects depict legal orders arising beyond the nation-state that comprise multiple actors, and involve hard and soft law rules and norms. For example, the Global Administrative Law project defines "global administrative orders" to include:

> (1) administration by formal international organizations; (2) administration based on collective action by transnational networks of cooperative arrangements between national regulatory officials; (3) distributed administration conducted by national regulators under treaty, network, or other cooperative regimes; (4) administration by hybrid intergovernmental – private arrangements; and (5) administration by private institutions with regulatory functions (Kingsbury, Krisch, & Stewart 2005: 25).

This project, however, is both broader and narrower in ambition and scope than the global administrative law project. The concept of transnational legal orders is broader because it is composed of more than administrative law principles and procedural rules, and includes substantive areas of law not traditionally touched by them, such as human rights trials (Sikkink 2011) and letters of credit used in the private sale of goods (Levit 2008). The concept of transnational legal ordering also does not (by its name) imply that it has a "global" reach. The project on transnational legal ordering is nonetheless narrower in that it does not mix positive and normative analysis. A distinct aim of the Global Administrative Law Project, in contrast, is to assess the relevance of traditional national administrative law tools to evaluate and improve the accountability of global governance mechanisms.[12] This book's assessment of transnational legal ordering is nonetheless complementary because of the normative implications raised by its empirical analysis.

[12] Kingsbury, Krisch, & Stewart 2005: 29 (focusing on "principles, procedural rules, review mechanisms, and other mechanisms relating to transparency, participation, reasoned decision making, and assurance of legality in global governance").

B. *State Change and Transformation*

For purposes of empirical study, we also need to specify what we mean by the state, state change, and state transformation, and to break down state change into different dimensions. For heuristic purposes, we refer to the conventional conception of a nation-state, as used by Max Weber (1978) and Charles Tilly (1992), which wields formal authority, exercises compulsory jurisdiction, and monopolizes the legitimate use of force within a territory.[13] We nonetheless recognize that such a conception is an ideal type because state institutions exercise varying degrees of actual authority, and one must disaggregate the concept of the state in order to assess empirically how the state changes over time (as addressed in Chapter 2). Most importantly, for our purposes, the very concept of transnational legal processes problematizes the idea of a state/transnational dichotomy. Although the nation-state remains central as a political unit, and thus central for purposes of sociolegal study, the state contributes to its own change through its active collaboration with and enabling of transnational forces. As Saskia Sassen (2006: 3) writes, "[t]he national is still the realm where formalization and institutionalization have all reached their highest level of development," but "the national is also often one of the key enablers and enactors of the emergent global scale." In other words, we do not live in a postnational world. Rather, states remain central, even when under constant transnational pressure to adapt new legal norms and associated organizational changes.

As regards change and transformation, we need to clarify what they comprise and what to assess. Transnationally induced change can affect the state generally or only discrete parts of the state. It occurs along different dimensions, such as legal, institutional, professional, and normative, which we typologize and examine in Chapter 2 (the *location* of change). It is thus a "differentiated process" (Sassen 2007: 34). Change can occur evolutionarily or revolutionarily, episodically, incrementally, or dramatically, as in Eastern Europe in the 1990s (the *timing* of change). The concept of *transformation* refers to a type of change that is significant or fundamental in its magnitude or scope.[14] The threat of transformation of the state can lead to a protracted politics, both transnationally and locally, to forestall or thwart such change. Diachronic empirical studies, as provided in this book, are thus important

[13] Charles Tilly, in his classic work *Coercion, Capital and European States: AD 990–1992* (1992: 2–4), defines "national states" as "states governing multiple contiguous regions and their cities by means of centralized, differentiated, and autonomous structures," and "states" as "coercion-wielding organizations that are distinct from households and kinship groups and exercise clear priority in some respects over all other organizations within substantial territories."

[14] For important studies on this question, see Campbell 2004 (chapter 2 on the problem of change); Grossman & Grossman 1971: 4–6 (on law and magnitude and scope of social change); Held et al. 1999; Leibfried & Zürn 2005; Sorensen 2004.

because we may not know the extent of change until after some struggle, possibly a protracted one.

The extent of change is always contingent, so that, at times, studies will speak of transnational influence, at times of transnational failure, at times of appropriation of transnational legal norms, and at times of significant transnationally induced change. The resulting legal change may occur *symbolically* (on the books in terms of constitutional, statutory, and administrative law revisions, or the creation or restructuring of agencies and courts), or *practically* (in terms of established patterns of organizational and individual behavior). While much of traditional law scholarship focuses on the symbolic (the law in the books),[15] the studies in this book address changes not only in formal law and organizational structures, but also in legal and organizational practice.

The effective importation of transnational legal norms and institutional forms often confronts a dilemma. While importation is facilitated if the legal norm can be translated and appropriated to fit the local context, the more that the norm is adapted, the less transformative it may be. As Sally Merry (2006a: 22) writes regarding human rights law and gender violence, legal norms "are more easily adapted if they are packaged in familiar terms and do not disturb established hierarchies, but they are more transformative if they challenge existing assumptions about power relationships." Because transnational legal norms interact with domestic institutional, political, and cultural contexts, changes are often evolutionary and incremental over time.

C. *Transnational Legal Process and Nonlegal Factors in State Change*

There are many transnational impacts besides law on nation-states, reflecting processes of economic and cultural globalization and global structures of political and economic power. Many earlier studies have examined these phenomena and their transnational impacts.[16] Transnational legal norms are, of course, affected by these larger political, economic, and social forces. As Lawrence Friedman (1996: 65) writes, "[c]ommerce, after all, is the most promiscuous crosser of national borders," and thus gave rise to the law merchant, an ongoing form of transnational law. Transnational legal ordering is driven in part by the mismatch between transnational markets and national law. It is thus difficult, if not impossible, to separate the impacts of law from other forces, and the accompanying studies do not attempt to do so.[17] Yet, at

[15] See, e.g., Watson 1974: 20 ("It cannot be doubted either that a rule transplanted from one country to another, from Germany to Japan, may equally operate to different effect in the two societies, even though it is expressed in apparently similar terms in the two countries. But our first concern will be with the existence of the rule, not with how it operates within the society as a result of academic or judicial interpretation").

[16] Campbell 2004; Held et al. 1999; Leibfried & Zürn 2005; Sassen 2006, 2007; Sorensen 2004.

[17] The purpose in this book is not to evaluate broader theories of the relation of law and social change in terms of whether law is primarily (or solely) a *product* of social forces and thus has little (or

the same time, counterfactually remove the technology of transnational legal norms from the story of state change and the story would surely be different.

However one views the relation of transnational legal norms to larger processes of globalization and the exercise of power, the focus on transnational legal norms and legal process provides us with a vehicle for assessing transnational influences on state change. Transnational legal norms embody prescriptions for the regulation of activities in particular domains. They can shape the perception and definition of problems and appropriate responses to them. They provide a framework for actors to weigh particular regulatory alternatives to address particular situations. They make available tools and models for reshaping institutional arrangements for the development, application, and enforcement of law to address these situations.

To understand change in regulatory fields requires an assessment of "the various processes by which institutions are continually reproduced and modified through . . . actors' practices" (Koslowski & Kratochwil 1994: 227).[18] Transnational legal processes engage relevant actors in an iterative process of interaction that can affect their practices, leading to incremental or more dramatic change. The study of transnational legal processes thus provides a window for assessing change in national legal norms, institutional organization, and practices. For those who prefer to work in terms of explanatory and dependent variables, transnational legal ordering, at a minimum, represents an intervening variable in affecting state change.

D. *Recursivity*

The sociolegal approach represented in this book combines the examination of transnational and national processes within a single frame by focusing inquiry on particular regulatory fields, as opposed to general global and transnational law principles, whether of an administrative or constitutional nature, or of a substantive or procedural one. In this way, the studies can assess how the transnational and national are interpenetrated within a field of activity. This dual focus is captured in the concept of *recursivity*, developed by Terence Halliday and Bruce Carruthers (2007; Halliday 2009). Recursivity connotes a multidirectional, diachronic process of legal change. From this perspective, transnational legal process is viewed not as unidirectional, but a process in which the transnational and local are held in tension, in which actors engaged in transnational legal processes seek to influence local lawmaking and practice, and in which national legal norms,

no) autonomy, or whether law is an independent *producer* of change. On the vigorous debates about legal autonomy and its limits, see Cotterrell 1992: 44–65. By assessing transnational legal processes, in other words, one need not privilege law and legal explanations for political and social ones.

[18] In a related vein, Sally Falk Moore (1974: 722) called for empirical assessment of distinct semi-autonomous social fields in terms of their processual characteristics.

adaptations, and resistances provide models for, and feed back into, transnational lawmaking.[19]

This conception of transnational legal process as recursive does not reify it as singular and absolute in content, but rather accounts for its historical specificity and provisional and changing nature. Some sort of settlement of legal norms may occur that persists over time until that settlement is destabilized. Transnational legal process is thus not reduced to a process of filling in "gaps" in law's implementation, but rather seen in dynamic terms in which national, international, and transnational political, social, and legal processes interact. The recursivity approach posits that changes and transformations of states will be a function of three processes operating concurrently and cyclically – a politics within international and transnational lawmaking, a politics within domestic lawmaking, and a politics between them.

2. STRUCTURE OF THE BOOK

A. *The Book's Analytic Framework*

The remainder of Chapter 1 lays out the analytic and theoretic framework for the study of transnational legal ordering and state change. This chapter has set forth the sociolegal conception of transnational law and legal ordering, comparing it with other existing ones. Chapter 2, in turn, conceptualizes and provides a map for what transnational legal ordering does. It gives specific examples from the case studies in the book (Chapters 3–7) to illuminate its points regarding common patterns and differences in state change.

The first part of Chapter 2 sets forth criteria to be assessed in terms of the dimensions and determinants of state change. It breaks down state change into five dimensions: (1) changes in substantive law and legal practice; (2) changes in the boundary between the state, the market, and other forms of social ordering; (3) changes in the institutional architecture of the state; (4) changes in professional expertise and expertise's role in governance; and (5) changes in associational patterns, institutionalized through transnational mechanisms of accountability with their accompanying normative frames.

The second part of Chapter 2 assesses the reasons for variation in the impacts of transnational legal ordering. It breaks them down into three clusters of factors: (1) the character of the transnational legal norm and legal process in terms of their

[19] For related conceptions focusing on the development of international law, see Waters 2005: 490 ("I argue that the relationship between domestic and international law is co-constitutive in nature – that is, a mutually constraining and mutually reinforcing relationship in which international norms not only shape domestic law and culture, but are in turn shaped by domestic law and culture"); Rajagopal 2003: 3 ("concerned with the role of international law in shaping the ideas and practices in the field of development and with the role of ideas and practices in the field of development in shaping international law"); and Ahdieh 2006.

legitimacy, clarity, and coherence; (2) the relation of the transnational legal process to the receiving state in terms of power and the place of intermediaries conveying the legal norm; and (3) the affinity of the transnational legal norm with domestic demand in light of domestic political contests, institutional path dependencies, legal culture, and the extent of change at stake. These factors respectively address law and politics at the transnational level, law and politics at the national level, and law and politics between them involving intermediaries and power asymmetries. Together, these factors determine the scope, timing, and limits of transnational legal ordering's impact, and thus what is normatively at stake.

The third part of Chapter 2 examines the dynamic relationship involving transnational legal ordering and state change from the perspective of recursivity theory (Halliday & Carruthers 2009). It notes that not only do international and transnational legal norms often come from national legal models, and, in particular, those exported from powerful states, it also shows that national responses to transnational legal processes, including in less powerful states, can spur reassessments of the transnational legal norm in question, resulting in dynamic, recursive processes affecting legal change.

B. *Application in Five Case Studies*

Chapters 3 through 7 present five comparative case studies of six different areas of law. Each study illustrates a sociolegal approach to how transnational legal processes work and interact with national law and institutions. Each is grounded in close attention to the interaction of transnational legal processes and domestic regulatory contexts. Through adopting a comparative framework, the studies examine variation in the reception and appropriation of transnational legal norms. They cover the following countries and regulatory domains:

- Anti–money laundering law in Brazil and Argentina, by Maira Machado;
- Corporate bankruptcy law in China, Korea, and Indonesia, by Terence Halliday;
- Primary education law and policy in more than seventy low- and middle-income countries, by Minzee Kim and Elizabeth Boyle.
- Patent, health, and competition law in South Africa, by Heinz Klug;
- Municipal water services regulation in Chile, Bolivia, and Argentina, by Bronwen Morgan.

The studies were chosen based both on their coverage of a range of legal domains in a range of countries in Asia, Africa, and South America, and the fact that they build from sustained empirical research projects in particular fields conducted over years. Most studies of law and globalization have focused exclusively on wealthy nations, which Twining (2005: 204) calls a "'Country and Western tradition' of comparative law," which applies "a naïve model of diffusion." These studies, with their careful attention to local practices in developing countries, thus help fill a major gap. The countries studied vary in terms of their institutional legacies, their political and cultural contexts, and their relations to sites of transnational lawmaking. The regulatory areas likewise vary from financial and business regulation to social and economic rights. Most importantly, each of the studies builds from long-term empirical research projects that engage with the interaction of transnational legal ordering and particular countries.

Each of the studies is conducted within a research design that examines the interaction of transnational and national legal processes in particular regulatory domains in different countries over time. Each study compares different countries' responses in a single regulatory field (or, in one case, that of Klug, a single country and transnational-national interaction in multiple regulatory areas), so that the authors can assess variation in transnational influence. Four of the studies entail field work involving participant observation and extensive interviewing of relevant actors. The fifth study (by Kim and Boyle) uses quantitative methods, together with a historical analysis, to assess the relative impacts across more than seventy low-income and middle-income countries of conflicting human rights and neoliberal development norms over a twenty-one-year period. Overall, the methods used include systematic interviewing, participant/observation, ethnography, documentary evidence, archival research, and surveys, as well as (in one case) quantitative regression analysis.

Although the case studies in this book focus primarily on a range of developing countries, the analytic framework used and the dimensions of change and factors assessed should apply across countries and regions, including the United States and the European Union (EU).[20] The primary difference between the United States and the European Union and the countries studied in this book lies in the general direction of transnational flows, with the United States and the European Union more likely being producers of transnational legal norms, as opposed to being appropriators of them. In a globalized world, much of law is subject to transnational influences and pressures, but more powerful states are the primary exporters of legal norms.

Chapter 3 consists of Maira Machado's study, *Similar in Its Differences: Transnational Legal Processes Addressing Money Laundering in Brazil and Argentina*. It assesses the development of transnational legal norms regarding money laundering and the reasons for their variable impacts within Brazil and Argentina. The transnational legal process started with US promotion of anti–money laundering norms

[20] On the migration of foreign and international law into the United States and European Union respectively, see, for example, Resnik 2006 (examining the history of migration of law into the United States and the multiple ports of entry, from the federal to the local); Resnik 2008: 46 ("as an empirical matter, one finds the frequent borrowing of words and text from elsewhere," noting constitutional borrowing of texts, rewriting of texts, and reinterpreting of texts); Scott 2009: 908–28 (describing the effect of the European Union's REACH program on chemical regulatory reform in the United States); Scott 2003: 228–32 (noting constraints on EU regulation imposed by WTO agreements); and Shaffer 2000 (examining the impact of European privacy law on US domestic privacy policies and practices).

within the Basel Committee on Banking Supervision, an institution created by the central bank governors of ten nations, moved to the Financial Action Task Force (FATF) created by the G-7, and then encompassed the United Nations (UN). The Basel Committee first adopted a relatively general statement of ethical principles for banks in 1998. In 1990, the FATF prepared more precise guidelines in the form of forty Recommendations on Money Laundering that are not formally binding, although many states consider them to be de facto binding if they are to remain in good standing before the organization. The FATF Recommendations and its reporting, monitoring, and peer-review processes create new forms of accountability not only for government bureaucrats but also for private financial institutions that must oversee and report on their customers' transactions. In 2002 and 2003, the FATF Recommendations became incorporated in two UN conventions that are formally binding, one against transnational organized crime and one against the financing of terrorism.

Machado's study assesses the variable impacts of the FATF's Recommendations on anti–money laundering in Brazil and Argentina. Although Brazil was certainly subject to transnational pressure, it also implemented the FATF Recommendations for its own domestic policy reasons. In contrast, the changes in Argentina have been largely reactions to transnational pressure and have had, as a result, less impact in practice. Machado shows how the Brazilian government found the FATF's policies useful for addressing the national problems of organized crime and corruption and their threat to the state, whereas there was little domestic demand in Argentina to implement them. The Brazilian state criminalized money laundering, and it created a new financial intelligence unit within the administration and a new interagency coordination and monitoring mechanism (named ENCCLA, or *Estratégia Nacional de Combate à Corrupção e à Lavagem de Dinheiro*) pursuant to which authorities interact over money laundering initiatives for the first time. It obligated financial institutions to identify customers, maintain records, and report on suspicious transactions, enlisting them as policing agents. It created a new Internet-based process (named *BacenJud*), which facilitates the exchange of financial information between financial institutions and judicial authorities. The result has been the creation of new hybrid public-private financial policing mechanisms and an overall shift in allocation of institutional authority from the judicial branch to the administration.

Chapter 4 consists of Terence Halliday's study, *Architects of the State: International Organizations and the Reconstruction of States in East Asia*. It examines the role of international organizations in restructuring corporate bankruptcy law in China, Korea, and Indonesia. Halliday starts by noting how "doggedly nationalistic" were the United States and England in initially developing and reforming their national models for bankruptcy in the 1970s and 1980s, without any reference to transnational or national legal norms. These models, however, later provided templates for the creation of global bankruptcy law norms promoted by international institutions.

Halliday examines how international and regional financial institutions and, eventually, the United Nations Commission on International Trade Law (UNCITRAL) drew from these national models in light of three sets of pivotal events: the fall of the Berlin Wall, a series of debt crises affecting pivotal developing and transitional economies, and the Asian financial crisis at the end of the 1990s. Clubs of nations, in particular the G-7 and G-22, with the United States playing a particularly influential role, first instructed international financial institutions, such as the World Bank and International Monetary Fund (IMF), to develop norms and create regulatory frameworks to address national credit crises more systematically and protect the global financial system. In the post-Washington consensus, the international financial institutions stressed the role of law and institutions, such as courts and regulatory agencies, as critical for effective policy, together with trained professionals who service them. International institutions, such as UNCITRAL, worked with international professional associations of insolvency practitioners, including the International Bar Association, to draw from their expertise in consolidating a model set of insolvency norms and practices that UNICTRAL adopted.

Halliday assesses the broader implications that these globalized legal norms raise within states and, in particular, the institutional architecture of states, including the relative roles of executive departments, legislatures, independent agencies, and courts. In Indonesia, in the midst of the financial crisis, the international financial institutions used their leverage to spur not only substantive and procedural legal reforms, but also the creation of entirely new state institutions, including a new commercial court that would be responsible for corporate bankruptcies, and an out-of-court agency for negotiations between debtors and creditors. In Korea, the state shifted power over corporate insolvency from executive departments to courts, which included functional equivalents of a US model of a specialized bankruptcy court. In China, the government adopted a law that outsources significant functions for the restructuring of companies to courts and private professionals, adopting global insolvency norms enunciated by the World Bank and UNCITRAL, albeit along China's timeline. Halliday nonetheless shows how the transnational promotion of legal and institutional reform, although seemingly technical, raises fundamental issues of state restructuring that implicates power configurations within states and spurs resistance to change. This resistance gives rise to recursive cycles of transnational and domestic lawmaking until some sort of settlement is reached.

Chapter 5 consists of the study by Minzee Kim and Elizabeth Boyle, *Neoliberalism, Transnational Education Norms, and Education Spending in the Developing World, 1983–2004*. It examines the relative impact on primary education policy of competing transnational regimes. One regime is composed of international human rights treaties that recognize a human right to free primary education, and relatively weak international institutions that promote its compulsory, universal provision. The authors trace the development of this legal regime, starting with the 1948 Universal Declaration of Human Rights, followed by the 1966 International Covenant on

Economic, Social, and Cultural Rights, and the 1989 Convention on the Rights of the Child. These treaties are monitored and promoted by international organizations, such as the United Nations Educational, Scientific, and Cultural Organization (UNESCO), and transnational nongovernmental organizations. The other regime is composed of international financial institutions which, in the 1980s and early 1990s, called for the adoption of market-oriented "user fees" for the funding of education. The international financial institutions emphasized free market principles, reductions in state spending, and balanced budgets as part of a neoliberal approach to development. When developing countries faced debt crises, the international financial institutions exercised considerable leverage, and, in particular, the IMF and World Bank through structural adjustment agreements and adjacent instruments that imposed de jure and de facto loan conditionalities. These "arrangements" were undertaken by the IMF and World Bank and numerous states, building from a common template of prescriptions. They do not fall within traditional conceptions of national or international law because the arrangements are not formally binding, but they are precise in their legal language, exercise de facto authority because the IMF can refuse to release successive "tranches" of a loan if a country fails to meet its undertakings, are clearly transnational in character, and implicate many countries. By 2000, according to a World Bank report, seventy-seven of seventy-nine countries studied had adopted some type of user fee for primary education.

The authors show that, despite the relatively weak position of the human rights regime compared with the coercive power of international financial institutions, the international human rights regime's approach to universal primary education has won out. The World Bank backed down and then denied that it had actually advocated user fees to fund children's education. The authors contend that it was the power of the greater legitimacy of the human rights regime, coupled with the activity of transnational nongovernmental organizations, which led to its success. Using data at yearly intervals for more than seventy low- and middle-income countries between 1983 and 2004, they show that the key factor in determining countries' per capita expenditure on education for children under fourteen and their percentage of state expenditure devoted to education was neither the ratification of human rights treaties nor the implementation of structural adjustment agreements. Rather, countries embedded in the transnational human rights regime through stronger linkages with transnational nongovernmental organizations were significantly more likely to increase their per capita educational spending on children and increase their relative spending on education. These transnational nongovernmental organizations operate as crucial intermediaries for the conveyance of international human rights norms regarding state expenditure on children's education. In sum, the authors find that transnational nongovernmental organizations were central to the resolution of the contest among competing transnational norms for primary education, as well as for national acceptance of the ideas promoted by the international human rights regime.

Chapter 6 consists of Heinz Klug's study, *Access to Medicines and the Transformation of the South Africa State*. It addresses the constraints and opportunities provided by international and transnational intellectual property, health, and competition law in post-apartheid South Africa. Klug notes how the transformation of South Africa was made in the context of opportunities and constraints created by international and transnational law and institutions, affecting competing political and economic factions within the post-apartheid state. As a result, some policy options gained salience, while others were foregone. Klug examines the interaction of the relative power of global and transnational institutions and models, on the one hand, and the confluence of local conditions and tensions among domestic policy sectors in light of domestic social problems, on the other. This interaction results in nonlinear and uneven processes of state change.

Klug assesses how the new post-apartheid government came into power at the time of the creation of the World Trade Organization (WTO) and inherited the commitments made by the previous regime. The bureaucracy within the government emphasized that South African law had long protected patents and contended that the new WTO Agreement on Trade-Related Aspects of Intellectual Property Rights (TRIPS Agreement) raised no significant issues for the country. The new health department, composed of activists of the African National Congress, felt otherwise. They found a transnational ally in the World Health Organization. Although competition law initially did not receive significant attention in South Africa, South Africa joined the International Competition Network in 2001 and strengthened its competition law institutions. It used these institutions and legal tools to address high levels of business concentration in South Africa, including in the pharmaceutical sector. Klug shows how the government and activists were able to use competition law norms to advance the government's "black economic empowerment" goals and challenge the drug pricing practices of pharmaceutical companies. In other words, transnational legal norms were appropriated to advance domestic aims.

Chapter 7 consists of Bronwen Morgan's study, *The Limits of Transnational Transformations of the State: Comparative Regulatory Regimes in Water Service Delivery*. It addresses both the influence and the limits of transnational legal norms in shaping state change in the field of municipal water services in South America. Powerful players developed a transnational epistemic community to address the issue of access to drinking water. The epistemic community consisted of international and regional financial institutions (the World Bank and the Inter-American Development Bank), multinational private water companies (particularly from the UK and France), and a transnational business-supported think tank, the World Water Council, which is supported by business-based nongovernmental organizations and large corporations. Interestingly, the United States is not central to transnational developments in this field, unlike France and the United Kingdom, because of the local and fragmented nature of US water delivery. This epistemic community promoted a shift in regulation to a "neoliberal" transactional model in which water services are provided by private companies, but overseen by independent regulatory authorities. The outsourcing of water service delivery from the public to the private sector, as a result, was accompanied by the development of new regulatory institutions. Conflicts that arose between the multinational investor and government authorities gave rise to international arbitration pursuant to a web of bilateral investment treaties, as well as bargaining in the shadow of potential international arbitration.

Morgan compares the national responses and implementation of this transactional model in Argentina, Bolivia, and Chile. She finds that, although each of the countries contracted out water service provision in a number of municipalities and formed new independent regulatory institutions, they did so in radically different ways. In Bolivia, the regulatory authority was politically marginalized. In Argentina, the authority's politicized role shifted erratically in light of economic crises and political tensions within a fragmented federal state. In Chile, it gained technocratic authority in stages that fit with priorities determined within the Chilean political context. Importantly in Chile, the "Chicago boys" – high-level government officials under the Pinochet government who had obtained their PhDs in economics at the University of Chicago – facilitated the transactional model's reception by acting as conduits and entry points for neoliberal policy norms. Morgan shows how the transnationally promoted transactional regulatory model reciprocally helped to catalyze new politics in Bolivia and Argentina that promoted an alternative regulatory model of participatory governance. This development, in parallel with others, affected transnational politics, such that international and regional financial institutions and foreign aid agencies reoriented their transnational programs.

C. *The Conclusion*

Chapter 8 summarizes the book's arguments and discusses the book's implications for the study of transnational legal ordering. It contends that the sociolegal conception of transnational law and legal ordering critically enhances our understanding of how international law and transnational legal processes work in light of the constraints they face. It highlights the multidirectional, recursive nature of transnational legal processes, as opposed to the unidirectional nature of most studies that focus solely on national "compliance" with international law. The conclusion discusses the role of transnational law and legal processes in playing a mediating role, together with configurations of power, so that changes in national law and institutions cannot be reduced to international *realpolitik*. We need more studies of transnational legal ordering in different domains along these lines.

Transnational legal processes can facilitate cooperation among states and their constituencies. It also can significantly constrain national policy space, whether for good or ill. Whatever be the normative goals actors have, whether they be constraining the risks of financial contagion or advancing human dignity, they can be more effective if they understand how processes of transnational legal ordering work and the challenges they face. Conversely, those wishing to resist transnational prescriptions in order to expand policy space within nation-states will likewise find critical the book's empirical assessments of how transnational legal ordering operates.

2

The Dimensions and Determinants of State Change

Gregory Shaffer

This chapter provides an analytic framework and a map for the empirical study of what transnational legal ordering does, and the limits it confronts. The first section examines five dimensions of state change that can be assessed empirically. Assessing these dimensions highlights the deeper implications of transnational legal ordering. The five dimensions are (1) changes in substantive law and practice; (2) changes in the boundary between the state, the market, and other forms of social ordering; (3) changes in the institutional architecture of the state; (4) changes in professional expertise and expertise's role in governance; and (5) changes in associational patterns, institutionalized through transnational accountability mechanisms with their accompanying normative frames.

The second section explains the factors that determine the extent, location, timing, and limits of state change, and organizes these factors into three clusters. It maintains that variation in the impacts of transnational legal ordering should be assessed as a function of three clusters of factors: (1) the character of the transnational legal norm and legal order in terms of their legitimacy, clarity, and coherence; (2) the relation of transnational legal ordering to the receiving state in terms of power and the place of intermediaries conveying the legal norm; and (3) the affinity of the transnational legal norm with domestic demand in light of domestic political contests, institutional path dependencies, legal culture, and the extent of change at stake. More succinctly, these three clusters entail law and politics at the transnational level, law and politics at the national level, and law and politics between them. These factors determine the extent and limits of transnational legal ordering's impact, and thus what is normatively at stake.

The final section applies recursivity theory in assessing the interaction of transnational lawmaking and national legal practice. On the one hand, it shows how transnational legal norms often come from national legal models and, in particular, from powerful states. On the other hand, it shows how national responses to transnational legal processes, including in less powerful states, can spur reassessments of

TABLE 2.1. *Dimensions of state change*

Dimensions of state change	Associated discipline
(1) Changes in national law and practice	Focus of Legal Studies
(2) Changes in the boundary of the state, the market, and other forms of social ordering	Focus of Institutional Economics
(3) Changes in the allocation of authority among state institutions	Focus of Comparative Institutional Analysis in Comparative Politics
(4) Changes in expertise and the role of expertise in governance	Focus of Sociology of the Professions
(5) Changes in associational patterns, institutionalized through transnational mechanisms of accountability with their accompanying normative frames	Focus of Organizational Sociology

the transnational legal norm, resulting in dynamic, recursive processes. Some sort of normative settlement may occur, until it again becomes destabilized, triggering new recursive processes. The chapter refers to the book's case studies (in Chapters 3–7) to illustrate how and why transnational legal ordering variably affects different dimensions of state change across substantive fields today, shaping law's meaning and practice.

1. THE DIMENSIONS OF STATE CHANGE

States are not monolithic, but differentiated. To assess the impact of transnational legal ordering on state change, we need to distinguish different dimensions of change. Besides shaping the substance of national law, transnational legal processes can have broader effects on the institutions and actors that apply law, and the normative frames in which they do so. Reflecting conceptually on the dimensions of state change at stake helps us to understand both the potential significance of transnational legal processes and their limits, both the opportunities they provide and the constraints they face.

This section provides a typology of five dimensions of state change affected by transnational legal ordering that can be assessed empirically. These dimensions are summarized in Table 2.1, together with the academic disciplines often associated with their study.[1] The listing of the associated disciplines highlights both the stakes

[1] This chapter breaks down the dimensions of state change into patterns of legal, institutional, professional, and normative change that can be identified across regulatory fields. Others have assessed the dimensions of the state and state change in terms of the normative goods that states provide, such as security, rule of law, democratic self-determination, and social welfare. See, e.g., Leibfried & Zürn 2005.

implicated by transnational legal processes, and the need for cross-disciplinary, sociolegal study of these implications.

The first dimension, changes in national law and practice, which is the focus of most legal studies, implicates the other four, which raise deeper structural and normative issues and thus bring to the foreground the stakes of transnationally induced legal change. The second and third dimensions involve shifts in the authority and architecture of state institutions, while the fourth and fifth involve shifts in professional expertise and associational patterns within particular normative frames. These dimensions are interlinked, because changes in one dimension can catalyze changes in others. For example, transnational legal processes can create new demands on the state by enhancing the authority of certain forms of expertise, which, in turn, creates pressure for shifts in the allocation of authority among state institutions, or in the boundary of the state and private ordering. It is nonetheless useful to disaggregate these dimensions for purposes of empirical study of the impacts and implications of transnational legal ordering.

A. *Changing National Law: Enactment and Practice*

To start with the traditional focus of legal scholarship, transnational legal ordering spurs changes across the spectrum of national law. It contributes to changes in constitutional law, with new and amended constitutions incorporating new human rights (Elkins, Ginsburg, & Simmons 2012; Klug 2000). It induces changes in criminal law, broadening its scope to address, for example, money laundering, human trafficking, cartels, and copyright and trademark violations.[2] As John Braithwaite and Peter Drahos (2000: 85) write, "[o]ne of the striking features of the evolution of intellectual property law is the increased involvement of criminal law. There has been no serious discussion of why the state should mete out criminal penalties in an area that has traditionally been a civil matter." US pressure for intellectual property enforcement possibly even led to capital punishment in China in a number of cases when China was negotiating its accession to the World Trade Organization (WTO) (Alford 1997: 91). Transnational legal processes spur changes in regulation across regulatory fields, as this book shows. National laws across the world, from South Africa to China, incorporate standards that are developed by international standard-setting bodies (Büthe & Mattli 2011). These processes can potentially lead to a "race to the top," a "race to the bottom," or ongoing divergence in regulatory stringency.[3] Actors are behind these processes, and determine their relative success, both in terms of the transnational construction of the legal standard and its local application.

[2] See, e.g., Machado, Chapter 3 (money laundering); Harding 2006; and Shaffer & Nesbitt 2011 (cartels).

[3] See Vogel & Kagan 2004, 31–32 ("the evidence . . . weighs heavily against the notion that globalization induces a general regulatory race to the bottom").

Implementation of transnational legal norms in a national legal system can be usefully viewed as a two-stage process. Formal domestic enactment of law (the focus of positivist legal scholars) is followed by actual legal practice, the law-in-action (the bread and butter of sociolegal theorists). Formal legal change can provide tools for actors to effect change in regulatory practice over time, but they do not necessarily do so. Binding national law could be formally enacted, but could have little to no practical impact, while changes in soft law norms potentially could have significant practical effects. The studies in this book address both the formal enactment and actual practice of law, but they focus their attention, in particular, on how transnational legal norms are applied, adapted, or rejected, in practice.

B. *Changing the Boundary of the State, the Market, and Other Forms of Social Ordering*

Transnational legal norms can have broader systemic effects within states. They provide rules and models that reconfigure the respective roles of the state, the market, and other forms of social ordering.[4] They can signal and call for the state to do more, or to do less. In some cases, the state devolves or outsources previous state functions; in others, it takes on new responsibilities; in yet others, it creates new public-private hybrid models of governance. These shifts involve both the state's direct engagement in economic production (reflected in privatization initiatives) and the state's regulation of production (reflected in regulatory and deregulatory policies). In sum, transnational legal ordering affects the allocation of authority between the public law of the administrative state, the private law of contract, and social practice, as well as interaction among them.

Transnational legal ordering induces states to assume responsibilities traditionally left to other forms of social ordering. Machado's study (in Chapter 3) documents the spread of state financial regulation and, in particular, the spurring of greater intervention of the criminal justice system over financial transactions so that financial secrecy and privacy are reduced. The study of Kim and Boyle (Chapter 5) shows how human rights law has been used to press developing countries to assume responsibility for providing free, universal primary education, increasing state expenditures in this domain. Klug (Chapter 6) highlights new pressures on the state to fund greater access to essential medicines on human rights grounds as well.

In other areas, however, transnational legal models have promoted shifts away from state administration toward privatization, deregulation, and greater regulatory flexibility, reflecting "neoliberal" policies following the collapse of the socialist model after the Cold War. Binding rules of the WTO and leverage exercised by the

[4] In practice, there is a blurred line between market and state and nonstate mechanisms of social control. The state/market dichotomy simply informs the assessment of governance choices along a continuum of government involvement.

International Monetary Fund (IMF) and World Bank have significantly constrained state regulatory choices over trade, intellectual property, and industrial policy. Klug, (in Chapter 6) for example, notes the constraints on the African National Congress's initial plans for industrial policy in South Africa when it took power.

Transnational legal processes can lead to the outsourcing of functions formerly performed by public institutions. Halliday's study (in Chapter 4) explains the shift toward courts and private professionals for corporate reorganizations in Korea and China. As he writes, the development of a more "sophisticated private profession . . . permitted the state to retract its interventions into the market because it could delegate with confidence to private professionals so long as they were ultimately accountable, usually to courts." Morgan's study (in Chapter 7), analogously, assesses the impact of new "transactional" models for the provision of municipal water services in South America. These changes were respectively promoted by transnational epistemic communities of consultants and practitioners working in coordination with international and regional financial institutions. The changes are supported by an array of international treaties governing investment disputes, which have served both to deregulate foreign direct investment controls and to denationalize dispute settlement through mandatory reference of disputes to international arbitration.

Where the state outsources traditional government responsibilities, state institutions do not leave the scene. Rather, the state shifts toward steering mechanisms, working through public-private hybrid and other governance mechanisms. As David Levi-Faur (2005: 15) writes:

> In regulatory capitalism, the state retains responsibility for steering, while business increasingly takes over the functions of service provision and technological innovation. This new division of labor goes hand in hand with the restructuring of the state (through delegation and the creation of regulatory agencies) and the restructuring of business (and other societal organizations) through the creation of internal controls and mechanisms of self-regulation in the shadow of the state.[5]

Outsourcing the provision of services to private entities simultaneously gives rise to new public agencies, new regulation, and new forms of dispute settlement in areas traditionally monopolized by the state (Morgan, Chapter 7). Levi-Faur (2005) has traced the proliferation of functional regulatory agencies around the world in areas where none previously existed, documenting the growth of material competencies of the state involving increased specialization and diversification of state administrations. Policymakers often introduce new governance concepts of benchmarking, soft law, information exchange, and best practices. Transnationally created

[5] See also Rhodes 1996; and Ayres & Braithwaite 1992. Cf. Loya & Boli 1999 (applying a world polity perspective regarding the proliferation of global standards through standard-setting bodies such as ISO).

indicators report on state practices and their effects, informing countries' regulatory strategies (Davis, Kingsbury, & Merry 2012). Machado (Chapter 3), for example, shows how information sharing, monitoring, and peer review lie at the core of the work of the Financial Action Task Force (FATF) on money laundering.

Although the concept of transnational legal ordering could suggest a conceptual link to the literature on the "retreat of the state,"[6] the state is arguably not retreating so much as being reshaped.[7] Transnational legal ordering has promoted particular structures for a market economy, shifting the boundary between the market, the state, and other forms of social ordering, affecting what the state does. These shifts can potentially have deep social repercussions over time.

C. *Changing the Institutional Architecture of the State*

Transnational legal processes affect not only what the state does; they shift allocations of authority among the state institutions that make, apply, and enforce law, whether they involve different branches or different levels of government.[8] These shifts can incite struggles between state institutions reluctant to cede or eager to gain power.

It is frequently argued that the expansion of international and transnational governance has empowered executives, leaving legislatures to rubber stamp the results of international negotiations.[9] Such shifts of institutional authority within states have indeed occurred in many domains, spurring analysis of ways to re-empower legislatures (Slaughter 2003). Yet, contrary to much of the conventional take on globalization's empowerment of the executive branch, legislatures can also be strengthened and executives weakened by transnational legal ordering. In many countries, the executive branch's discretion has been reduced, and the legislature's power enhanced. This shift is particularly salient when comparing allocations of authority under state-development models of economic growth in which power was concentrated in executive branch bureaucracies. Katharina Pistor and Philip Wellons (1999: 6–7) note the increase in legislative activity and the reduction of discretion of state bureaucrats in Asia. Halliday (in Chapter 4) discusses these shifts in his study of transformations of bankruptcy law in that region. The executive's authority is similarly curtailed when regulatory power is delegated to independent agencies operating at greater remove from executive power. These processes are captured in

6 See, e.g., Glenn 2003. See also Ohmae 1995; Strange 1996. Cf. Sassen 1996: xii ("globalization under these conditions has entailed a partial denationalizing of national territory and a partial shift of some components of state sovereignty to other institutions, from supranational entities to the global capital market").

7 See also Campbell 2004; Leibfried & Zürn 2005; Sorensen 2004.

8 See, e.g., Kelemen 2004, 269, 270 (contending that international legal integration encourages centralization of regulatory power, but finding that the impact has been modest).

9 See, e.g., Richardson 2001, 94–5 (arguing that globalization decreases the power of legislatures); Brewster 2003; Scheppele 2011 (on 9/11 and the ensuing rise of global security antiterror law has empowered executives in relation to legislatures and courts); Zürn 2004: 264 (on "executive multilateralism").

Morgan's study (in Chapter 7), which documents a shift toward independent agencies for the regulation of water services in Latin America spurred by transnational legal processes.

Transnational legal ordering also affects the role of courts within national systems, sometimes providing courts with new leverage to increase their authority in relation to executives. Courts have been traditionally weak in many developing countries, and transnational legal processes provide them with new tools to assert themselves. Halliday (in Chapter 4) notes the enhancement of judicial power over corporate bankruptcy in South Korea, as well as its potential in China and Indonesia. Klug (in Chapter 6) shows how judges have been empowered to force the hand of state bureaucrats regarding state-provided medical treatment. Morgan (in Chapter 7) shows the increased role of courts in disputes over municipal water services in Argentina. Yet, transnational legal processes do not invariably enhance judicial power. They can also shift authority away from courts, and allocate power to executive branches or to independent agencies because of perceived failures of courts. National administrations, for example, have asserted new authority over criminal justice policy vis-à-vis judicial authorities in the area of money laundering, as shown in Machado's study (in Chapter 3).

Transnational legal ordering, in other words, promotes the construction of new architectures of the state. It provides rules and models for the creation of entirely new state institutions and the reconfiguration of relations among existing ones. These institutional changes can exhibit isomorphism across states, although the actual practices of these institutions may vary considerably.[10] The law of the WTO, for example, requires the creation of new specialized state institutions for handling patent applications, resulting in the formation and expansion of patent offices in developing countries. Yet, how these offices operate in practice varies.[11] The direction of change in institutional authority within states, and what drives these changes, calls for ongoing empirical work.

D. *Shaping Professional Expertise and Expertise's Role in Governance*

In spurring the enactment of new law and the reconfiguration of state institutions, transnational legal ordering gives rise to new professional specializations and shifts in professional authority, creating incentives for individuals and institutions to

[10] On isomorphic changes across states, see Boyle & Meyer 1998; Meyer et al. 1997. However, the actual practice of these institutions may diverge. See, e.g., Halliday, Machado, and Morgan, this book, regarding the regulation of bankruptcy, money laundering, and municipal water services.

[11] Drahos 2010; Drahos 2008; Drahos 2009. Article 8(a) of the TRIPS agreement states that WTO members must "provide as from the date of entry into force of the WTO Agreement a means by which applications for patents for such inventions can be filed." Agreement on Trade-Related Aspects of Intellectual Property Rights, art. 70.8(a), April 15, 1994, Marrakesh Agreement Establishing the World Trade Organization, Annex 1C, 1869 U.N.T.S. 299; 33 I.L.M. 1197 (1994).

adjust to them. These developments can trigger changes toward more technocratic forms of governance, away from other forms of authority,[12] such as representative government.[13] They enhance the prospect of experts exercising authority, and create incentives for individuals and institutions to invest in expertise in specialized areas. New professions develop, professional markets are shaped, and existing career paths adapt to new opportunities. Individuals, and, in particular, elites in societies, invest in them to gain or retain material welfare, social capital, and authority (Dezalay & Garth 2002b).

These domestic shifts in governance occur within state institutions, in private ordering, and in public-private hybrid forms of governance. State restructurings unleash competition for new expertise when the state regulates new activities, creating new positions within the state. They do so as well when the state outsources traditional governmental tasks. New private governance regimes have law-like features and demand the services of professionals.[14] These professionals monitor business behavior and state institutional practice in light of state adaptations to transnational legal ordering, as Machado shows regarding anti–money laundering law (in Chapter 3). In turn, when individuals invest in professional expertise, they have stakes in supporting particular national legal and institutional changes. Different forms of expertise are often in competition with each other, such as law, economics, and accounting, so that professional stakeholders advocate divergent institutional changes that will enhance and protect their relative positions (Dezalay & Garth 2002b). In other words, this dimension of change interacts with others, both responding to changes in the architecture of the state and driving it.

This book's case studies depict the development of new specializations in the fields of bankruptcy law, anti–money laundering law, intellectual property law, competition law, and the regulation of the provision of municipal water services. New professional expertise has developed for bankruptcy services in Asia (embracing lawyers, accountants, and insolvency specialists), and for urban water services in South America (involving economists, management consultants, and lawyers), as shown respectively by Halliday (Chapter 4) and Morgan (Chapter 7). Machado (Chapter 3) shows how private actors perform new functions when they police financial transactions for money laundering pursuant to new obligations to report suspicious behavior to authorities, creating new professional positions, and resulting in new hybrid public-private governance models for financial regulation. Trade,

12 These shifts can be viewed in terms of Max Weber's ideal type of rational-legal forms of authority. Weber 1978, 212–301 (regarding ideal types of traditional, charismatic, and rational/legal forms of authority).

13 Kennedy 2005; Picciotto 1996. See also Aman 2004.

14 See, e.g., Nonet & Selznick 1978 (writing in the US context). See more recently, Meidinger 2009 (on private food safety regulation); and Calliess & Zumbansen 2010 (on corporate governance and *lex informatica*).

intellectual property, and competition law are new fields of specialization in South Africa, India, and Brazil, creating new vested interests, and shifting industry orientations. As I wrote earlier regarding trade law and policy in Brazil:

> Changes at the international level have helped unleash competition for new expertise to take advantage of the opportunities offered by international trade law, involving law schools, policy institutes, law firms, consultancies, think tanks, business associations, and different government ministries. . . . The participants in these networks have formed a community of trade policy specialists within Brazil, one that is transnationally linked to a broader trade policy field (Shaffer, Ratton-Sanchez, & Rosenberg 2008: 389).

Individuals who invest in such expertise play important roles in national governance in specialized domains, whether they are employed in the public or private sector, or revolve between them. These individuals serve as conduits for the conveyance, adaptation, and potential embedding of transnational legal norms. They form part of specialized circuits of knowledge diffused through hybrid networks of public and private actors.

E. *Changes in Associational Patterns and Normative Frames*

Transnational legal ordering generates shifts in patterns of association, institutionalized through mechanisms of accountability that convey particular normative frames. Individuals and groups inside and outside of government account to institutions outside of national borders (Keohane & Nye 2003). They form new patterns of association through ongoing interaction. New relations of authority develop. The normative frames that are reflected in these accountability mechanisms can affect loyalties, influence legal understanding and practice, and reshape the legal culture and legal consciousness of elites and (potentially) broader publics. They can shape the way individuals "conceive of the 'natural' and normal way of doing things, their habitual patterns of talk and action, and their commonsense understanding of the world" (Merry 1990: 5).

A central transnational accountability mechanism consists of monitoring, surveillance, and reporting obligations that trigger peer pressure. International organizations directly monitor national processes; governments must report to them, and these reports are formally reviewed. WTO members, for example, report to a series of WTO committees and councils on their compliance with WTO trade and intellectual property commitments. Those reports are prepared and evaluated within the normative frame of WTO rules. The FATF similarly monitors compliance with financial disclosure requirements, creating new forms of accountability not only for government bureaucrats, but also for private financial institutions that oversee and report on their customers' transactions (Machado, Chapter 3). The Committee on the Rights of the Child likewise monitors compliance with the Convention on the Rights of the Child, harnessing input from both government officials and nongovernmental organizations (NGOs) (Kim & Boyle, Chapter 5).

The construction of transnational indicators has become an important part of transnational accountability mechanisms (Davis, Kingsbury, & Merry 2012). These indicators increasingly define how international legal commitments are construed and measured. The construction of such indicators facilitates further monitoring, potentially shaping national understandings of goals, exercising a form of discipline within particular normative frames.

National institutions are created and developed to respond to transnational accountability demands. Governmental agencies and civil society organizations receive resources through technical assistance and capacity building programs. Peter Drahos (2010), for example, shows how domestic patent offices have become part of a globally integrated network in which the offices of Europe, the United States, and Japan, and the interests of multinational companies, are central. Sometimes new national agencies are designed and even staffed by consultants from transnational institutions. Morgan (in Chapter 7) notes how national water agencies in developing countries frequently are designed and (in the case of Bolivia's water regulatory agency) staffed by consultants who work for international organizations and are seconded to national state institutions. Klug (in Chapter 6) notes how the World Health Organization (WHO) seconded an official to work with the South African Health Department. Over time, new associational communities form as "clubs" in functionally disaggregated legal areas.

These processes have implications for how state representatives and civil society organizations view themselves and their roles, as they mediate relations between transnational and national sites of governance. Transnational networks engage national policymakers within particular normative frames. They can shape elite perspectives on the appropriate role of institutions, such as markets, independent agencies, and courts. Local claims are viewed in transnational context. Through transnational patterns of interaction and practice, new conceptions of meaning are conveyed that may be gradually accepted as normal and authoritative. These conceptions can affect both the definition of particular goals and the means to further them.

These shifts in patterns of association, institutionalized through mechanisms of accountability with their accompanying normative frames, can shape the identities and subjectivities of elites and potentially (over time) of broader publics.[15] They can, in the process, affect the legal consciousness and legal culture of elites and broader publics, influencing the demands that elites and publics put on the state. This

[15] As Mead (1934) explains, individuals' sense of identity is shaped by social interaction. See also Friedman 1997 (on legal culture).

TABLE 2.2. *Explanatory factors that determine state change*

Three clusters of factors	Components within each cluster
Nature of the Transnational Legal Process and Norm	(i) Legitimacy of the Transnational Legal Processes (ii) The Clarity of the Transnational Legal Norm (iii) The Coherence of the Transnational Legal Processes
Relation of the Transnational Legal Process and the Receiving State	(i) Power asymmetries and the receiving state (ii) Role of intermediaries (iii) Ability to Harness Historic Events
Context of the Receiving State	(i) Domestic demand (ii) Domestic configurations of power (iii) Domestic institutional capacities and path dependencies (iv) Domestic cultural frames (v) Extent of change at stake

pressure can spur other dimensions of change, such as the allocation of institutional authority within the state. Once more, we see how these different dimensions of state change interact.

2. THE FACTORS EXPLAINING THE LOCATION, EXTENT, AND LIMITS OF STATE CHANGE

Transnational legal processes operate in the context of institutional path dependencies, social histories, and domestic contests over national law and policy, factors that mediate the extent of state change. The results of transnational legal processes are thus not homogeneous across countries, because they can affect different dimensions of the state within different countries. Therefore, to understand the impact of transnational legal processes on state change, we need to specify the factors that explain its location, timing, and extent. This section provides a typology of three clusters of factors that determine the impact of transnational legal processes, which are enumerated in Table 2.2. Each of these factors can be isolated for purposes of subsequent study, but the purpose here is to provide an overall framework regarding the factors that shape the timing, extent, location, and limits of state change.

The first cluster involves the transnational legal norm-making in question; the second cluster the relation of transnational legal ordering to the receiving state; and the third cluster the context of the receiving state. The case studies in Chapters 3–7 illustrate how these clusters of factors operate and interact in different fields, affecting the location, extent, timing, and limits of state change.

A. *The Nature of the Transnational Legal Norm-making: Legitimacy, Clarity, and Coherence*

These three clusters of factors can be broken down into different components, as summarized in Table 2.2 and explained below. To start with transnational legal orders, this first cluster can be disaggregated into three aspects: (1) the legitimacy of the transnational legal process that contributes to the norm's authority; (2) the clarity of the transnational legal norm; and (3) the coherence of the transnational legal norm(s) in reflection of whether different transnational legal processes complement or are in conflict with each other. Collectively, the legitimacy, clarity, and coherence of a transnational legal norm affect its impact.

1. The Relation of Transnational Legal Norm-making's Legitimacy to Its Authority

Scholars from various disciplines increasingly have engaged with the concept of legitimacy in evaluating the impacts of international law and institutions.[16] Legitimacy, as used in a sociological sense, refers to the subjective belief of actors that a rule or institution should be obeyed. Legitimacy consists of "a generalized perception or assumption that the actions of an entity are desirable, proper, or appropriate within some socially constructed system of norms, values, beliefs, and definitions" (Suchman 1995: 574). The concept of transnational law's legitimacy is thus a relational one, because it depends on whether actors regard the institutions and processes that promulgate and convey it as "rightful," and thus authoritative.[17] Where political and social struggles over regulatory norms exist, actors attempt to use law strategically to advance their aims through harnessing law's potential legitimating authority. The more that a transnational legal order and its norms are perceived to be legitimate, the more likely it will exercise normative pull.

A transnational legal order's legitimacy can be assessed along three dimensions in terms of inputs (who participates in a process), throughputs (the quality of procedural fairness and deliberation characterizing such process), and outputs (perspectives on how a process substantively responds to a problem).[18] Overall, national actors are more likely to perceive transnational legal ordering to be legitimate where they have a voice in its formulation; where the process is procedurally fair and characterized by noncoercive, reasoned argument; and where they perceive such ordering to be efficacious. In sum, the perception of the legitimacy of a transnational legal process should vary along these three dimensions of representativeness, procedural fairness,

[16] See, e.g., Bodansky 1999 and Franck 1990 (in law); Halliday 2009; Halliday & Carruthers 2009; Hurd 2007 (in international relations); and Suchman 1995 (in sociology).

[17] An institution acquires authority when it is perceived to be legitimate (Hurd 2008).

[18] Cf. Bodansky 1999 (legitimacy in terms of sources, procedures, and outcomes); Halliday & Carruthers 2009, 11; and Scharpf 1999, 2 (distinguishing input and output legitimacy).

and perceived effectiveness. We refer to "perceived effectiveness" because it is only ex ante perceptions of efficacy that shape actors' views of a legal norm's legitimacy.

Legitimation is an aspect of power, and neither legality nor legitimacy should be viewed in contradistinction to power, as in some conceptions in the legal literature. Transnational legal orders exercise power and authority through different mechanisms, which can be typologized as coercion, reciprocity, persuasion, and acculturation.[19] Stated in other terms, states and nonstate actors may adopt or otherwise adapt to transnational legal norms because they are coerced to do so, they find it to be in their self-interest through a reciprocal exchange or through being persuaded, or they are normatively induced to comply with it in light of its perceived legitimacy (Hurd 1999). Those scholars who focus on the role of sanctions highlight law's coercive aspects, but law also exercises considerable power (if not its greatest power) through normative processes in which law is accepted as legitimate because it reflects norms of proper social behavior (Tyler 1990). As Merry (2006: 4) writes, "law's power to shape society depends not on punishment alone but on becoming embedded in everyday social practices." In short, these mechanisms are ideal types, and in practice they interrelate, affect, and build upon each other.[20]

These mechanisms all depend in different ways on legitimacy. Sanctions are more likely to be effective if the relevant transnational legal order is accepted as legitimate and thus authoritative. The sanctions will thus be more difficult to resist, avoid, and counter through enlisting third-party assistance. Where transnational legal processes are perceived to be legitimate, they are also more conducive to facilitating dialogue that leads to persuasion, as well as to reciprocal exchange. Mechanisms of acculturation most directly depend on transnational legal processes' perceived legitimacy because, here, actors do not formulate their interests in relation to the legal norm.

Michael Barnett and Raymond Duvall (2005) have provided a useful framework of four conceptions of power in international governance that they label as agency, institutional, structural, and productive power.[21] Each of these conceptions applies

[19] See Ginsburg & Shaffer 2010 (discussing the links between these mechanisms with those discussed in Braithwaite & Drahos 2000 (seven mechanisms); Halliday & Osinsky, 2006 (eight mechanisms); and Goodman & Jinks 2004 (three mechanisms). There are, as noted in Chapter 1, other mechanisms that induce legal and institutional changes in states that are not directly linked to transnational legal processes, such as market competition among states. See, for example, Simmons, Dobbin, & Garrett 2008 (four mechanisms of diffusion, highlighting the roles of competition and emulation).

[20] As Hurd (2007, 40) writes, "the relationship between coercion, self-interest, and legitimacy is complex, and each is rarely found in anything like its pure, isolated form. Further, they are probably sometimes related in a patterned, systematic fashion, in that many social structures that are eventually legitimized emerged first from relations of coercion or from individual self-interest."

[21] Peter Digeser (1992, 980) summarizes these four conceptions of power as follows: "Under the first face of power the central question is, 'Who, if anyone, is exercising power?' Under the second face, 'What issues have been mobilized off the agenda and by whom?' Under the radical conception, 'Whose objective interests are being harmed?' Under the fourth face of power the critical issue is, 'What kind of subject is being produced?' "

to the assessment of transnational legal processes and their effects, and each has implications for understanding the way legitimation operates in these processes. First, from an *agency perspective* of power, actors have variable resources that affect their ability to shape and mobilize transnational legal ordering (Dahl 1957, 1968). They likewise have variable resources to deploy offers of rewards and threats of sanctions to induce third parties to comply with it. Because actors have stakes in the perception of a transnational legal norm's legitimacy, they have incentives to mobilize resources to legitimize or delegitimize transnational legal norms and processes. Powerful players, such as the United States, are typically best positioned to use transnational legal norms and processes to legitimize policies that they want, and to delegitimize those that they do not want. Yet, less powerful actors also invest in contests over law's legitimacy. Within the legal academy, critical legal studies can be viewed as an attempt to delegitimize accepted law on account of perceived structural biases.

Second, from an *institutional perspective*, transnational institutions shape the type of issues and arguments that parties may effectively raise. As Peter Bachrach and Morton Baratz (1962: 948) contend, "power is also exercised when A devotes his energies to creating or reinforcing social and political values and institutional practices that limit the scope of the political process to public consideration of only those issues which are comparatively innocuous to A." International institutions and transnational policy networks structure choices, in particular, for less powerful states (Gruber 2000). They provide frames that organize deliberation over the conceptions of problems, their diagnoses, and strategies to address them. Institutional power is more likely to be effective where institutional processes are accepted as legitimate. Actors invest in (and forum shop for) international institutions, in part, because of the legitimation they can provide.

Third, from a *structural perspective*, transnational legal ordering materially affects how actors calculate the costs and benefits of alternative policies, shaping actors' perceptions of the worth of pursuing or even conceiving of alternatives (Lukes 1974). In this way, they can affect actor's understandings of their interests. Fourth, from a *productive (or constitutive) perspective*, social discourse and knowledge systems can shape actors' subjective understandings of their identities and their capacities (Foucault 1984; Guizzini 2000). Transnational legal ordering propagates certain conceptions of identity and choice with the result that public and private stakeholders are more likely to accept a given order as normal and inevitable. Although these latter conceptions of power do not focus on actors, those able to benefit from these forms of power, through the legitimation that transnational legal norms can provide, are in privileged positions.

These latter conceptions of power find their reflections in the transnational legal process theories of Harold Koh, Ryan Goodman, and Derek Jinks within the legal academy. Koh (1998: 642) contends that "[r]epeated participation in the transnational legal process . . . helps to reconstruct the national interests of the participating nations." He sees "transnational legal process" as "seeking to shape and transform personal identity" so that political elites and broader societies "internalize" international law norms.[22] Similarly, Goodman and Jinks (2012) analyze acculturation processes through which states are socialized without reflecting if the norms they adopt are in their interests. Although Koh, Goodman, and Jinks are generally positive in their assessments of these processes, one does not need to assume a normative stance to accept their power and influence. For our purposes, where transnational legal processes are accepted as legitimate, they are more likely to shape actors' interests and identities, and thus have transformative effects.

The studies in this book commonly highlight how the power of a transnational legal norm's perceived legitimacy exercises influence in affecting domestic legal change, and how coercion is less successful when a legal norm's legitimacy is challenged. International financial institutions, for example, were successful in using their coercive financial leverage during the Asian financial crisis to press Indonesia to enact bankruptcy law reforms, as shown in Halliday's study (in Chapter 4). However, these formal changes were not implemented in a way that changed outcomes in the directions or degree that the IMF anticipated. In contrast, the United Nations Commission on International Trade Law (UNCITRAL) has exercised much greater authority in national bankruptcy law reform efforts because the processes of representative deliberation, which gave rise to its "model rules" and "legislative guides," are deemed more legitimate. The national actors who participate in the UNCITRAL process take home models that they had a voice in drafting and approving, models that can become part of a national agenda to enhance financial stability and economic development. Similarly, Kim and Boyle's study (in Chapter 5) shows how the World Bank's structural adjustment policies initially pressed developing countries to shift toward requiring user fees for primary education (with seventy-seven of seventy-nine countries studied for a World Bank report having adopted some type of user fee for primary education by 2000). However, these efforts were rebuked following nongovernmental actors' challenges to their legitimacy, which pressed the Bank to revise its policies. As Kim and Boyle write, "[by] 2001, the World Bank quietly indicated to countries that it did not support user fees for education. . . . By 2006, the World Bank was considered the leading global advocate for greater public spending on education."

2. Variation in Transnational Law's Hard and Soft Law Nature and the Coherence of Transnational Legal Ordering

The impact of transnational legal ordering varies in terms of different features that affect its authority. Variations in the features of transnational legal norms have

[22] Koh 1998, 629. Cf. Hurd 2007, 388 ("the operative process of legitimation is the internalization by the actor of an external standard. Internalization takes place within the actor's sense of its own interests and is partly constituted by a force outside itself, that is, by the standards, laws, rules and norms present in the community"); and Koh 1997.

been usefully conceptualized in terms of hard and soft law, which contrast across the dimensions of obligation, precision, and delegation. Hard law "refers to legally binding obligations that are precise (or can be made precise through adjudication or the issuance of detailed regulations) and that delegate authority for interpreting and implementing the law" (Abbott & Snidal 2000: 421–22). Soft law, in contrast to hard law, refers to legal arrangements that are weaker along one or more of these three dimensions. Variations along these dimensions can affect a legal norm's clarity. Beth Simmons (2009: 12), for example, observes how "[n]ormative as well as rational theorists have explored the quality of law precision as an influence on compliance," citing the work of legal scholar Thomas Franck from a normative perspective and of political scientist James Morrow from a rationalist one. Where a transnational legal norm is clearer and less ambiguous, there is less room for significant variation at the domestic level when it is formally adopted.[23] Similarly, where a transnational legal norm is elaborated over time through delegated dispute settlement or through different forms of delegated monitoring, peer review, and reporting, these processes can enhance the legal norm's clarity.[24] It is striking, for example, how competition law in South Africa, for which there are transnational soft law principles but no binding international law obligations, has developed in a more indigenous manner than patent law, which is subject to the relatively precise and binding rules of the Trade-Related Aspects of Intellectual Property Rights (TRIPS) Agreement of the WTO. Although precise legal norms may, in some cases, be ignored or evaded, and vague legal norms can be applied in similar ways, clearer legal norms generally provide less ambiguous signals regarding the legal change sought, and thus provide better tools to local actors at the stage of domestic implementation of the legal norm.[25] Overall, the more that a transnational legal norm is clear, binding, and its meaning is interpreted, elaborated, and applied by a third party regarding particular contexts, the more compelling its signal should be to states and other constituencies. Actors promote these features to enhance the impact of a transnational legal norm.

Transnational legal processes, however, can also complement or conflict with each other, affecting their coherence.[26] Different transnational legal orders, such as

[23] In an experimental study of the impact of legal imprecision on compliance, Yuval Feldman and Dorion Teichman (2009) find that people are less likely to comply in situations where uncertainty stems from imprecision than from imperfect enforcement.

[24] See Sandholtz & Sweet 2004 (on dynamic processes of elaboration of international law over time).

[25] For an example of the problems for implementation of vague transnational environmental law rules, see, e.g., Talitman, Tal, & Brenner 2003. Nonetheless, the link between rule precision and legal certainty is a debated one in a world of complexity, rapid change, and high economic stakes where legal entrepreneurs can manipulate bright line rules to evade broader policy goals captured in principles (Braithwaite 2002). Franck (1990) also notes that bright line rules may sometimes be less important than principles that accommodate diverse situational contexts.

[26] See, e.g., International Law Commission 2006; Raustiala & Victor 2004, 279; Shaffer & Pollack 2010. Franck (1990, chapter 6) also discusses coherence in his study of the power of international law's legitimacy, but he largely focuses on coherence in the application of a single rule. The rise of the

a trade-oriented one and a human rights-oriented one, can address a single regulatory question. Where they complement each other, their leverage can increase. Where they conflict, transnational legal norms may be in tension, or even contradictory, affecting their overall coherence. In this latter case, states and constituencies within them could have greater policy discretion in relation to a particular transnational legal process. In other words, even where a transnational legal norm is precise and obligatory by its terms, if it is in significant tension with another transnational legal norm, domestic actors can more easily find means to evade it. Conflicts among transnational legal processes often reflect political struggles both among and within states. Transnational and domestic struggles can become intermeshed, as different local actors view competing international organizations and transnational networks as their allies.

Chapters 3–7 illustrate the processes of complementarity, conflict, and consolidation of transnational legal norms over time in different domains, affecting their clarity and coherence. The legal norms promoted by the FATF became increasingly precise over time, and eventually became reflected in binding UN conventions, as Machado illustrates in Chapter 3. UNCITRAL built on the recommendations and guidelines of the international financial institutions for national bankruptcy law when it created a Legislative Guide and Model Law that were adopted by its members, as Halliday shows in Chapter 4. In contrast, the study of Kim and Boyle (in Chapter 5) illustrates how two transnational legal orders advocated different approaches toward user fees in primary education, but one of those (the UN human rights regime) prevailed over the other (the international financial institutions' structural adjustment policies promoted through financing conditionalities). In Klug's work (Chapter 6), different transnational legal orders again provided conflicting frames regarding the interaction of intellectual property and public health protection. This time, however, the tensions between these transnational legal orders remain. Even though the WTO TRIPS Agreement's provisions are binding, relatively precise, and subject to third-party dispute settlement, activists in South Africa were able to harness international human rights and transnational competition law norms against demands for pharmaceutical patent protection. They were thus able to counter somewhat the pressure for higher pharmaceutical prices through monopoly patent rights in the context of struggles over access to medicines.

B. *The Relation of the Transnational Legal Process to the Receiving State*

The second cluster of factors affecting a transnational legal norm's impact involves the relation of the transnational legal process to the receiving state. We can look at this relationship from a top-down perspective in terms of structure, and a bottom-up

WTO, and the literature on the challenges posed by the fragmentation of international law, have developed since his study.

one in terms of agents and intermediaries. Macrosociological theories, such as world systems theory and world polity theory, take a top-down approach, focusing respectively on material and ideological power. World systems theory has a materialist orientation in which structural power, whether exercised by dominant states or transnational capital, is the primary mediator of international relations, and in which such power is determined by a division of production between "core" and "peripheral" states (Robinson 2001; Wallerstein 2004). World polity theory, in contrast, has a normative-ideological orientation, and "stresses the embeddedness of nation-states in a wider world cultural context of meaning and models" (Kim & Boyle, Chapter 5). Microsociolegal studies address the patterns of interaction between local and global actors, focusing on the role of intermediaries. They help us to "map the middle," in Merry's phrase (2006), to understand the mechanisms and dynamics of state change.

1. Power Asymmetries and the Receiving State

Structural power asymmetries have long driven transnational flows of legal norms, as reflected in Roman, Napoleonic, and colonial conquests.[27] The United States and Europe are the major producers of transnational legal norms today, and they have the means at their disposal to circulate them and induce their adoption globally. They diffuse regulatory approaches through the strength of their know-how and experience, coupled with technical assistance, capacity building programs, and other inducements. They control the budgets of the IMF and World Bank, affecting their policy prescriptions. Their national regulations and the private standards adopted by their private sectors set requirements for products around the world simply because of the economic importance of their markets (Snyder 2002).

Structural power asymmetries create opportunities for transnational actors to use leverage, such as economic coercion, in reshaping institutions and legal norms in target states. Particular events, such as financial crises, enhance their ability to do so. Powerful states are often behind these transnational processes, and they work through and in conjunction with international and transnational institutions. Only states in structurally weaker positions are subjected to mechanisms of economic coercion. The international financial organizations exercised much more leverage over Indonesia during the Asian financial crisis than they did over Korea, and they exercised no leverage over China, as shown in Halliday's study in Chapter 4. They have often exercised leverage over developing countries in shaping social policies, such as educational policy as depicted in the study by Kim and Boyle in Chapter 5. Economic coercion is most tempting to use when regulation has asymmetric financial implications, benefitting some countries at the expense of others. Such is the case with intellectual property regulation, as Klug's study (Chapter 6)

[27] Cf. Whitman 2009 (stressing the missionary influence in Christianity); and Mattei & Nader 2008 (stressing material interests).

shows regarding the US government's attempt to threaten South Africa with trade sanctions, including the withdrawal of tariff preferences and the cutting off of foreign aid, which it hoped to legitimize in part by the claim that South Africa was in violation of WTO legal requirements.

The studies in this book, nonetheless, address the limits of the use of coercion, calling into question how much real transformation occurs at the implementation stage where only coercive mechanisms are used. Coercive measures can de-legitimate a transnational legal process because they generate resentment. Coercive measures may initially be successful in inducing symbolic legal change (in terms of legal enactments), but ultimately be thwarted at the stage of actual implementation – the law-in-action. The case studies highlight both the use of coercive measures and their limits. Indonesia made significant changes to its bankruptcy law in response to IMF conditions during the Asian financial crisis, but implementation was often foiled in practice, as Halliday shows (in Chapter 4 and Halliday & Carruthers 2009). Kim and Boyle (in Chapter 5) similarly show the limits of structural adjustment conditionalities on education policy in developing countries, and Klug explains the eventual withdrawal of US legal challenges against South Africa regarding its patent law (in Chapter 6; and Klug 2008).

2. The Role of Intermediaries

Second, for transnational legal processes to be effective, they require intermediaries who are cognizant of both the processes of transnational lawmaking and national settings. Intermediaries are the carriers, conduits, and points of entry for the circulation of transnational legal norms.[28] They can operate at the national or subnational levels, and consist of public or private actors, thus offering (to borrow from Judith Resnik) multiple "ports of entry" for transnational legal norms.[29] They help to diagnose national situations, monitor national developments and responses, and translate, adapt, and appropriate transnational legal norms for local contexts. Through their links with international institutions and transnational networks, they form part of transnational epistemic communities. They play central roles across areas of law, from human rights law to business regulation. Regarding human rights, Merry (2006: 1) highlights "the role of activists who serve as intermediaries between different sets of cultural understandings of gender, violence, and justice." On business law, Kuk Woon-Lee (2007: 245) notes how, in the four largest Korean law firms, three-quarters of the lawyers who passed the bar between 1980 and 1990 had studied abroad, primarily in the United States. Intermediaries, in the words of

[28] Transnational legal norms depend on "the international circulation of experts and knowledge between the North and the South" (Garth & Dezalay 2009, 123).

[29] Resnik 2006 (on ports of entry in federalist systems); Resnik, Civin, & Frueh 2008 (discussing the role of Transnational Organizations of Government Actors, or TOGAs); Sassen 2007, 190–212.

Bryant Garth and Yves Dezalay (2010 :113), are "essential to produce the credibility and legitimacy of these transnational norms."[30]

The impacts of transnational legal processes are, in part, a function of the positions of intermediaries. Bruce Carruthers and Terence Halliday (2006: 529–32) have typologized intermediaries in terms of their competencies, power, and loyalty. Intermediaries may, for example, have greater competence in legal or economic expertise, have variable power to translate international legal scripts into national contexts, and have variable loyalties to actors at the national and international levels. These intermediaries include cosmopolitan government representatives, professional service providers, academics, think tank policy analysts, NGOs, and social movement leaders. Where a country is culturally distant from the transnational legal norm, local intermediaries tend to be fewer and more difficult to locate, rendering implementation of the norm more challenging (Carruthers & Halliday 2006: 529).

Local intermediaries can be empowered by transnational legal processes so that they have a professional stake in them. Through their national and international connections, they are able to inform themselves of developments both at home and abroad, which provides them with informational advantages. International organizations depend on them to convey transnational legal norms to work in local settings, bridging cultural divides and, where necessary, indigenizing transnational norms. National governments and organizations rely on them to present national positions in international fora and within transnational networks. When these intermediaries have a stake in the national adoption of transnational legal norms, they become important allies in attempts to embed them, whether the norms are human rights or business ones.

The studies in this book depict the key roles played by intermediaries. National intermediaries, respectively, played key roles in the adoption, adaptation, and application of transnational bankruptcy, financial transparency, and competition law norms, as shown in the chapters by Halliday, Machado, and Klug. Kim and Boyle also show statistically the relation between the number of transnational NGOs operating in countries and their adoption of international human rights obligations to provide universal primary education, controlling for other factors.

3. Harnessing Historic Events

Particular historic events create opportunities where actors can capitalize to convey transnational legal norms to change domestic law and institutions. Events such as

[30] Dezalay and Garth (2002b, 34) refer to them as brokers and double agents, noting how elites "use international credentials, expertise and connections to build capital that they can reinvest in domestic public arenas."

the fall of the Berlin Wall and the major debt and financial crises striking Latin America and Asia provide such openings. Crises create uncertainty that destabilizes background assumptions and perceptions of interest regarding legal and institutional change. As John Campbell (2004: 21) writes, historic events can lead to processes of change involving "punctuated equilibria," where "a crisis upset[s] the institutional equilibrium and precipitate[s] a search for a new . . . order that, once institutionalized, usher[s] in a new period of institutional equilibrium."[31]

Each of the studies in this book grapples with transnational legal processes within their historic contexts. The Asian financial crisis created openings for transnational actors to press Asian states to restructure their bankruptcy laws and institutions, as demonstrated by Halliday (in Chapter 4). The development and conveyance of a "transactional model" for the provision of municipal water services reflected a shift in the 1990s toward neoliberal policies and the reappraisal of economic development models, following the fall of the Berlin Wall, as noted by Morgan (in Chapter 7). As Machado shows (in Chapter 3), the terrorist attacks of September 11, 2001 on the World Trade Center catalyzed new developments before the Financial Action Task Force and the United Nations through pressure from the United States. These studies each illustrate how transnational legal processes harness and are constrained by historic contexts.

C. *The Domestic Context: Domestic Demands, Domestic Struggles, and the Extent of Change at Stake*

Although intermediaries are necessary, and the legitimacy, clarity, and coherence of transnational legal ordering are important, they are not sufficient. To understand transnational legal ordering and state change, the study of domestic factors remains central. Arguably, the most important determinant of state change is the affinity of the transnational legal reform efforts with the demands and discursive frames of domestic constituencies and elites in light of domestic configurations of power and the extent of change at stake. This third cluster of factors involves domestic demand, domestic political struggles, domestic institutional capacities and legacies, and domestic cultural frames. Together, these factors shape how transnational legal norms are received and implemented in practice, affecting the extent of state transformation. Sometimes they lead to the rejection of transnational law, sometimes to significant institutional and legal change, and sometimes to an appropriation for purposes initially not considered.[32]

First, transnational legal norms are more likely to be successfully implemented where there is *local demand* for them. Sometimes domestic elites will support their adoption because the elites believe that legal reforms will spur foreign direct

[31] Campbell 2004, 21 (citing the work of Neil Fligstein). See also Hall 1993.

[32] As Moore (1974, 723) writes, "the social arrangements are often effectively stronger than the new laws."

investment and promote economic growth, possibly in relation to interstate competition.[33] Sometimes professionals or commercial interests promote them because reforms enhance their career and business prospects (Dezalay & Garth 2010). Sometimes domestic activists support them as leverage against current government or private practices (Klug, Chapter 6).

Second, transnational legal processes ultimately meet *configurations of power* within national political contexts. Legal and institutional change advocated by international organizations and transnational networks that seem rather technical, such as over bankruptcy law, can upset careers and power configurations in domestic orders, creating incentives for factions within governing elites and affected domestic constituencies to thwart the reform efforts. Such transnational legal reform efforts are difficult to implement because they can represent "the restructuring of the state itself" (Halliday, Chapter 4). As Dezalay and Garth (2002b: 5) write, the "success of import is inevitably tied to domestic palace wars and to the international competition to export state expertises." Transnational legal processes will be most successful if they are useful to national actors as tools in these political contests.

Third, *institutional path dependencies and capacities* place constraints on national change.[34] In many cases, countries, especially poorer countries, lack the institutional capacities to carry out transnational legal prescriptions. In other cases, the reception of transnational legal processes is mediated through domestic institutional structures that have their own interests and their own long-standing ways. Institutionalized practices do not change without sustained pressure. Dezalay and Garth (2002b: 14) thus conclude, "the results of particular exports of state expertises depend on the extent to which there are structural homologies in the respective fields of the importers and exporters."

Fourth, transnational legal norms are more likely to have an impact if they resonate with local norms. Discursive frames that are consonant with *prevailing cultural and institutional norms and practices* are most likely to be accepted as legitimate within a domestic setting, whether the norms comprise human rights, business, or regulatory norms.[35] Activists thus construct frames that will appeal in national contexts, such as the use of human rights frames as opposed to feminist frames in challenging discrimination against women (Keck & Sikkink 1998; Merry 2006).

[33] See, e.g., Berkowitz, Pistor, & Richard 2003; Halliday & Carruthers 2009, 339; Simmons, Dobbins, & Garrett (2008).

[34] See Campbell 2004, 28–9, 118 (stressing the role of institutional path dependencies); Peerenboom 2006, 833 ("Even when there is no ideological barrier to transplantation, local institutions may lack the institutional capacity to implement reforms"); Fourcade-Gourinchas & Babb 2002 (providing a historical institutionalist account of variation in the reception of neoliberalism in four countries).

[35] See Berkowitz, Pistor, & Richard 2003, 174 ("legal intermediaries . . . can be more effective when they are working with a formal law which is broadly compatible with the preexisting order, or which has been adapted to match demand"). Cf. Watson 1974; and Teubner 1998 ("[l]egal irritants cannot be domesticated; they are not transformed from something alien into something familiar, not adapted to a new cultural context, rather they will unleash an evolutionary dynamic in which the external rule's meaning will be reconstructed and the internal context will undergo fundamental change").

Where discursive frames and policy prescriptions resonate in the domestic setting, local actors can more effectively harness the transnational legal norm to further their goals. Where the distance between the transnational legal regime and the local cultural and institutional context is considerable and the extent of change at stake great, then transnational legal processes are less likely to have a transformative impact.

Local populations have their own interests and ideas and do not simply accept and reject transnational legal norms. They also exercise agency in translating, reshaping, and appropriating transnational legal norms for their own uses in their own contexts, shaping their own histories.[36] The norms may often be transformed for purposes that were not contemplated by their transnational promoters. Klug (in Chapter 6) illustrates this point regarding the use of competition law in South Africa.

> While the new competition law in South Africa is modeled on European Union, United Kingdom and Canadian statutes, and draws on legal concepts developed in the United States, it also represents a hybridization of global norms and rules designed both to accommodate international restraints as well as take advantage of the opportunities these norms and rules provide to pursue particular national goals that are peculiar to the history and social context of South Africa.

In Klug's case, local authorities use competition law norms developed in the United States to rein in pharmaceutical prices charged by US-owned pharmaceutical companies, as well as to empower new black ownership of capital.[37] Transnational legal processes do not simply convey legal requirements that are internalized without reflection of domestic interests and domestic stakes. They rather provide tools that national actors use to advance particular policies. In this way, transnational legal norms cross-pollinate and hybridize.

The studies in this book each focus on the role of domestic factors in explaining the location, extent, timing, and limits of state change. On the one hand, they address the power of local actors to thwart and foil transnationally promoted legal change at the implementation stage. Weak actors at the level of international negotiations and domestic ratification can become strong in foiling actual implementation of transnational prescriptions. Indonesia may have been more easily subject to economic coercion to carry out bankruptcy reforms advocated by international

[36] Campbell uses the concepts of "bricolage" and "translation." Campbell 2004, 71, 80 ("the concept of bricolage focuses our attention on a creative process in which actors make decisions about how to combine the institutional elements at their disposal"). As Merry (2006, 3) writes regarding the issue of women's rights, local actors "appropriate, translate, and remake transnational discourses into the vernacular," that is, into terms that resonate in local settings. She stresses "a process of appropriation rather than imposition." See also Dezalay & Garth 2002b, 6 (finding "[i]nternationally generated imports success only where the local situation allows them to be nationalized – made part of indigenous structures and practices. Local histories determine what can be assimilated into local settings and how what is assimilated will affect long-standing local practices").

[37] As Klug elsewhere writes, "South African actors drew on foreign sources of legitimacy to try to support their own points of view in the process" (Klug 2002, 276). See also Hirsch 2005 (on competition law and the black economic empowerment program).

TABLE 2.3. *Transnational legal orders (TLOs) and the synchronicity of the domestic context*

	HIGH (TLO coherence)	LOW (TLO coherence)
HIGH (Synchronicity of domestic demand)	Corporate bankruptcy (Korea, China); Money laundering (Brazil); Competition law (South Africa)	Municipal water services regulation (Chile)
LOW (Synchronicity of domestic demand)	Corporate bankruptcy (Indonesia); Money laundering (Argentina); TRIPS and patents (South Africa)	Municipal water services regulation (Bolivia; Argentina)

TRIPS, Trade-Related Aspects of Intellectual Property Rights.

financial institutions than Korea and China, but these changes were often thwarted at the implementation stage, as illustrated in Halliday's work (Chapter 4). Similarly, Latin American social movements have successfully resisted municipal water service reforms in weak states such as Bolivia, as Morgan documents (in Chapter 7). Klug (in Chapter 6) addresses the partial success of NGOs in the fight over patent protection and access to medicines in South Africa.

Yet, the studies also address where transnational legal processes help precipitate significant institutional and legal developments within countries. In Brazil, a government concerned over organized crime used the transnational recommendations of the FATF to tighten banking regulations in order to accomplish domestic goals to combat organized crime and corruption, as Machado shows (in Chapter 3). The government was less interested in US and European concerns over terrorist networks, which had spurred an intensification of FATF activity. In contrast, financial reform efforts were less successful in Argentina because no domestic demand was mobilized. Similarly, the three Latin American countries studied by Morgan (in Chapter 7) each "partially ceded [regulatory control] to semi-independent regulatory institutions that strongly resemble the institutional recommendations of the transnational consensus" for water services regulation. However, analysis of "the implementation dynamics of these institutions . . . reveals significant national differences." Chile, for example, implemented a transactional model promoted by transnational actors, but it staged its urban water reforms in reflection of Chilean government perceptions of national priorities. Transnational models likewise provided templates for China in its bankruptcy reform efforts studied by Halliday (in Chapter 4), but China adopted them at its own pace following extensive internal debate.

The interaction of the relative coherence of a transnational legal order (TLO) and the degree of synchronicity of domestic demand for the legal changes envisaged can be mapped as shown in Table 2.3, which plots the different subject areas and countries covered in this book.

TABLE 2.4. *Dynamic cycles of recursive change*[38]

Flow a: National regulatory models are conveyed to, and appropriated by, international and transnational institutions and networks giving rise to transnational legal norms.
Flow b: Transnational legal norms are conveyed to receiving states, but often encounter resistance at the stage of enactment or implementation.
Flow c: National resistance spurs a new transnational politics that triggers a reevaluation and modification of the transnational legal norm.
Flow d: A modified transnational legal norm is conveyed to national institutions and processes

3. THE RECURSIVITY OF THE TRANSNATIONAL LEGAL PROCESS

Transnational legal processes are dynamic and recursive, involving the interaction between national and transnational law and policymaking. National law often provides the models that are then exported to other nations through transnational legal processes. Even when these models become accepted within international and transnational institutions, their adoption is often resisted within countries at the stage of implementation, which can trigger reassessments of the transnational legal norm. This resistance can spur new counter-politics of transnational coordination, organization, and lawmaking, leading to competitive transnational legal processes. Table 2.4 provides a summary of a simplified dynamic cycle of recursivity between national and transnational lawmaking processes.

This depiction is a stylized one, as the processes are multifold and multidirectional, both top-down and bottom-up, composed of competition and conflict as frequently as coordination and cooperation, and involving ongoing interaction between national and transnational legal norms. The intensity of this interaction varies in light of the degree of normative settlement (if any) that is reached. A range of actors are involved, including key intermediaries serving as conduits and conveyors of transnational and national legal norms, who use a range of mechanisms, such as coercion, persuasion, reciprocal bargaining, and acculturation, discussed above.

To break down the processes' complexity, we can think of it, for heuristic purposes, in terms of stages. First, a domestic policy export often provides a model for a transnational legal order so that many transnational legal norms represent globalized (or transnationalized) localisms (Santos 2003). The United States and the European Union most frequently provide the models (Braithwaite & Drahos 2000). When their models are not promoted through transnational legal orders, US and European resistance to transnational legal prescriptions is often transparent. Yet, their prominent role in providing models tends to be overlooked in much of traditional international law scholarship that focuses on the texts of international law. For example, US

[38] For an expanded figure summarizing the exogenous and endogenous factors that drive recursive processes, see Halliday & Carruthers 2009.

and European intellectual property law became the basis for the WTO TRIPS Agreement, their competition law norms the basis for the International Competition Network's principles and recommended practices, their anti–money laundering legal prescriptions the basis for the FATF's recommendations, and their bankruptcy law the basis for the UNCITRAL Model Law and Legislative Guide. These national models are disseminated through transnational legal processes, including through technical assistance, capacity building, benchmarking, monitoring, and enforcement measures. Transnational legal processes help to legitimize these legal exports.

Second, however, these transnational legal norms and institutional prescriptions often encounter resistance when the models are implemented in receiving states. Powerful actors may prevail in international negotiations as well as in the domestic enactment of transnational legal norms. Yet, actors who are weak (or unrepresented), whether in international negotiating fora or before executives and legislatures, can be powerful at the stage of actual implementation, as Halliday discusses in Chapter 4 (see also Halliday & Carruthers 2007). Such resistance to transnational legal norms can trigger reassessments of transnational strategies, as well as of the norms themselves. Domestic implementation challenges send signals to international organizations over what legal norms will be accepted and what rejected. Both positive and negative signals flowing from the national to the transnational can compel the latter to reassess the appropriateness of the transnational legal norm, triggering further iterations of transnational lawmaking.

Third, national resistance to the implementation of transnational legal norms can spur a new politics that catalyzes new transnational organizing and lawmaking. Transnational pressures to apply neoliberal regulatory models, for example, can incite the creation of new political coalitions to advance social welfare and human rights concerns, as Klug shows regarding access to medicines (in Chapter 6), Morgan regarding municipal water services (in Chapter 7), and Kim and Boyle regarding primary education (in Chapter 5). Although international and transnational institutions tend to reflect the interests of the dominant powers, developing countries and activist groups can also influence transnational legal ordering through their choice among international and transnational institutions in a fragmented international system (Helfer 2004). They often do so to create policy space for themselves.

As a result, many cycles of lawmaking may occur as international and transnational institutions find that carefully crafted transnational legal norms are unacceptable or unworkable in national regulatory settings. International and transnational institutions are thus pressed to reassess the norms and institutional models that they promote, as well as the mechanisms that they use to diffuse them. Many iterations of transnational legal norms may be produced until some settlement is reached, including tacit agreement to live and let live. Nonetheless, as states are transformed along the dimensions we have discussed, and as intermediaries are empowered, these state changes and intermediaries can facilitate the conveyance and appropriation of the transnational legal norm over time, potentially leading to a greater embeddedness of the transnational legal order. That settlement, depending on one's politics, may be progressive or regressive.

Each of the studies captures these processes, but let us turn to Halliday's work to provide a brief example. Halliday (in Chapter 4, and in Halliday & Carruthers 2009) theorizes the following four mechanisms that drive recursivity: (1) the indeterminacy of law; (2) contradictions introduced into the law; (3) diagnostic struggles over how the problems are construed to be resolved through law; and (4) "actor mismatch." Actor mismatch occurs when those actors who wield power in the domestic implementation of transnational legal norms are not represented at the international negotiation stage. If their interests are not taken into account, the resulting agreement is less likely to be implemented effectively, potentially triggering a new recursive cycle. Similarly, if domestic actors integral to implementation of a transnational legal norm are not represented in domestic lawmaking, they will be less invested in the law's implementation. In Halliday and Carruthers' study of bankruptcy law, international institutions such as the IMF, World Bank, and regional development banks looked predominantly to US and UK national models in devising international bankruptcy law norms in light of a series of financial crises that raised concerns of a risk of global financial contagion. These financial institutions peddled their bankruptcy law reform models to states in East Asia, using different mechanisms, ranging from coercion to persuasion to modeling, in light of the situation of the receiving state and the availability of intermediaries. These bankruptcy law reform prescriptions, however, were often successfully resisted by actors within the receiving states, even when they were actually enacted into domestic law, as in Indonesia, because local actors who were not represented in the international and national enactment processes retained power at the implementation stage. This resistance led to the reformulation of prescriptions at the international level, with legal norm-making power shifting from the international financial institutions to UNCITRAL, an organization in which developing countries were better represented, and with the models themselves offering greater flexibility while retaining precision regarding alternatives.

In sum, transnational legal norms and institutional models are negotiated over time as part of dynamic, multidirectional, transnational legal processes. The studies in this book illustrate when and why transnational legal norms are resisted, adapted, and appropriated. They do so through the empirical study of legal and institutional change in countries varying in their relation to centers of global political and economic power. Many of these countries are quite distal from these centers, but their politics nonetheless can trigger reassessments of transnational legal norms.

3

Similar in Their Differences

Transnational Legal Processes Addressing Money Laundering in Brazil and Argentina

Maíra Rocha Machado

A decade ago Brazil and Argentina were invited to join the Financial Action Task Force (FATF), which previously was a select club of Organization for Economic Co-operation and Development (OECD) countries. At that time, the two countries shared very similar positions regarding foreign interests in the implementation of anti–money laundering norms and were both taking the first steps toward compliance with international standards. Almost ten years later, Brazil is the first Latin American country to assume the presidency of FATF, and Argentina is facing one of the worst evaluations for a FATF member country. These different trajectories raise questions on the role played by membership in transnational legal processes. Relying on the comparison of these processes in Brazil and Argentina, this chapter contends that membership in international standard-setting bodies has only limited implications for state change. Nevertheless, membership has been dominating the debates regarding the legitimacy of the transnational legal order to address money laundering.

This chapter argues that full membership as a guarantee of representation (input legitimacy) and participation in the decision-making process (throughput legitimacy) is not sufficiently decisive to convey state change. Rather, such a focus tends to disguise the asymmetries of power among the members, and the minor contribution of some of them, such as Brazil and Argentina, to the reevaluation and modification of transnational legal norms. Therefore, this chapter downplays the "members vs. nonmembers" dichotomy to make other distinctions visible within FATF membership, such as north-south, or developed countries and developing countries. Despite the different indicators each of these dichotomies addresses, this chapter suggests that the study of Brazil and Argentina sheds light on other aspects of legitimacy in transnational legal processes other than formal representativeness (or input legitimacy).

This chapter also addresses the debate on the output legitimacy (i.e., the effectiveness) of transnational legal orders addressing crime and punishment. The output legitimacy of the anti–money laundering order has, on the one hand, been taken for granted and, on the other hand, been an issue of great concern for scholars seeking to identify how effectiveness should be assessed and measured. In assessing the effectiveness of transnational legal orders, the features of the enforcement system of this transnational legal order are at the core of the debate. This chapter contends that the transnational legal order to address money laundering is built on two legal fields: criminal law and the administrative law for finance. Both fields are used to affect behavior, even if sometimes involving different targets (individuals, corporations, and law enforcement agencies) and strategies. Criminal law, as a "closed field," focuses on individuals' imprisonment (Delmas Marty 2004a: 33; Pires 2001, 2008),[1] whereas administrative law for finance tends to rely on reputation and market sanctions, monitoring processes, and a range of regulatory techniques (Brummer 2011: 307).

During the past two decades, money laundering has become an issue addressed by most of the international financial bodies. Chris Brummer (2011: 273) identifies a "regulatory division of labor" in international financial law "through which authorities across a spectrum of domestic and international institutions interact with one another both cooperatively and competitively to promulgate global rules and standards." From the financial administrative law perspective, this dynamic accurately describes the transnational legal order addressing money laundering. As this chapter shows, financial intelligence units (FIUs) centralize national regulatory efforts, devise rules locally, implement legislative products, and represent the country before international standard-setting bodies. At the same time, the FATF shapes the functions of "interagency forums," and monitors and evaluates compliance. Observing the same transnational legal processes through the criminal law lens, another set of institutions, concerns, and discourses has been mobilized. The United Nations – its General Assembly, Security Council, and Specialized Offices – as well as transnational cooperation and security policies orbit around the traditional national criminal law triad of police-courts-prison.

This chapter focuses on the bordering issues – or to employ the inspiring formulation by Georg Simmel (1994: 5) – on the *bridges* between these two legal fields. It aims to shed light on the way transnational legal norms are constructing and combining legal mechanisms and ideas that are commonly associated with *only one* of the two legal fields. Focusing on the bridges draws our attention to the flows across the two banks of the river. This chapter identifies several connections between the criminal

[1] Delmas Marty and Pires introduce the concept of "modern penal rationality" to draw our attention to the system of ideas that the modern theories of punishment emphasize (retribution, deterrence, and rehabilitation in prison), which leads to the conceptual exclusion of sanctions and solutions provided by other branches of law. See also Machado (2011: 684–8).

and administrative law fields, and suggests that the flow from the criminal law to the administrative law field has been more visible and intense than the other way around. As this chapter shows, the anti–money laundering order provides conceptual and institutional bridges between the two fields. Our interest in the bridges between the criminal and financial fields contributes to narrowing the issues discussed in this chapter. Accordingly, several interesting topics arising both from criminal law (e.g., the predicate offenses, *mens rea*, and the burden of proof) and financial law (e.g., the professional and economic sectors committed to anti–money laundering rules, the role played by the G-20, and the cooperation and competition among financial institutions) will not be addressed.

The study presented in this chapter relies on public documents and in-depth interviews conducted from 2007 to 2010 with public officials working on behalf of governments and international organizations.[2] The reports produced by the bodies and institutions that take part in the transnational legal processes have been reviewed, and the major newspapers in both countries searched to understand the terms through which the transnational legal processes informed the local audience.

These two Latin America countries were chosen for two primary reasons. First, the literature discussing the reception and implementation of anti–money laundering norms in nondeveloped countries is scarce. There are studies that are not devoted to Latin America in particular,[3] or when Latin American countries are included, the studies focus on the comparison among a wide range of countries in a particular area, but without the same detail or focus.[4] Outside the money laundering domain, there are interesting studies comparing Brazil and Argentina (and sometimes other Latin American countries) in a transnational context from a historical, sociological, or economic perspective, but they do not address the conveyance and development of money laundering norms.[5] These earlier studies nonetheless have contributed to

[2] More specifically, 12 interviews were conducted in Brasilia, Rio de Janeiro, Buenos Aires, Paris, and Vienna. The research also makes the most of several informal talks with public and private actors who, for different reasons, refused the formalities of the interviewing process. Some of the interviews were conducted again, by phone, in January 2010 to update and explore recent events, such as the 2010 FATF Report of Brazil and Argentina. Audio files are in the author's possession.

[3] See, for example, Gathii (2010) (focusing on Sub-Saharan Africa), Wessel (2007) (presenting a case study on the Cayman Island), Sharman (2008) (focusing on Barbados, Mauritius, and Vanuatu), and Tang and Ai (2010) (discussing the phenomenon of "adopt but not enforce" in several "transition countries" from East Europe and Central Asia).

[4] See, for example, Jorge (2010) (comparing the reports of the mutual evaluation processes conducted by FATF or regional bodies in ninety-five countries) and Passas (2009) (comparing the reports from fourteen countries concerning, specifically, terrorism financing).

[5] For example, Fausto & Devoto (2004) (an essay on comparative history of Brazil and Argentina from 1850 to 2002); Dezalay & Garth (2002b) (on the internationalization of human rights and business law and institutions in Argentina, Brazil, Chile, and Mexico from the 1960s to 2000), Salama (2009)

understanding and interpreting the results of the comparison between Brazil and Argentina.

Second, the two countries selected in this chapter were similarly diagnosed in terms of the "risk of experiencing money laundering" and, therefore, received the same level of interest from powerful countries such as the United States to require action "to stem and prevent money laundering" (General Accounting Office [GAO] 1996: 29–30). Yet, despite this common starting point, the transnational legal processes that the two countries underwent and in which they are still engaged, are substantially different, for the reasons discussed in this chapter. Briefly put, although Brazil and Argentina share similarities in their interactions with transnational forces, they differ significantly in terms of their internal developments in this domain. Therefore, the comparison of these processes provides useful insights to discuss the location, extent, and limits of state change within this field.

The chapter proceeds in three sections. Section 1 provides an overview of the transnational anti–money laundering order, focusing on three of its distinctive features: (1) the interaction between soft and hard law, (2) the interaction between public and private actors and interests, and (3) the requirement of global acceptance of the transnational legal order's rules. Section 2 of this chapter provides a comparison between the transnational legal processes that Brazil and Argentina underwent during the last decade. This comparison focuses on the three central pillars of the anti–money laundering order: criminalization, administrative obligations imposed on the financial sectors, and the creation of an FIU as a new national institution. Section 2 additionally offers examples of substantive internal change fostered by transnational processes, but which respond to national demands. Section 3 discusses the evidence gathered in this study in view of the theoretic framework of "transnational transformations and state change" (Shaffer, Chapter 1). The chapter examines five dimensions of state change, and discusses the legitimacy of this transnational legal order and the recursive flows between the creation and implementation of legal norms in the Brazilian and Argentinean cases.

1. THE ANTI–MONEY LAUNDERING ORDER: AN OVERVIEW

Most recent theoretic efforts to explain regulation in contemporary societies in a global context have discussed, or at least mentioned, the area of anti–money laundering (Braithwaite & Drahos 2000; Delmas Marty 2004b, 2006; Kingsbury, Krisch, & Stewart 2005; Slaughter 2004). Reflecting the authors' particular disciplinary backgrounds and theoretic interests, the money laundering phenomenon has been explored through the lens of "global governance" (Wilke 2008), "international law"

(discussing the impacts of the international financial crisis in 2008 in Argentina, Brazil, and Mexico), and Lafer & Peña (1973) (exploring the role played by the two countries in international relations).

(Doyle 2002), "financial regulation" (Brummer 2011), "global administrative law" (Wessel 2007; Gathii 2010), and "international relations" (Hulsse & Kerwer 2007).

As part of a research project on "transnational legal process and state change" (Shaffer, Chapter 1), this chapter examines a wide set of anti–money laundering normative and political efforts as a *transnational legal order*, defined as "a collection of legal norms and associated institutions within a given domain that order behavior across national jurisdictions" (Shaffer, Chapter 1). What has been earlier referenced in the literature as "a regime," "a system," or "a policy" will be assessed in this chapter as a transnational legal order that will be called the "anti–money laundering order" (AMLO).

One of the main distinctive features of the AMLO is how it combines financial regulation and enforcement obligations to serve crime control strategies. The AMLO's proclaimed aim is to change individuals' behavior. Its core idea is to counter criminal activities through depriving persons of the profits these activities generate. Its hope is that, without the proceeds of their criminal activity, individuals will lose their main incentive for engaging in them.[6] Put in these terms, the AMLO is supposed to deter a wide range of illicit activities – trafficking in drugs, armaments, and human beings; terrorism; corruption; and organized crime in general.

The so-called "follow the money" rhetoric bridges "regulatory laws" and "a destructive, often bloody reality," to employ the terms of William Wechsler (2001: 40). As explained in the literature, the "follow the money" strategy was built from the systematic failure of other forms of crime control, specifically related to drug trafficking.[7] Since the policies' beginnings, it has been clear that the traditional criminal law approach ("police-court-correction") was far from sufficient to reach anti–money laundering goals (Alldridge 2008: 439; Levi & Gilmore 2002: 340; Sharman 2008: 640). The regulation of private financial intermediaries was a *sine qua non* condition to locate and recover illegally obtained funds. Therefore, to guarantee that states would enact and enforce the rules directed at individuals and corporations, states created a new set of legal norms.

Building from Shaffer's definitions, this chapter will describe the AMLO as a "collection of legal norms" that lay out behavioral prescription for individuals, corporations, and states themselves. This collection of norms is issued by different authoritative sources that vary from strictly legally binding rules to memorandums of understanding. They are backed by a broad enforcement system that includes long prison sentences, fines, and corporate liability (for individuals and

[6] The UN Convention Against Illicit Traffic in Narcotic Drugs and Psychotropic Substances (1988) illustrates the tone of the official argument for anti–money laundering rules in its preamble ("determined to *deprive* persons engaged in illicit traffic *of the proceeds of their criminal activities* and thereby *eliminate* their *main incentive* for so doing").

[7] See, for example, Alldridge (2008: 440); Andreas & Nadelmann (2006: 147) Levi & Reuter (2006: 290). For a skeptical perspective of the costs and benefits of "following the money," see Braithwaite (1993).

corporations), and political and economic sanctions (for states). Table 3.1 relates the three different recipients of the transnational legal norms and the AMLO's prescriptions, authoritative sources, and enforcement systems.

As Table 3.1 demonstrates, the concept of transnational legal order – unlike the concepts of "regime" or policy" – captures the wide range of interacting legal and institutional pieces that play key roles. Sources and enforcement systems that otherwise would be considered "purely national," such as criminal legislation and the functioning of the courts, are conceived as an integral part of the transnational legal order. National criminal laws, observed through the transnational legal norms lens, shed light on the variety of sources that took part in the norm production process. In the Brazilian case, as Section 2 shows, the authors of the Brazilian legislation took great advantage of foreign legislation and international documents. The same is true with the adoption of criminal proceedings: exchange of information, international cooperation, and also the fact that, in a certain way, through the mutual evaluation procedures, the courts' activities are meant to be accountable to transnational institutions.

What Table 3.1 might not show is that the AMLO has a protagonist: the FATF. Created by the G-7 heads of state and the president of the Commission of the European Communities, the FATF initiated its activities with the preparation of a document entitled *Forty Recommendations* (FATF 1990). In 1990, the FATF's objective was to establish guidelines for an anti–money laundering regime based on the improvement of national judicial systems, increased participation of the financial sector in monitoring and enforcement, and strengthened international cooperation. Subsequent to the document's publication, all OECD member countries joined the group, and some non-OECD countries were also invited to participate in the program. The membership of the FATF was increased in 2000 with the addition of Brazil, Argentina, and Mexico. In the following years, the Russian Federation, South Africa, China, the Republic of Korea, and India also joined (FATF 2010).

Instead of systematically presenting each of the sources and institutions mentioned in Table 3.1, this section is organized analytically around the framework of Shaffer (Chapter 2) concerning the likelihood of a transnational legal order's being effective in producing domestic legal and institutional change. He posits that one of three clusters of factors affecting the impact of a transnational legal order in a country is the clarity and coherence of the transnational legal order's norms, and the acceptance of the transnational legal order as legitimate, leading to normative consensus (Chapter 2). Besides their usefulness as conceptual tools to assess the limits and extent of changes the AMLO produced in Brazil and Argentina (Section 2 below), the ideas of clarity, coherence, and acceptance provide interesting entries to present an overview of the AMLO.

The clarity and coherence of legal norms can be assessed and discussed in different ways. In view of presenting the main developments toward the consolidation of the

TABLE 3.1. *Anti–money laundering order: an overview*

	Individuals	Corporations	State
Prescriptions	• Legal prohibition of money laundering and "terrorism financing" (criminalization)	• Customer due diligence and record keeping • Know your customer (KYC) and suspicious transactions report (STR)	• Create a financial intelligence unit (FIU) • Enact and enforce the norms directed at individuals and corporations. • Produce and provide information for evaluation procedures
Main authoritative sources	• Legislation enacted by congress	• Legislation enacted by congress and/or the administration • Regulatory rules, internal corporate compliance rules	• 40+9 Financial Action Task Force (FATF) Recommendations • Egmont Group • UN and Regional Conventions
Enforcement system	• National criminal justice system (Police-court-correction) • Prison sentences, fines, and confiscation of the proceeds of crime.	• National administrative law: fines and administrative sanctions • Compliance, "cost of capital for firms," sanctions and shame	• FATF mutual evaluation process – political and economic sanctions.

AMLO, this section covers three topics. The first is related to variations in the dimensions of obligation of AMLO norms, frequently covered in the literature through the concepts of "hard law" and "soft law" (Shaffer & Pollack 2010). The second concerns the intensification of the participation of private actors in the construction of the AMLO. The third deals with the peculiarities of the high demand for worldwide acceptance of this set of norms. Each of these developments addresses the origins and main developments of the prescriptions of the AMLO, respectively, targeting individuals, corporations, and states as highlighted in Table 3.1. The next three sections sketch the expansion of the AMLO in the past twenty years in terms of these three aspects: the interaction of hard and soft law, the interaction of public and private actors, and the goal of worldwide coverage.

A. *The Interaction between Hard and Soft Law*

The AMLO norms encompass a wide range of obligations as a consequence of the various sources shaping the transnational legal process: UN conventions, UN Security Council resolutions, recommendations, standards, declarations of principle, national legislation, and so forth. We could further include other types of documents that play non-negligible roles in these processes, such as the name and shame lists and the national reports detailing lack of effectiveness that are widely broadcast through institutional press releases and media coverage. Focusing on the Forty Recommendations and the FATF process, the literature frequently tries to conciliate two apparently contradictory features: its lack of legally binding force and its strong enforcement capabilities (Brummer 2011: 304).[8] In other words, the AMLO norms are often pictured as an illustration of the "many varieties" between hard and soft law (Abbott & Snidal 2000: 422; Shaffer & Pollack 2010: 716).

This section takes a different direction, using the hard and soft law distinction to present aspects of the AMLO's consolidation and development over time. More specifically, this section seeks to describe the dynamic relationship between soft and hard norms in the construction and flow of transnational legal norms. This interaction between soft and hard law can be identified at different levels of the AMLO. We first focus in this section on the process of complementarity between UN conventions and the FATF Forty Recommendations. We then address a second level of complementarity between hard and soft law in Section 2 by noting the predominant role played by nationally enforced hard law in this transnational legal order.

The first international document in this policy area was the UN Convention Against Illicit Traffic in Narcotic Drugs and Psychotropic Substances (UN 1988), strongly promoted by the United States. The Convention mentions for the first time "money laundering" and mechanisms for the confiscation of values equivalent to the proceeds obtained from criminal practice. Following this Convention, economic and financial concerns played an increasing role in the justification of the application of criminal law to financial transactions. The confiscation of the proceeds from criminal activities became central to the intervention model as a complement to criminal punishment. By threatening to confiscate property obtained through activities considered criminal, policymakers hoped to make these activities less economically attractive. Deterrence was to result not only from punishment, but also from eliminating the benefits of crime.

At that time, the link between money laundering and drug trafficking alone was perceived to be an obstacle to the effectiveness of the anti–money laundering order (Stessens 2000: 11–14). The FATF Forty Recommendations took the lead to foster the

8 Brummer refers to *"hard" soft law* and discusses the flaws of the traditional approaches that rely on the hard and soft dichotomy. See also Wilke (2008: 519), and Levi & Gilmore (2002: 359).

expansion of the predicate offences to which money laundering would be attached. In 1996, the first FATF revision of the Forty Recommendations was expanded to cover "serious offences" and in 2003 to cover the "widest range" of offences possible (FATF 2004b: 13). Only in the early 2000s, following significant changes brought about through the FATF process, did the UN Conventions against transnational organized crime (UN 2000a) and the financing of terrorism (UN 1999) provide formal *hard law* status to this criminal policy. In addition, they require the adoption of a group of complementary noncriminal measures in respect to each crime under their jurisdiction. Both Conventions reproduce the same policies adopted as soft law by the FATF since the early 1990s with regard to money laundering: the requirements that financial institutions identify customers, maintain updated records, and report suspicious operations, and that a national "financial intelligence unit" be created "to serve as a national center for the collection, analysis and dissemination of information" (UN, 2000a: Article 7.1. a, b; UN, 1999: Article 18.1.b). In addition, the two Conventions contain long articles regulating the freezing or seizure of proceeds, funds, or equivalent value, and the domestic and international procedures for this purpose (UN 2000a: Article 12 and 13 b; UN 1999: Article 8). These issues were also regulated, although in a less detailed manner, by the Convention Against Illicit Traffic in Narcotic Drugs (UN 1988: Article 5).

In sum, part of the construction of the AMLO encompasses a complementary process between hard law and soft law instruments. The UN convention on trafficking drugs paved the way to the criminalization of money laundering. The expansion of the predicate offences was maintained as a "soft law" rule through the Forty Recommendations until the approval of the UN conventions on organized crime and financing terrorism. This complementary interaction fully supports Shaffer and Pollack's (2010: 765) hypothesis on the likelihood of hard and soft law "to work as complements in an evolutionary manner." According to the authors, it requires "a broad policy consensus among the most powerful actors within a given issue area" (Shaffer & Pollack 2010: 765), which is definitely the case in the AMLO.

B. *The Interaction of Public and Private Actors and Interests*

A second distinctive feature of the AMLO is the interaction between private and public actors in the construction of transnational norms, in this case as applied to the financial sector (Table 3.1). As Mark Pieth and Gemma Aiolfi (2003: 360) explain, the rules directed at the financial sector in the Forty Recommendations were a product of the combination of national strategies – from Switzerland, the United Kingdom, and the United States, and an international recommendation of the Basel Committee from 1988, drafted by the United States. In the background, it was assumed that the monitoring functions developed for the private sector could never be effectively accomplished directly by the states alone (Levi & Gilmore 2002: 340). From the Basel Committee's perspective, preventing the banking system from being used as an intermediary for funds derived from criminal activities was a response to systemic issues. The main concern was that banks' inadvertent associations with criminals could undermine public confidence in banks, and hence the stability of the entire banking system. The Basel principles acted as a base for subsequent transnational legal obligations imposed on the financial industry. However, the FATF formalization of these principles was perceived as insufficient to guide the implementation process. Pieth and Aiolfi depict the 1990s as a decade of struggle among bank supervisors and banking communities to implement the regulations. The outcome, according to them, "was the creation of a patchwork of rather diverse rules which had the effect of immediately increasing regulatory competition and regulatory arbitrage, thus enabling the money launderer to profit from these discrepancies between the various financial centers" (Pieth & Aiolfi 2003: 360).

In addition, Marie Wilke (2008: 516) calls attention to the fact that the vagueness of the Forty Recommendations played an important role in facilitating the increasing interaction of the private sector with the AMLO. The main initiative came almost a decade later (in the late 1990s) when "facilitators talked to key US and European banks to convince them that getting together and defining a common anti–money laundering standard could be beneficial for the banks as well as wider society" (Pieth & Aiolfi 2003: 361). In light of this initiative, and as a result of exchange and discussion of their own internal compliance rules, a group of major banks published in 2000 the Wolfsberg Anti–money Laundering Principles for Private Banking.[9] Several other documents concerning mutual funds, correspondent bank customers, and trade finance, among others, have been published by the Wolfsberg Group since then.

The move toward the private sector's active participation in the construction of the AMLO helps to explain a shift from a "rule-based" regulation to a "risk-based" approach. Banks were accordingly allowed to monitor transactions in a simpler and cheaper fashion, unless they detected certain indicators of risk. In 2003, the FATF undertook a revision process and took into account the Wolfsberg Principles (Wessel 2007: 188; Wilke 2008: 518).

C. *The "Everybody In" Mantra*

A third distinctive feature of the AMLO is its global scope, conceived in terms of a requirement of full compliance with a set of rules in every single financial center in the world for the legal order to be effective (Doyle 2002: 295).[10] The FATF's Forty Recommendations first gave expression to the idea that a regular assessment would

[9] Wolfsberg documents are available at http://www.wolfsberg-principles.com (accessed February 28, 2011).

[10] Doyle (2002), while discussing the effectiveness of the FATF, mentions the "organization's oft-repeated mantra that the regulations are not working only because they have not yet been adopted across the board." See also Sharman (2008: 641) and Alldridge (2008: 458).

"stimulate countries to give to these issues a high priority," although money laundering control was already the highest priority to the United States (FATF 1990: 28).[11] The worldwide requirement of acceptance of the AMLO is frequently justified by the "borderless nature of the threat" (FATF 2010: 9).[12] According to this view, there is no point in having anti–money laundering rules only in some countries, because the lack of compliance of some would raise obstacles to the work of others in criminal investigations and money tracing. During the past twenty years, the FATF has developed different programs to assess compliance, implementation, and effectiveness of the AMLO norms, explicitly recognizing that formal compliance through the enactment of legislation is far from sufficient (FATF 2004b: 8).

The FATF uses two major formats to assess compliance, one involving "rule making among members" and the other "rule making applied to nonmembers." This formal dichotomy reflects the idea of legitimacy, that is, that countries must take part in the production of – or, at least, voluntarily accept – the norms applied to them. Although the "members vs. nonmembers" dichotomy might describe well the first thirteen years of FATF activity, after 2004, transformations in the FATF membership and monitoring rules blurred this scheme.

Since the beginning of its activities, the FATF has established two different procedures, with different rules and methodologies, for members and nonmembers. Members used to be evaluated according to the Forty Recommendations and through "self-assessment" and "peer pressure" mechanisms. Two rounds of mutual evaluation were conducted for members in the 1990s. A nonmember country, in contrast, risked being included in a widely disseminated list of "noncooperative countries or territories" (NCCT), and it could be subjected to counter measures aimed at preventing FATF member countries from engaging in transactions with natural corporations from that country. The NCCT process started in 2000 and was widely discussed in the literature.[13]

Since 2004, the FATF has been changing this scenario. First, the FATF started granting "associated membership" status to the "FATF-style regional bodies" (FSRBs) that have been created throughout the world.[14] The FSRBs include, as members, most of the countries that used to be evaluated through the NCCT regime. This new scenario extends the peer pressure and self-assessment mechanisms

[11] For a detailed description of US predominance in this regard, see Wechsler (2001: 48–51), and Braithwaite & Drahos (2000: 105).

[12] See also Sharman (2008: 640) and Van Duyne, Groenhuijsen, & Schudelaro (2005: 120, 139): providing a critical analysis of the "threat imagery," the authors state that "the policy of anti-money laundering has been disseminated with a zeal befitting a messianic message of 'Apocalypse Now.'"

[13] See, for example, Alldridge (2008: 444–5); Blazejewski (2008: 18–25); Doyle (2002: 295–8); Hulsse & Kerwer (2007: 626); Levi & Gilmore (2002: 353–4); Mugarura (2011: 65–6); Sharman (2008: 644–6); Wechsler (2001: 48–51); Wessel (2007: 175–7, 195); and Wilke (2008: 513–15).

[14] There are nine FSRBs with associated membership status. Together, they encompass 181 countries and territories, but some among them are members of more than one FSRB (FATF 2010: 10–11). See also Blazejewski (2008: 23–45) (detailing FATF's institutional partnerships).

to cover more than 100 new countries and territories. It does so without interfering in the FATF decision-making process and yet, arguably, while reducing the so-called legitimacy deficit of the NCCT mechanism.

Second, the FATF launched in 2004 a document of general applicability called *Methodology for Assessing Compliance*, defined as "a tool to assist assessors to determine whether countries are in compliance with the Forty Recommendations" (FATF 2004b: 5, 82). The third round of mutual evaluation, starting in 2005, was conducted under the new rules. Some international organizations, such as the International Monetary Fund and the World Bank, started to play an active role in conducting evaluations of nonmember countries based on the FATF Methodology for assessing compliance.

The NCCT process was maintained for nonmembers until 2006, when all countries were considered to have progressed sufficiently to become de-listed. In 2007, the FATF launched a new strategy to deal with countries that, according to the FATF, represented a high risk to anti–money laundering efforts. The so-called International Co-operation Review Group (ICRG) has been analyzing and recommending specific actions regarding those jurisdictions. The ICRG's concerns are systematized and disseminated through public statements issued by the FATF. When a jurisdiction failed to address the identified deficiencies, "FATF took the additional step of calling upon its members and urging all jurisdictions to apply counter-measures to protect their financial sectors from money laundering and terrorist financing risks emanating from it" (FATF 2010: 28).

As a result, after 2004/2005, the FATF membership started to include, in an already diverse group, associated members (FSRB countries) and observer members. This expansion was conceived to provide representativeness (or input legitimacy) to the widest range of countries possible. At the plenary meetings (which constitute the FATF decision-making body), each FATF member country has one vote, just as does each of the nine FSRBs.[15] As pointed out during my interviews, the FATF thus became a "global body" without destroying the decision-making process. Even after granting a "second class membership" to more than 100 countries, the FATF plenary meeting is still able to reach decisions.

Besides formal representation, the number of experts each country is able to send to the FATF meetings is decisive for the decision-making process. For some countries, such as the United States, the FATF delegation includes experts from a wide range of specializations and backgrounds. Brazil and Argentina, in contrast, normally send smaller missions – Brazil between eight and twelve, and Argentina only half of that.[16] The characteristics of the missions are important not only to the defense of

[15] Therefore, Latin America is represented by four votes: Brazil, Argentina, Mexico, and GAFISUD (also representing the other seven countries that are not FATF members).

[16] Also according to interviews, to the plenary meetings that approved the mutual evaluation reports Brazil sent twenty-two delegates and Argentina ten.

the countries' interests generally, but in particular for allowing participation in the working groups.

Through these different mechanisms of assessment, the FATF concluded that its standards have been "endorsed by more than 180 jurisdictions around the world" (FATF 2010: 10). The level of acceptance of these norms in different jurisdictions varies considerably, however, as this chapter's assessment of Brazil and Argentina illustrates.

2. STATE CHANGE IN BRAZIL AND ARGENTINA

This section provides a chronology of the main aspects of the process, including documents issued and evaluated, and the legal and institutional changes entailed. It then compares how Brazil and Argentina responded to, and implemented, the three central pillars of AMLO: (1) the criminalization of the offence of money laundering; (2) the obligation of certain economic sectors to identify customers, maintain records, and report transactions considered to be suspicious; and (3) the creation of a national FIU. The section concludes by exploring relevant changes identified in Brazil that can be observed as consequences of the AMLO, without having been required by it.

A. *Transnational Legal Processes*

Table 3.2 summarizes the interaction between FATF membership and monitoring activities, and the legal and institutional changes arising in both countries. This table provides a map for understanding the numerous international and regional organizations that act as nodes in transgovernmental regulatory networks that help to diffuse anti–money laundering norms and shape institutions and policies within countries.

Our story begins in 1995, when the US State Department identified Brazil and Argentina as "medium-high" countries "on the basis of the degree to which they are at risk of experiencing money laundering activities" (GAO 1996: 29–30).[17] Even though the countries' formal engagement with the FATF came five years later, some efforts toward the criminalization of money laundering took place in the meantime.

According to the authors of the 1998 Brazilian law, the FATF's Forty Recommendations was one influence, among others, for the establishment of Brazil's national policy, which included a broad definition of money laundering, the creation of an FIU, and a mandatory reporting system for suspicious transactions. My interview

[17] Brazil and Argentina were listed at the "Major Money-Laundering Countries in 1995" as "medium-high" priority countries. High and medium-high priority totalized thirty-three countries that the document considered to be "locations in which action is needed to stem and prevent money laundering in order to make headway into the international money-laundering problem."

TABLE 3.2. *Anti–money laundering order (AMLO) in Brazil and Argentina*

	Brazil	Argentina
1988: UN Convention Against Illicit Traffic In Narcotic Drugs and Psychotropic Substances		
1990: FATF 40 Recommendations		
1995: Egmont Group is established.		
1995: The US report lists Brazil and Argentina as "high-risk" jurisdictions.		
1996: CICAD/OAS (Inter-American Drug Abuse Control Commission) creates a money laundering regulation	1996: The Minister of Justice prepares the anti–money laundering legislation according to "international standards."	
	1998: Anti-Money Laundering Law 9613. Criminalizes laundering of proceeds of a list of serious crimes and creates the Financial Intelligence Unit (COAF).	
1999: FATF invites Brazil, Argentina, and Mexico to join as observers at a Plenary Meeting. 1999: CICAD/OEA creates an Anti-Money Laundering Unit.	1999: COAF (Brazilian FIU) becomes an Egmont Group member.	
2000: FATF invites the first countries in Latin America (Brazil, Argentina, and Mexico) to become members. 2000: FATF starts NCCT policy	2000: First FATF evaluation in Brazil. FATF considers Brazil fully compliant with the recommendations then in effect, with one exception: the regulation regarding financial secrecy.	2000: Anti-Money Laundering Law 25246. Extension of the money laundering offence to include all existing crimes in the Penal Code. Formal creation of FIU. 2000: First FATF evaluation in Argentina. FATF considers Argentina compliant

(*continued*)

TABLE 3.2 *(continued)*

	Brazil	Argentina
		with the minimum conditions to become a member, although several deficiencies are pointed out.
2001: FATF makes Eight Special Recommendations concerning terrorism financing.	2001: New bank secrecy law (LC 105/2001) eliminates the deficiencies identified by FATF.	2001: FATF issues threat because of noncompliance.
2002: Wolfsberg Principles and Statement on the Suppression of the financing of terrorism are published. 2002: UN Convention for the suppression of the financing of terrorism enters into force. 2002: GAFISUD starts operations.		2002: UN Convention against transnational organized crime ratified. 2002: FIU starts operations (Decree 1038/03)
2003: UN Convention against transnational organized crime enters into force.	2003: Terrorism financing is considered a predicate offence of money laundering (Law 10.701/03). 2003: The Specialized Federal Courts were created. (Resolution 314/2003 of the Federal Council of Justice). 2003: FATF "on-site" visit for the second evaluation (November).	2003: FATF "on-site" visit for the second evaluation (October 20). 2003: Criminalization and forfeiture rules amended, partially complying with Recommendations. 2003: FIU becomes an Egmont Group member.
2004: FATF, WB, and IMF agree and approve the *Methodology for Assessing Compliance*.	2004: UN Convention against transnational organized crime ratified. 2004: FATF/GAFISUD second evaluation report approved by the FATF Plenary Meeting.	

	Brazil	Argentina
	2004: Creation of DRCI – Brazilian Central Authority (Ministry of Justice). 2004: Creation of ENCCLA (described below).	2004: FATF/GAFISUD second evaluation report approved by the FATF Plenary Meeting. 2004: Follow-up Progress Report is presented at October Plenary Meeting.
	2005: UN Convention for the suppression of the financing of terrorism ratified.	2005: Follow-up Progress Reports are presented at February, June, and October Plenary meetings. 2005: UN Convention for the suppression of the financing of terrorism ratified.
	2006: ENCCLA initiative includes corruption.	2006: FATF High Mission visits Argentina to verify its improvement (March 30). 2006: FIU receives unrestricted access to bank and securities records (Law 26087 – April, 24). 2006: Board of FIU restructured (Law 26119 – July, 26) 2006: Financing Terrorism draft law sent to Congress (December, 20). 2006: "National Coordination Office" was created to prepare the "national agenda." 2006: Resolution 130/2006 created the Fiscal Unit for the Prevention of Money Laundering and Financing of Terrorism with the Attorney General's Office (*UFILAVDIN*).

(*continued*)

TABLE 3.2 *(continued)*

	Brazil	Argentina
2007: A new FATF initiative on nonmembers is launched (International Co-operation Review Group [ICRG]).	2007: COAF's Resolution on terrorism and "politically exposed persons."	2007: New legislation on Money Laundering and Financing Terrorism (Law 26.268/07). Added a chapter to the criminal code called "Terrorist criminal association and financing of terrorism."
		2007: FATF Plenary Meeting approves the progress report and closes the second mutual evaluation.
		2007: The president approves a national agenda on money laundering (Decree 1225/2007).
	2008: Brazil becomes the first Latin American country to assume FATF Presidency.	
2009: G-20 explicitly concerned with money laundering (FATF Annual Report 2009: 5).	2009: FATF/GAFISUD "on-site visit" for the third evaluation (October, 26–November 07).	2009: FATF/GAFISUD "on-site visit" for the third evaluation (November 16–27).
	2010: Third mutual evaluation. FATF Plenary Meeting adopts the Mutual Evaluation Report of Brazil (June 25).	2010: Third mutual evaluation. FATF Plenary Meeting adopts the Mutual Evaluation Report of Argentina (October 22).
		2010: Argentina receives a high-level FATF mission (December).

with the Minister of Justice at the time of the creation of the law indicates that Brazil's interest in the policy was determined more by contacts with US representatives on drug issues than by the FATF's initiative. The FATF report formalizing Brazil's invitation to become a FATF member recognized that "Brazil has, in a relatively short time, developed and begun implementing a comprehensive anti–money laundering program" (FATF 2000: 10). The only problem identified at that time was the lack of successful prosecutions and convictions, which the FATF attributed to "the relatively recent establishment of the Brazilian anti-money laundering regime" (FATF 2000: 11).

In contrast, Argentina's efforts to implement broad rules on money laundering began only after its invitation to join FATF meetings as an observer. Before that time, the money laundering offence in Argentina only related to drug crimes, reflecting the UN Convention (1988). The FATF viewed the passage of Law 25246 in April 2000 as a first sign of Argentina's commitment, although one in need of great improvement (FATF 2000: 9). The decision to invite Argentina to become a member was made despite the many Argentinean deficiencies identified by the FATF in 2000.

The FATF and GAFISUD (Grupo de Accion Financiera de Sudamérica – South America Financial Action Task Force), the FATF-style body created in 2000 to conduct the evaluation process in Latin American countries, closely monitored both countries after they became FATF members. As of May 2011, the FATF had evaluated both Brazil and Argentina three times. The FATF's first evaluations took place at the beginning of 2000 to review each country's respective fulfillment of the minimal requirements for admission to the FATF. FATF and GAFISUD representatives conducted the second evaluations in 2003, with the objective of identifying each country's level of compliance with the anti–money laundering regime and providing recommendations for its improvement. In 2009, FATF and GAFISUD held the third evaluations of both countries. The last two reports were adopted at the FATF plenary meeting and published on the FATF website in 2004 and 2010, respectively.

In its Annual Report of July 2004, the FATF published an "executive summary" of the second evaluations of the anti–money laundering regimes in Brazil and Argentina. The evaluations were based on information collected by FATF assessors who visited both countries in 2003 during meetings held with judicial and executive branch agencies, financial institutions, and private sector organizations. The process includes "on-site visits" from a commission of experts from FATF member countries, the preparation of a report detailing progress and deficiencies, and the report's approval by a plenary session of the FATF. When the FATF considers it necessary to encourage national action strongly, a "high-level mission" visits the country to reinforce the importance of compliance with the FATF's recommendations (FATF 2004a).

Argentina received a 'high-level mission' in March 2006.[18] The high-level mission is one of the five steps that should be taken to encourage jurisdictions to take the necessary measures. This step precedes the application of Recommendation 21, which demands "special attention to business relationships and transactions with persons, including companies and financial institutions, from countries which do not or insufficiently apply the FATF Recommendations" (FATF 2003: Recommendation 21). The next step is expulsion from the FATF.

[18] Marteau 2010: 121; UIF (2006: 19) and interviews.

The main problem identified in the Argentine regime, which was subject to the high-level mission, was the nonexistence of a law criminalizing the financing of terrorism. After several follow-up reports were presented, the second mutual evaluation was closed a few days before the FATF Meeting on June 3, 2007, in view of the approval of the legislation on terrorism by the Argentina Congress (Marteau 2010: 119).

Brazil has also been closely monitored, but has never been subject to noncompliance measures. At the first evaluation, the FATF considered Brazil fully compliant with the recommendations then in effect, with one exception: the regulation regarding financial secrecy limited access by the Conselho de Controle de Atividades Financeiras (COAF) to communications of suspicious transactions, and it required that the exchange of information with other countries be made via rogatory letter (FATF 2000: 10–11). Just over six months after publication of the FATF evaluation report, the Brazilian Parliament enacted Complementary Law No. 105 dated January 10, 2001, which eliminated the specified deficiencies. The rapid approval of the new legislation concerning banking secrecy only changed the venue of contestation over access to banking information by anti–money laundering authorities. Five days after the approval, a small conservative party filed a claim of unconstitutionality of Complementary Law 105/01 before the Supreme Federal Court. We are still waiting for a decision as of May 2011.[19]

A few years later, Brazil urgently expedited its procedure for the approval of the UN Convention for the Suppression of the Financing of Terrorism (1999) by Brazil's National Congress due to FATF's next "on-site" visit.[20] In April 2004, the Commission of Foreign Relations and National Defense, where the approval was then being handled, received and approved Request No. 25/2004, which requested a public hearing that would include the president of the COAF, on the need for urgent handling of the Convention. The justification for this request noted that nonratification of the Convention by Brazil "represents one of the main gaps in the Country's evaluation before [the] FATF," and that the proposal should be accepted "in view of the proximity of the evaluation of Brazil by [the] FATF" (Request No. 25/2004). Despite the pressure for action, the Convention was not approved by the National Congress until June 30, 2005.[21]

The FATF's second evaluation report of Brazil indicates those items in Brazil's anti–money laundering regime that have completely fulfilled FATF recommendations as well as those actions that should be taken to improve the legal and institutional framework. The report finds that Brazil's procedures for monitoring operations and information maintenance fulfill the FATF Recommendations. In contrast, the FATF report recommends that Brazil extend access to information

[19] ADI 2390, from January 15 2001, presented by the "Partido Social Liberal."

[20] The Legislative Bill No. 986 aiming to approve this UN convention was presented to the Congress on November 10, 2003, a few weeks after the FATF visit.

[21] The Request No. 25/2004 is available at www.camara.gov.br (accessed May 15, 2011). The Convention was then enacted by the President of the Republic on December 26, 2005 (Decree No. 5640/05).

regarding the financial industry's communications of suspicious transactions to the Securities Commission (CVM, Comissão de Valores Mobiliários); this information was formerly subject to secrecy. The FATF also recommends eliminating the threshold of minimal amount that triggers reporting obligations, so that all suspicious operations must be reported (FATF-GAFISUD 2004: 88). COAF and the Brazilian Central Bank have since addressed all of these issues (COAF 2008: 10, 22).

In July 2008, Brazil assumed the presidency of the FATF. The position was previously held by two other noncore members: Hong Kong (China) in 2001, and South Africa in 2005. The appointed senior official is Antonio Gustavo Rodrigues, the head of Brazil's FIU since 2004. For Rodrigues, "regional balance" and "democratization of ideas" are the main reasons why the FATF presidency "was offered" to Brazil (Costa 2008: 36). One of Costa's interviewees explicitly stressed the relevance of alternating the presidency, especially between European and non-European countries. The Brazilian presidency represented a "natural progression" as the country explicitly "volunteered to hold the position." Recognizing that each presidency defines its own agenda, the interviewee welcomed the diversity of approaches. Another interviewee considered the "regional balance" less important than the award that the FATF presidency represented both to Brazilian efforts regarding the AMLO and to Mr. Rodrigues himself. From his standpoint, it was the proactive work of the Brazilian senior officer that won Brazil the presidency.

Rodrigues minimized the importance of holding the presidency, because the decision power of FATF is held by the plenary meeting, but considered that Brazil is able to contribute "with our style and the things Brazil believes are important" (Costa 2008: 36).[22] In this regard, the Foreword of the FATF 2009 Annual Report, signed by him, highlighted the enhancement of cooperation with non-FATF jurisdictions as "one of [his] key objectives" (FATF 2009: 5).

In 2009, the third mutual evaluation started in both countries. The reports published in 2010 consist of long and detailed explanations of the achievements and deficiencies regarding each of 40+9 recommendations; they total more than 558 pages. This evaluation was the first for both countries under the new methodology (adopted in 2004) and was, therefore, more stringent and broader in scope than the previous ones.

The introductory section provides useful insights regarding what the national authorities consider to be the relevant national problems for the AMLO to address. In this regard, according to the 2010 Report, "Argentinean authorities identify tax evasion as the domestic offence that generates the largest amount of criminal proceeds." The paragraph continues regarding the significant proceeds generated by drug trafficking and by smuggling, corruption, and different types of fraud (MER of Argentina 2010: 17). In the Brazilian report, on the other hand, a whole section is devoted to the "long-standing issue" of corruption in the country. The main sources

[22] Costa quotes an interview with Rodrigues, who defined the presidency as the "swallow that alone does not make a summer."

of proceeds of crime in the country were considered to be "corruption and crimes against the national financial system, including fraud and capital flight," as well as "drug trafficking, weapons trafficking, organized crime, smuggling and embezzlement of governmental money" (MER of Brazil 2010: 10). Note that terrorism and terrorism financing were not part of the list of problems.

A team of seven experts from different nationalities and with different background expertise from the FATF and GAFISUD Secretariat and FATF member countries assessed Brazil and Argentina. The assessment team subjected both countries to a two week, on-site inspection. It met with representatives from almost fifty bodies from government, the financial industry, and other private sector bodies in each country (MER of Argentina 2010: 238; MER of Brazil 2010: 288).

Table 3.3 summarizes the 2010 evaluation reports' assessments of the compliance of Brazil and Argentina with the forty-nine recommendations. It breaks down the recommendations into five categories: (1) "legal system" (concerning the offences and the confiscation measures), (2) "preventive measures" (recommendations directed at the financial system and particular economic sectors), (3) "institutional and other measures" (concerning the FIU and other authorities), (4) "international cooperation," and (5) nine special recommendations on terrorist financing. According to the FATF (2004b), the rating of compliance is organized into four levels: (1) C (compliant); (2) LC (largely compliant), "there are only minor shortcomings"; (3) PC (partially compliant), "the country has taken some substantive action and complies with some of the essential criteria"; (4) NC (noncompliant); and finally (5) NA (not applicable).

Both countries are only partially compliant with a large number of FATF recommendations. The reports list many technical shortcomings in Brazil and Argentina, noting that several aspects of the AMLO "lack effectiveness" in these countries, and that, for some issues, the evaluators "lack information to assess effectiveness." Yet, overall, Table 3.3 depicts how Brazil is evaluated as being much more compliant than Argentina. Moreover, although Brazil was considered to be "working to address deficiencies" to "enhance its legal and institutional AML/CFT (anti–money laundering/combating the financing of terrorism) framework," Argentina was considered not to have "made adequate progress in addressing a number of deficiencies identified" in the previous evaluation (MER of Argentina 2010: 6; MER of Brazil 2010: 25). The report on Brazil pointed to several factors that have been contributing to the improvement of Brazil's performance. The next section provides an overview of Brazilian and Argentinean compliance with the three central pillars of the AMLO.

B. *The Three Central Pillars of AMLO in Brazil and Argentina*

Brazil and Argentina differentially responded to the transnational legal order's three central pillars: (1) the criminalization of the offence of money laundering and terrorism financing; (2) the obligation of certain economic sectors to identify customers,

TABLE 3.3. *Compliance according to the 2010 mutual evaluation report (MER) of Argentina and Brazil*

	Legal system		Preventive measures		Institutional measures		International co-operation		Terrorist financing		Total	
	ARG	BRA	ARG	BRA	ARG	BRA	ARG	BRA	ARG	BRA	ARG	BRA
C			1	2			1	1			2	3
LC				10	1	4		4		3	1	21
PC	3	3	11	6	3	4	4	1	5	2	26	16
NC			10	3	5		1		4	4	20	7
NA				1		1					0	2
Total	3		22		9		6		9		49	

maintain records, and report transactions considered to be suspicious; and (3) the creation of a national FIU. These pillars cover the main demands that the AMLO makes of the state, the economic and financial sectors, and individuals (Table 3.1).

1. The Criminal Offenses

Assessments by FATF address the legal elements of each country's money laundering offence (concealment, disguise, conversion, transfer, acquisition, possession, use, and self-laundering), the definition of proceeds, the list of predicate offences, and the scope of liability. The reports also evaluate the effectiveness of anti–money laundering measures as documented in available statistics regarding investigations and convictions.

Both Brazil and Argentina similarly define the money laundering offence and the main exceptions to it, but there are some differences.[23] First, self-laundering is not criminalized in Argentina, which is considered to be one of the main technical deficiencies of Argentina's criminal legislation. In other words, Argentine money laundering offences only apply to third-party launderers, and not to the perpetrators of the predicate offences (MER of Argentina 2010: 33, 37). Second, in Argentina the money laundering offence refers to assets originating from any criminal activity, whereas Brazil specifies a list of predicate offences. The FATF itself strongly supports extension "to the widest range of predicate offences," and indicates the minimal standard for a country to be considered in compliance with the Forty Recommendations (FATF 2004b: 7). A new Brazilian law on money laundering was being discussed (as of May 2011) that would eliminate the list of offences, so as to reach all criminal activity.[24] In Argentina, on the other hand, the FATF evaluation called attention to actions that are not defined and punished by criminal law, although considered civil violations, such as insider trading and market manipulation (MER of Argentina 2010, 33).

Regarding punishment, the FATF advocates proportionality and deterrence. The FATF reports for both countries consider the range of two or three to ten years of imprisonment to be "proportionate" (MER of Argentina 2010: 35; MER of Brazil 2010: 34). The Brazilian report found that the punishment established was sufficient to assert its dissuasive character, despite its lack of effectiveness (MER of Brazil 2010: 34). The Argentine report, however, found that the six months to three years range applied to some elements of the money laundering offence was "low." The latter report's discussion of the deterrence effect of the prescribed penalty was coupled with assessment of the actual application of the penalties; the report did not focus

[23] The basic money laundering offences are described at the "framing laws" 9613/1998, section 1 (Brazil) and 25.246/2000, section 3 (Argentina). Full versions of these laws are available in English at the respective FIU websites: www.coaf.fazenda.gov.br and www.uif.gov.ar (accessed January 28, 2011).

[24] These modifications of the anti–money laundering legislation were being discussed at the Brazilian Parliament as of May 2011 (Bill Project 3443/2008).

only on the existence of the criminal offence as in the Brazilian report (MER of Argentina 2010: 35).

The report found that the main Brazilian deficiency in this pillar was the lack of criminalization of terrorist financing. Since the UN convention for the suppression of financing terrorism came into force in the country, in 2005, units within the government have intended to create a broader offence of "terrorism" than the one from the 1980s, as well as a specific offence for the financing of terrorism. In an effort to avoid a "not compliant" evaluation in this regard, Brazilian authorities have mentioned the last of several "national securities laws" issued during the military dictatorship. However, the evaluation report considered that this law "focused on deterring a violent overthrow of Brazil's government" and, therefore, only covers much narrower circumstances than those referenced in FATF Special Recommendations. The report also states that during the on-site visit, most authorities "expressed the view that terrorism and financing terrorism is not a problem in Brazil" as an explanation for the lack of implementation of the international obligations embodied in both the UN convention for the suppression of financing terrorism and FATF Recommendation (MER of Brazil 2010: 43, 45). My interviewees provided another explanation: the administration could not reach an agreement on the definition of the terrorism offence. Despite a huge effort from COAF to adopt a definition as broad as the international documents required, other units of the government feared that this definition could be used to criminalize legitimate social movements, specifically the "Movimento dos Sem-Terra" ("Movement of the Landless").[25]

Argentina, on the other hand, amended its money laundering legislation in 2007 to criminalize both terrorism and the financing of terrorism. Nevertheless, the FATF evaluation found that the provisions were not fully in line with the FATF Recommendations (MER of Argentina 2010: 38–9).

Besides the technical deficiencies, the main concern of both evaluations regards the "lack of effectiveness" of existing measures. Both reports use the number of investigations, prosecutions, and convictions as indicators of effectiveness. A section called "statistics and effectiveness" presents and discusses the information presented by the national authorities to the evaluation team (MER of Brazil 2010: 34–9; MER of Argentina 2010: 35–6). The reports found that both countries did "not maintain comprehensive statistics" on the matter, and they raised several concerns regarding data collection.

In Brazil, the available information provided by the authorities for the purpose of the evaluation comes mostly from the specialized federal courts created in 2003. In Argentina, it comes from the units created in 2006 at the Attorney General's Office. The FATF reports find that, although the statistics are limited and incomplete, those

25 For an approach of the movement and its impacts on the Brazilian legal and social fields, see Houtzager (2005).

available have raised "serious concern about the overall effectiveness of implementation, given the size of the financial system and level of money laundering risk in the country." There have been only four prosecutions and no convictions in Argentina, and only eleven cases resulting in final convictions in Brazil (MER of Brazil 2010: 36; MER of Argentina 2010: 35).

The FATF report for Brazil finds that the main deficiency comes from the fact that each institution involved in the criminal justice system – police, public prosecutors, and the judiciary – is responsible for keeping its own statistics (MER of Brazil 2010: 34). The report points to systemic problems within the Brazilian judicial system and not to the anti–money laundering measures themselves (MER of Brazil 2010: 36). In the Argentine case, the report states that that self-laundering is not criminalized in Argentina, and the low penalties for some laundering through third parties are among the several factors leading to a finding of deficiency (MER of Argentina 2010: 37).

2. The Obligations of the Economic and Financial Sectors

The second pillar of the AMLO is mandatory reporting of suspicious transactions. According to the FATF's recommendations, each country should delineate a list of persons subject to the obligations of identifying customers, keeping updated records of those customers, and reporting transactions.

In Brazil, different supervisory agencies are in charge of adopting specific regulations within their jurisdictions, such as the Central Bank, CVM (Securities Commission), SUSEP (Superintendência de Seguros Privados; Agency of Private Insurances), and SPC (Secretaria de Previdência Complementar; Secretary of Complementary Social Security). The FIU (COAF) is responsible for regulating all other areas, subject to underlying legislation.[26]

In both countries, the legal frameworks provided by the AMLO set out only the general requirements regarding preventive measures for finance and other areas. These requirements are complemented and elaborated by various types of regulatory instruments issued by the different authorities. The report of Brazil sets forth an organizational chart of sixty-nine instruments in force (MER of Brazil 2010: 92).

The 2010 Reports of both countries show that regulatory authorities in Argentina have been much more reluctant in implementing the requirements for the financial and economic sectors. Of the four FATF recommendations concerning these measures, Argentina was considered to be "noncompliant" with two of them and "partially compliant" with two others. The report most frequently notes lack of provisions of law as a deficiency (MER of Argentina 2010: 10, 104–8).

[26] Brazil defines these areas in Law No. 9613/98, section 9–11. Argentina defines them in Law No. 25246/00, section 20.

The picture is quite different in the case of Brazil. In the years that followed the enactment of Law No. 9613/98, the supervisory agencies issued norms and regulations detailing obligations applying within their respective jurisdictional areas. These norms specify the type of information that reference files should provide, which records should remain stored at the institution for a period of five years, the information to be entered in these records, and the category of operations that should be reported to the COAF and other supervisory authorities.

The 2010 Report considered Brazil "largely compliant" with three of the four recommendations and "partially compliant" with one of them. The main deficiency identified was that many customers' due diligence obligations are not set out "in law or regulation"; rather "other enforceable means" are used, which are considered to be insufficient for full compliance (MER of Brazil 2010:126).

The AMLO addresses the scope of the reporting obligations, which create a bridge between the criminal and financial fields as to what is to be reported. The FATF provides two recommendations: (1) to report when there is suspicious activity or "reasonable ground to suspect that funds are the proceeds of a criminal activity"; and (2) to report "all domestic and international currency transactions above a fixed amount" (FATF 2003: Recommendations 13 and 19). Both countries were considered in compliance with the last recommendation, although Brazil implemented this system years ago, and Argentine authorities only demonstrated that this reporting system is "currently under consideration" in the country (MER of Argentina 2010: 127).

3. A New National Institution: The Financial Intelligence Unit (FIU)

The FATF considers the creation of a national agency to centralize the functioning of the AMLO to be a key element in a national regime. In this critical regard, Brazilian and Argentine experiences differ considerably. Although both countries formally created an FIU in their AML Laws, the Brazilian FIU (COAF) started to operate immediately, in 1998, whereas the Argentine FIU started operating in 2002, two years after its formal creation. This difference is reflected in the interaction of both FIUs with the Egmont Group, an informal meeting of 120 FIUs, established in 1995 to encourage international cooperation in the areas of information exchange, training, and sharing of expertise. COAF and the Argentine FIU joined it in 1999 and 2003, respectively (Egmont Group 2010: 7; MER of Argentina 2010: 9; MER of Brazil 2010: 66.).

In the 2010 Report, the Argentine FIU was considered "ineffective" because of technical deficiencies, as well as a lack of adequate human and material resources to accomplish its goals (MER of Argentina 2010: 60). Regarding human resources, the Report states that at the time of the on-site visit, FIU staff had 74 employees but only two in a "permanent position," whereas the others were under temporary contract. The Argentine media has also highlighted the lack of adequate human resources at the FIU, pointing to the intensive changes during 2010, when eleven persons assumed the coordination.[27]

On the other hand, COAF was considered to be "an important institution in Brazil's AML framework" and also "an effective and well-regarded FIU." Several improvements were highlighted in the report "to ensure that this continues" (MER of Brazil 2010: 71). The Brazilian authorities, unlike their Argentine counterparts, were able to provide detailed information regarding the number of suspicions transaction reports (STRs) and currency transaction reports (CTRs) received by COAF, the exchange of information with local and foreign authorities, their budget, and even the number of hours of training the staff received (MER of Brazil 2010: 60–71).

Many factors have contributed to the disparities in the operation of the two FIUs. One important factor seems to be that Argentina took many years to pass a law authorizing the financial sector to submit information requested by the FIU. When the Argentine FIU started operating in 2002, banking institutions and the Federal Administration of Public Revenue maintained that bank and tax secrecy precluded submitting the information requested by the FIU. In many cases, it became necessary to start a judicial case to ask for the removal of bank or tax secrecy. In April 2006, Law 26087 provided that the economic and financial sectors were obliged to report and could not argue bank or professional secrecy, or even legal or contractual commitments of confidentiality, to avoid their reporting obligations. The law also provided that the Federal Administration of Public Revenue could only remove tax secrecy when the organ itself reported the suspicious transactions, and only in relation to persons (natural or juridical) directly involved in the reported transaction. In all other cases, the FIU must ask a federal judge for tax secrecy removal, and the judge has at most thirty days to decide the matter (MER of Argentina 2010: 60).

Brazil had to change its tax and bank secrecy law as well to permit FIU operation. The FATF requested this change during its first evaluation of Brazil, when the country became a member. Brazil passed a new law a few months later, in 2001, which provided the COAF, Brazil's FIU, with unrestricted access to information.

The most consistent explanation for the differences between Brazil and Argentina seems to be the way each country has responded to the issue of public intervention regarding financial activities. In the case of Argentina, my interviews show that money laundering has been regarded as an external phenomenon, and that public control over financial activities is not a priority for the country. Argentina would never have established its measures without FATF pressure. In fact, it took six years for Argentina even partially to remove the secrecy restrictions that prevented the FIU from functioning. The Argentine process has been consistently blocked by conflicting internal interests, with the result that Argentine policy changes have

[27] This was reported in *La Nacion* on December 29, 2010. The information was confirmed through interviews.

consisted largely of improvised reactions to FATF pressures (Machado & Jorge 2009).

C. *Beyond AMLO: Brazil's Initiatives*

Brazil, in contrast to Argentina, has actively developed its own strategies and adapted its institutions accordingly. The implementation of its anti–money laundering norms has been taken seriously by Brazilian administrations, even when facing budgetary restrictions and internal policy disputes. A number of institutional changes in the Brazilian state were necessary. They can be divided into two groups: the creation of new institutions and rules, and the adoption of new tasks in existing institutions. The first set of changes is exemplified by the creation of an FIU (in the Ministry for the Economy) and a central authority (in the Ministry of Justice), the shift of international cooperation responsibilities from the judiciary to the administration, and the creation of specialized groups on financial crime in Brazil's federal judiciary and its Central Bank. Regarding the second change, existing government institutions have produced and reorganized their databases and provided statistics about their activities in light of FATF Recommendations. It is clear that the FATF evaluation policy has strongly encouraged both sets of state changes.

Brazil, however, adopted its own initiatives to address national deficiencies that it identified internally in light of domestic policy challenges. The first example is the development of the *BacenJud*, an Internet information request system that allows for information exchange directly between judicial authorities and the financial sector. It was introduced in 2001. Prior to this, the Central Bank received these requests from the judicial branches and forwarded them to the financial institutions. The financial institutions would then make copies of account statements or other requested bank documents and send them to the requesting judicial authority. This procedure entailed extensive paperwork and was very time consuming. The introduction of *BacenJud* permits judges with previously registered passwords to request financial information that is automatically forwarded to the respective financial institutions. Using data encryption technology, the system recognizes orders for the lifting of financial secrecy, as well as for freezing and unfreezing bank accounts (BACENJUD 2005).

A second example is the creation of a new National Strategy to Combat Money Laundering (ENCLA, Estratégia Nacional de Combate à Lavagem de Dinheiro) through coordination of the judiciary and the relevant ministries and administrative agencies. The Minister of Justice commenced an initiative at the end of 2003 to remedy the lack of coordination among Brazil's various government institutions. At the time, there were no common training programs for public agents or uniform database policies and technological standards. Since then, a group of high- and middle-range representatives of these public institutions has met annually to discuss internal deficiencies, identify overlapping tasks, and formulate plans of action. This group is open to civil society input and participation. At the end of 2006, a "C" was added to the ENCLA (which is now known as ENCCLA) to reflect the formal addition of the mandate of combating corruption. More than seventy Brazilian organs attend the ENCCLA meeting. The 2010 FATF Report on Brazil highlights that ENCCLA has been functioning as a "mechanism for consultation between the competent authorities and the private sector," (MER of Brazil 2010: 226) and, therefore, is an "important factor contributing to Brazil's progress" (MER of Brazil 2010: 26).

Argentina has noted the development of ENCCLA, although the Argentine process still appears to be driven primarily by the need to respond to the FATF. In its 2006 report, the Argentine FIU notes the creation of a "national coordinator" to represent Argentina in the FATF and GAFISUD. Among its activities is the formulation of a national project to deal with money laundering issues. The idea is to invite public administrative organs to participate in the process. My interviews have shown that Argentine representatives have closely followed the ENCCLA process. Nonetheless, when, in 2007, the Argentine government approved a "national agenda to combat money laundering and terrorism financing," it appeared to track primarily FATF recommendations. The document establishes twenty goals, and the organs responsible for implementing them. Each goal mentions one or more FATF Recommendations as a reference. This aspect suggests that the goals were defined to obtain compliance with the Forty Recommendations, and not to establish a national program according to Argentine needs.[28] One year after the approval of the agenda, none of the goals was accomplished (Marteau 2008).

Right after the adoption of the 2010 Report, Argentine authorities engaged in a strategy directed at strengthening the FIU. On December 1, 2010, Argentina decided to concentrate within the FIU all supervisory powers, as well as the representation of Argentina to FATF and other international bodies. According to Argentine newspapers, confirmed through my interviews, this change is one of the packages of measures through which Argentine authorities are preparing to address the deficiencies highlighted in the 2010 FATF Report.

3. TRANSNATIONAL TRANSFORMATIONS OF THE STATE

A. *Five Dimensions of State Change*

The transnational legal order to address money laundering resulted in extensive changes in national law in both countries. Three sets of prescriptions analyzed above – directed to individuals, financial and economic sectors, and the state – were

[28] On the contrary, according to the author's interviews, the main purpose of the national agenda was to define a national strategy to deal with financial crime and money laundering problems, and fulfilling FATF recommendations was a consequence of that.

implemented through the enactment of legislation by the national parliaments. The norms directed at the private sector provide an example of the range of legal instruments that this transnational legal order generated in both countries. Changes in law were symbolically very similar within all three pillars of the transnational legal order. The same can be said of the practical dimension of these changes: both countries are making efforts to investigate and prosecute money laundering offences; financial and economic sectors are producing suspicious transaction reports; and FIUs now exist to centralize the exchange of information. The transnational legal process to address money laundering has provoked changes in Brazilian and Argentine laws, both symbolically and practically. However, a number of concerns can be raised regarding the extent and limits of these changes to reach the goals established by the FATF. According to the standard-setters, much remains to be done at the legal, and most importantly, institutional level.

This transnational legal order benefited from other processes in place long before the money laundering phenomena. The AMLO's call for criminalization has found fertile ground owing to the solid foundations of modern penal rationality in Western countries (Pires 2008). Argentine and Brazilian experiences at this point are very similar. Both countries have interpreted "proportionate and dissuasive sanctions" to constitute a minimum punishment of imprisonment for two or three years and a maximum penalty of ten years. In other countries, there might have been differences regarding the existence of minimum punishments or the amount of the maximum penalty, but certainly not the definition of imprisonment as "the" sanction.

The transnational legal process also provoked changes in the boundaries of both states. These changes support the argument that states are not retreating, but rather are been reshaped (Shaffer, Chapter 2). First, the AMLO illustrates strong public-private hybridism. The financial and economic sectors were central targets of the anti–money laundering norms. Because of the "know your customer," "record keeping," and "suspicious transactions report" mechanisms, these sectors are, so to speak, in the front line of investigations of money laundering. The participation of private actors in decision-making processes regarding legal and institutional reforms can be identified not only at the transnational level but also at the national level, as the increasing presence of private actors at ENCCLA meetings demonstrates. Second, changes in the boundaries of the state can also be observed in what Shaffer identifies as growth in "material competencies of the state involving increased specialization and diversification of state administration" (Shaffer, Chapter 2). Beside the creation of the FIU and central authorities for international cooperation, several bodies within the administration developed their own money laundering departments to deal with regulatory and implementation issues. In the judicial branch, courts and public prosecutors in Brazil and at the Attorney General's office in Argentina developed specialized expertise.

The third dimension of change concerns the institutional architecture of the state. Both the interactions between the legislature and administration, and between the courts and the administration, are not particularly conclusive regarding "who is being empowered over whom." Nevertheless, the evidence gathered in this project is quite clear concerning the creation of new institutions and the reconfiguration of existing ones (Shaffer, Chapter 2).

The transnational legal processes may appear, at first sight, to support the argument of empowerment of executives, "leaving the legislatures to rubber stamp the results of international negotiations" (Shaffer, Chapter 2). As mentioned, the administration – through FIUs or national ordinances – leads the production and permanent reform of AMLO legislation.[29] At least in the Brazilian experience, however, we have no evidence that the empowerment of the executive vis-à-vis the legislature is a distinctive feature of the transnational legal process addressing money laundering. On the contrary, the Ministry of Justice has been playing a central role in many areas. Moreover, the legislature, even though it lacks influence in the production of the norms, determines the timing of the normative changes. The Forty Recommendations are insistent on the importance of the "legal status" of the normative changes they support. The legislature is always seen as "a reference" for national administration, as it determines what is likely to pass and what is not appealing.

The creation of the FIU as one of the central pillars of the AMLO has visible impacts on the allocation of power among the different branches of government. Although the standard definition of FIUs encompasses different shapes – judicial, law enforcement, administrative, and hybrid – the units in both countries share the characteristics of the "administrative model," as defined by the Egmont Group (2004: 2): an "administrative authority, which receives and processes information from the financial sector and transmits disclosures to judicial or law enforcement authorities for prosecution." The Brazilian COAF, within the Ministry of Finance, and the Argentinean FIU, within the Ministry of Justice, function as "a buffer between the financial and the law enforcement communities" (Egmont Group 2004: 2). Observing FIU activity as a "buffer" or a "bridge" between the financial and criminal fields undermines the argument that they are shifting authority away from courts. Pursuant to the "follow the money" approach of the AMLO, FIUs are providing new tools to the courts to strength their capacity for handling certain criminal activities. The argument of the empowerment of judges is also illustrated by the creation of *BacenJud* in Brazil, where judicial authorities now have easy, fast, and direct access to banking information. In the opposite direction, however, the granting of "investigative powers" and the wide access of financial information to the administration provide examples of some authority being shifted away from courts.

A fourth dimension of state change concerns the shaping of markets for professional expertise (Shaffer, Chapter 2). As recognized by a number of authors, owing to the specificity and wide coverage of AMLO norms, a new market of expertise

[29] The two mains examples are the Brazilian legal frame (Law 9613/98) that was conceived by the Ministry of Justice, and the discussion on the Project of terrorism financing.

for lawyers, accountants, economists, and business administrators has emerged.[30] In particular, the AMLO demands experts in the private sector to monitor and report transactions in an ever-growing number of economic sectors; to assist the FIUs to process and exchange the information received; to start and conduct investigations and prosecutions within specialized units; and finally, to represent the country at several international forums.

The role of expertise in the transnational legal processes is strongly demonstrated by the characteristics of the FATF mutual evaluation process. This process leaves room for negotiations among the national team and the assessment team regarding the interpretation of laws and institutional practices that have an impact on the ratings. The participation of the national experts in foreign evaluations is decisive for capacity building and development of epistemic know-how across countries.

Finally, a fifth dimension of state change regards the shifts in patterns of association and mechanisms of accountability that convey particular normative frames (Shaffer, Chapter 2). The AMLO is built upon the idea of monitoring, surveillance, and reporting obligations on at least two levels: from the economic and financial sectors to the FIUs, and from the whole set of state institutions to the international standard-setters. The engagement of Brazil and Argentina with these transnational accountability mechanisms has had a huge impact on both states.

However, the countries' degree of political will and institutional commitment to respond to these accountability demands differs considerably. Brazil's creation of ENCCLA illustrates its greater national commitment to combat money laundering in light of Brazil's own internal concerns. The ENCCLA mediates between internal and external demands for accountability. On the one hand, ENCCLA is explicitly recognized in the 2010 FATF Mutual Evaluation Report as a relevant tool for Brazilian progress. ENCCLA's goals, monitoring activities, and databases are quoted many times throughout the FATF Report. On the other hand, ENCCLA aims to respond to national interests and concerns even if they are not part of transnational priorities. The expansion of ENCCLA's activities to cover corruption, when terrorism financing was "the cue ball" for the US-driven transnational legal order, shows that external demands are relevant, but are not the only ones that matter.

B. *Legitimacy*

The legitimacy of the AMLO and, specifically, of FATF activities, has been discussed almost exclusively by distinguishing between member and nonmember countries. The FATF policies toward NCCTs and its mechanism of expansion through the FSRBs have attracted most of the attention in the literature. The comparison between two FATF member countries in this chapter sheds light on some aspects that are not

[30] On the role of experts at the mutual evaluation process, see Wilke (2008: 520). See also Sharman (2008: 642) (emphasizing the "lucrative industry for AML consultants").

addressed by the "member vs. nonmember" dichotomy. We thus need to deepen the comparison between Brazil and Argentina by building from Shaffer's proposal for assessing a transnational legal order's legitimacy "in terms of inputs (who participates in a process), throughputs (the quality of procedural fairness and deliberation characterizing such process), and outputs (how a process substantively responds to a problem)" (Shaffer, Chapter 2).

Input legitimacy is commonly described as "having a voice" (Brummer 2011: 307; Wilke 2008: 520). From Brazilian and Argentinean points of view, concerns over formal representativeness could have been raised before 2003/2004, when both countries became full members. After that, both countries had not only a voice but also the right to vote, even if the actual participation was asymmetric when compared with FATF core members. The distribution of voting power might be relevant for input legitimacy, but tells little about the quality of the decision process. The number and technical capacity of the experts play a decisive role in the preparation of the national reports, in the negotiation with the assessment team, and in the political discussion of the evaluation during its adoption at the FATF plenary meetings.

Finally, output legitimacy is the most sensitive and complex dimension of the transnational legal processes studied in this chapter. This topic is widely discussed in the criminal law literature under the concept of "effectiveness." The major difficulty derives from debates over the definition of the problem to which the process is responding, and, consequently, what goals are established to respond to it.

When criminality is defined as "the problem," the main goal is crime reduction, and the skepticism regarding how AMLO responds to this problem is normally great. The skepticism starts with uncertainty regarding the phenomenon itself (behavior compared to formal regulation)[31] and the actual harm of the social problem AMLO norms are to address.[32] It becomes much stronger when concerns are raised about the lack of evidence that the goal is being accomplished. Authors vary at most between finding "little evidence" and "no evidence at all" of effectiveness.[33] This way of approaching effectiveness faces some methodological challenges that have been discussed in the criminological literature for a long time. The concern is that the crime phenomena – increase or reduction – are frequently assessed through the official statistics of the criminal justice system: the number of investigations

[31] "Money laundering remains legally and empirically a hazy area. This is partly due to the phenomenon itself and partly to the way it is approached by politicians and policy makers" (Van Duyne, Groenhuijsen, & Schudelaro 2005: 135).

[32] "Money laundering has become one of the great morals panic of our day. A range of sources, including mass media, assert it is bad, very interesting, and slightly daring, but do not deal so much with what it is, how it is done, or why (otherwise than as a form of complicity in some previous offence) it is so damaging" (Alldridge 2008: 437).

[33] For example, Sharman (2008: 636) states that "there is very little evidence to show it actually works." The same concern can be found in Braithwaite (1993: 667–8), and Levi (2002: 190). Levi & Reuter (2006: 347–65) provide a broader discussion on the problem of assessing the effectiveness of the AMLO, and conclude that "how well the system works in suppressing crimes and preventing terrorist acts is entirely a matter of speculation."

started by the police, the number of prosecutions started by the public prosecutor, and the convictions made by the courts. The FATF measures the effectiveness of the AMLO criminal rules in this way. Our concern is not with the lack of statistics, which the FATF reports on Brazil and Argentina repeatedly critique, but of the limited role of official statistics to inform about the problem and about the accomplishment of the goals. The criminological literature on the methodological issues regarding "counting crime" lists several shortcomings of the data collection process, and concludes that these numbers do not measure crime in itself, but only the functioning of the institutions that are providing the data.[34] From this perspective, the effectiveness, or output legitimacy, of the anti–money laundering order is being reduced to a questionable effort to measure by statistics the impact of its prohibitive norms on individual behavior.

The problem that the AMLO is addressing can also be defined in view of the two other categories of prescriptions presented in Table 3.1 regarding the obligations placed on the financial sector and the creation of national FIUs. The problem might be defined as a lack of control over economic and financial activities, a lack of coordination among enforcement authorities, or a lack of mechanisms for the exchange of information. When these are characterized as "the problems," the way AMLO substantively responds to them is enthusiastic.[35] In this regard, qualitative information gathered through the mutual evaluation process is useful for providing information on how norms are enforced and how private and state institutions are addressing issues. But also, in this case, the impact of the enforced norms on individual behavior cannot be taken for granted, although it usually is.

Ideas regarding the mediation between "legal norms" and "individual behavior" have been dominated since the eighteenth century by the so-called 'modern theories of punishment' (Pires 2001, 2008). The concept of deterrence has been systematically used as a theoretic tool to express the effects of national enforcement of transnational norms on individual behavior. The FATF Reports on Brazil and Argentina have shown that the evaluation of the deterrent effect is attributed to different things. Sometimes the legislative message seems to be sufficient and the deterrent effect is assigned to the criminalization of the activity in itself or, more frequently, to the quality or quantity of the punishment. Other times, the deterrent effect is deemed to be conditioned on court decisions, specifically on the number of convictions (MER of Argentina 2010: 35).

Nevertheless, the deterrent effect of criminal punishment is highly contested. A huge literature focusing on the existence of associations between levels of crime and

34 Evans & Himelfarb (2000: 62) conclude that the "further you go into the system, the more obvious it becomes that you are counting something about how the system itself operates; you are counting official decisions about crime . . . ." See also, Muncie (2001: 196), and Walker (1983: 292).

35 Brummer (2011: 303) considers the FATF a case "where high adjustment costs were met by strong disciplining mechanisms" that have been "far from perfect." These mechanisms "seem to have incentivized coordination and most degrees of implementation among blacklisted countries."

sentencing practice has been produced and systematically reviewed. Focusing on the studies produced in the past twenty-five years, Anthony Doob and Cheryl Webster (2003: 147) state that "the majority of the reviews examined do not support the claim that harsher sanctions deter."[36] These studies focus on the relation between severity of sanctions and crime rates, and not on the capacity of the whole justice system to deter individual behavior. In other words, it is not exactly the deterrence ideal that is at stake here, but the impact of variations in the levels of punishment.[37] In the case of anti–money laundering, the deterrence idea is associated not exclusively with criminal law. The expectation that a legal norm will be able to deter both those directly participating (specific deterrence) and others who become aware of legal norm enforcement (general deterrence) is also associated with administrative sanctions, financial controls, and even civil proceedings.[38] The FATF reports on Brazil and Argentina also assign deterrent effect to others branches of law.[39]

The demonstration of the inadequacy of relying on deterrence is far beyond the objectives of this chapter. Our main purpose at this point is twofold. First, we emphasize that all efforts to include individual behavior in the argument of output legitimacy or effectiveness presupposes the acceptance of the highly contested idea of deterrence. Second, deterrence through criminal law sanctions is not the only way to assess the legitimacy of the transnational legal process from an enforcement perspective. Rather, one can also assess the enforcement of rules directed at the financial and economic sectors, and at regulatory agencies, that together make it possible to hold individuals accountable for violations of the law.

C. *Recursivity*

Transnational legal processes addressing money laundering in Brazil and Argentina involved dynamic interaction and tension between national and transnational

[36] See also Braithwaite & Petit (1990: 3), who assert that "the deterrence literature also failed to produce the expected evidence that more police, more prisons, and more certain and severe punishment made a significant difference to the crime rate."

[37] The deterrence ideal is being challenged both conceptually and practically. See, in this regard, Pires (2008) (on the deterrence theory as formulated by Cesare Beccaria); Doob & Webster (2003: 191) (referring to several Western sentencing systems that "do not subscribe to general deterrence – in part or in whole"); and Tonry (2008).

[38] See Brummer (2011: 290), who states that "an effective monitoring system can also have important deterrent effects," and also Levi & Reuter (2006: 297), who describe an anti-money laundering regime "as having two basic pillars, prevention and enforcement" and assert that "the prevention pillar is designed to deter criminals from using institutions to launder the proceeds of their crimes."

[39] The MER of Argentina (2010: 12) states that "the SSN [Superintendence of Insurance] also lacks clear supervisory powers; the range of sanctions at its disposal is not dissuasive and its sanction regime is not effective." The MER of Brazil (2010: 39), discussing the constitutional obstacles to introducing corporate criminal liability in Brazil, concludes that "Brazil should take legislative action to establish direct civil or administrative corporate liability for ML and ensure that effective, proportionate and dissuasive sanctions may be applied to legal persons."

policymaking. Following the conceptualization of dynamic cycles of recursive change noted by Shaffer (Chapter 2), evidence gathered in this research strongly supports some of the flows and raises questions and concerns regarding others.

The first flow emphasizes the role played by the export of national regulatory models to form a transnational legal order. In this regard, the United States' predominance is very clear (Andreas & Nadelman 2006: 10; Braithwaite & Drahos 2000: 27; Dezalay & Garth 2002a: 58; Nadelman 1993: 477). The whole set of anti–money laundering norms owes much to the United States, from the definition of the social problem to the creation of a detailed legal system to address it, although the support of other countries should not be neglected (Andreas and Nadelman 2006: 147; Levi & Gilmore 2002: 342). Moreover, the emphasis on monitoring techniques and "white" or "black listing" for noncompliance is part of national US policy and is widely embraced by FATF (Braithwaite 2005: 329). Besides the very well documented US participation in the lawmaking process and enforcement efforts, the United States is at least an observer member in virtually all FSRBs.[40]

A second flow of recursive change involves the resistances the transnational legal norms might face during the national implementation processes (Shaffer, Chapter 2). In this regard, the Brazilian and Argentine experiences demonstrate that resistance might be observed on many levels. In the Brazilian case, the first example of resistance discussed in this chapter was the extension of access of banking information to the FIU (COAF) without a court order, which is required by the Constitution. Under the pressure of the FATF's first evaluation, a new law was approved very quickly.[41] However, the process of implementation of the new legislation has not been completed. Opponents of the law moved to obtain a declaration of unconstitutionality. While this file has waited for the Supreme Court's decision for years, a number of projects to reform this legislation were presented to the Congress and are being closely monitored by ENCCLA (ENCCLA 2010: Action 7). A second example from the Brazilian experience comes from the lack of consensus within the administration regarding terrorism financing legislation. According to my interviews, the main explanation of the prolonged tension around this issue is the technical impossibility of defining "terrorism" without opening a door to the criminalization of legitimate social movements.[42] After seven years of debate, in 2008, the project to reform the Brazilian legal framework (Law 9613/98) creates a specific crime of "financing

[40] Of eight existing FSRBs, the United States is an observer in four, including GAFISUD, a "co-operating and supporting nation" at the Caribbean Group, and a full member of the Asian Pacific Group. The other two FSRBs only have members.

[41] According to the author's interview, the government – that was the author of project – had the support of the Central Bank, the Ministry of Justice, and the "international community."

[42] One of the interviewees added that the obstacles presented by the sectors of the administration on the proposal prepared to "satisfy FATF demands" could only occur in view of the left-wing nature of the Lula administration. "Another government, between international pressure and the social movements, would certainly choose the first."

terrorism" without using the word "terrorism." This solution is expected to satisfy FATF requirements without compromising the activity of legitimate social movements.

The Brazilian experience can be described as punctual resistance from social forces that are managing to keep the tension alive through the shifting of battlefields. In Argentina, however, it is hard to identify and describe punctual resistances, especially in the past years, when Argentina is perceived as a country that has decided to quit the game. According to my interviews, the 2010 evaluation shows that "the money laundering problem was totally out of the Argentine agenda." As Table 3.2 shows, Argentina took almost three years to conclude the second evaluation. The several follow-up reports required internal efforts and changes, the last of them being the approval of the national agenda in September 2007. After that, Argentine policy to address money laundering experienced a further setback.[43]

Finally, although the evidence gathered in this chapter strongly supports the two first flows of recursive change, it is scant regarding the others. The third and fourth flows address the possible impacts that national resistance might have "to trigger reevaluation and modification of the transnational norm" that is then, again, conveyed "to national institutions and processes" (Shaffer, Chapter 2). No evidence indicates that any of the changes that the AMLO underwent during the last decade were spurred by the resistances noted here. The overall impression of the transnational legal processes in Brazil and Argentina indicates that both countries are too concerned with the huge lists of demands to comply with the AMLO to make voluntary contributions to the transnational agenda. The Brazilian presidency of the FATF, which could have presented an interesting opportunity to trigger modifications based on the Latin American experience, has been described within Brazil as extremely relevant for making Brazil stronger in the international community, but not for having an impact on the transnational legal norms themselves.

4. CONCLUSION

This conclusion highlights three points. First, this chapter illustrates the *conceptual benefits* of the analytical framework developed in this book to capture the complex, diversified, myriad rules and institutions created in the past twenty years to tackle money laundering. The concept of transnational law has been usefully developed as a complement to that of international law to capture the diverse legal norms that address cross-border transactions. Yet the conventional concept of transnational law as "law applying to transnational situations" fails to capture the dynamic multilevel

[43] The expectations for the following years mirror Argentine experience after the second mutual evaluation reports. Several follow-up reports will be presented in the next FATF Plenary Meetings, which will continually stress the importance of its commitment to the international standards. Nevertheless, foreign and local interviewees do not believe that FATF would apply, for the first time, Recommendation 21 to a member country or suspend Argentine membership.

character of transnational legal processes that involve not simply traditional international law or new private or hybrid forms of lawmaking across borders. As this chapter illustrates, the concept of transnational law as transnational legal ordering, or the transnational construction and flow of legal norms, captures the construction and reconstruction over years of legal norms that can constitute a transnational legal order, but whose implications nonetheless depend on national contexts. Shaffer's concept, by focusing on the creation and conveyance of legal norms through transnational legal processes, is sufficiently comprehensive to encompass norms produced and rearticulated by transgovernmental networks, international institutions, national parliaments, national administrations, and private banks, including declarations of formally nonbinding principles, formally binding UN treaties, working practices, and a diversified set of monitoring and enforcement mechanisms. The concept of "transnational legal order" provides a powerful analytic tool for assessing the development and impact of transnational legal norms in a particular functional domain, in this case, that of anti–money laundering.

Second, this study calls into question perceptions of *legitimacy*, which rely on representativeness in an international institution. Measures of "input legitimacy" of FATF activities in terms of national representation elide the different capacities of actual participation in the structuring of global agendas and the development of global rules. "Throughput legitimacy," which focuses on procedural fairness, is important, but it is difficult to assess empirically in practice. Although document analysis provides helpful information on who participates in the process, only interactive methodologies, such as direct observation and in-depth interviews, can provide better evidence of the quality and fairness of the deliberation process. In this regard, the huge body of information provided by the FATF's mutual evaluation reports is of little help. As this study shows, they are much more concerned with measuring the implementation of transnational legal norms in a country than with the gathering of information regarding this country's participation in decision making. The disparate impact of transnational legal processes addressing money laundering in Brazil and Argentina confirms that membership strategies to foster the acceptance of transnational norms are not decisive in conveying state change. Literature that focuses on "members vs. nonmembers" dichotomy to present the asymmetries between the anti–money laundering order and the receiving states, and to address FATF rule-making strategies and legitimacy concerns, are insufficient.

Third, this chapter highlights the need for an analytical framework to assess the *effectiveness* of transnational legal orders empirically. This study shows that how a country formally responds to a particular transnational legal process is insufficient to frame an assessment of "output legitimacy" in the anti–money laundering domain. One must assess the national context and bottom-up factors, especially of national institutional capacities and political will, to explain state trajectories. Countries may transform the objective of a transnational legal norm in their implementation, as Brazil has done in focusing on corruption as opposed to terrorist financing, or they may not engage significant resources for actual implementation, as in the case of Argentina. This study opens rich venues for further research in this domain and others related to crime control strategies. How should a transnational legal order's output legitimacy be assessed? What should be considered "material results" to call a transnational legal order effective?

Working within the conceptual framework provided in this book, this chapter has examined the transnational legal order for money laundering in relation to the targets of behavioral prescription (states, state institutions, corporations, and individuals) and shown how these prescriptions have been differentially harnessed by Brazil and Argentina. The evidence gathered supports Fausto and Devoto's (2004: 20) claim that the "history of each of the countries had been much more attached to western political and economic centers than between each other." The GAFISUD experience and the institutional interaction between the countries' FIUs provide an empirical field to explore this claim.

4

Architects of the State

International Organizations and the Reconstruction of States in East Asia

Terence C. Halliday

Since the fall of the Berlin Wall, and even more, after the Asian Financial Crisis, international financial institutions have committed themselves to an enormous enterprise of legal institution-building (World Bank 2002b). Backed by negative and positive economic sanctions, the Legal Departments of the International Monetary Fund (IMF), World Bank, and regional development banks have broken out of their straitjackets of transactional legal work to spearhead many initiatives to build legal foundations for markets (Carruthers, Babb, & Halliday 2001; Carruthers & Halliday; forthcoming; Halliday & Carruthers 2009). In this enterprise, they have been joined by international organizations (IOs), such as the United Nations Commission on International Trade Law (UNCITRAL) and the Organisation of Economic Cooperation and Development (OECD). The goal of this enterprise is nothing less than to create an international financial architecture that is firmly grounded on globally authorized national legal systems (G-22 1998a, 1998b), that is, transnational legal ordering.

There is nothing new in the recognition that law and development involve state-building or state-restructuring (Salacuse 2000; Santos 2000). In the first wave of law and development, public law was harnessed to centralized states that drove economic change from above. In law and development's second wave, private law has been championed in order to devolve responsibility for the economy away from state agencies and toward private economic actors. Each wave presupposes states with differing structures, not least the power of courts. In the second wave of law and development, however, the implication of law reform for state reconstruction is often invisible or opaque, either because it is buried beneath so-called technical law reforms or because IOs cannot be seen to be interfering in national politics. Thus, law reform manifests itself in arcane, commercial, and ostensibly market-related changes that are intended to appear far removed from power and its redistribution (Halliday 2010).

Corporate bankruptcy law is one such locus of highly technical global norm-making, a body of law and institutions that international financial institutions (IFIs) have sought to propagate across transitional and developing countries. Precisely because it is the realm of small numbers of technical experts and specialist organizations, it is a valuable exemplar of how ostensibly technical commercial law can convey within it substantial consequences for state structures.

Between 1998 and 2006, a plethora of initiatives emanated from sovereign states and multilateral transnational organizations to enable the orderly handling of cross-border bankruptcies (Clift 2002; Flaschen & Silverman 1994; 1998; Fletcher 1997; Westbrook 2000)[1] and to erect national corporate bankruptcy systems (Halliday, Block-Lieb, & Carruthers 2009; Halliday & Carruthers 2009).[2] These were urged on countries in the Global South[3] with varying degrees of vigor, persuasion, inducements, and even economic coercion (Halliday & Carruthers 2007, 2009).

Fifteen years after the Asian Financial Crisis, and more than twenty years after the collapse of former Soviet command economies, the IFIs concede that many of their efforts have stimulated resistance, distortion, and rejection. It is not surprising, therefore, that the Legal Departments of IFIs and other trade lawmaking organizations identify the implementation gap as an acute problem.

This chapter argues that the implementation gap occurs because the magnitude of reforms far exceeds narrow technical reforms and, in fact, reaches to restructuring of the state itself. Under the guise of trade lawmaking, IFIs are acting as architects of the state.

The chapter elaborates the argument in five steps. First, I show that national precedents in the United States and Britain for global norm-making presaged the principal institutional contours of state restructuring. Second, I describe how transnational and global designers of corporate bankruptcy norms elaborated and modified precedents in the United States and Britain for global dissemination. Third, overviews of reforms in China, Indonesia, and Korea demonstrate how a shift of bankruptcy-related functions in and around the state amount to a restructuring of the state itself – and with varied and often unsuccessful consequences. Fourth, I show that failures of state architects to produce significant settled reforms result from complex dynamics of recursivity. The final section identifies four sets of conditions that determine the ultimate efficacy of transnational legal ordering by global architects of the state.

[1] We draw a distinction in this chapter between "transnational" norms and processes, which refer to the universe of all sets of norms and processes that exist above the sovereign domain of states (and include bilateral, regional, multilateral, and global regimes), and "global" norms and processes, which either do, or are intended to, cover all nations in the world. See Shaffer, Chapter 1.

[2] A fully defined corporate bankruptcy system can include six elements: (1) substantive law; (2) procedural law; (3) courts; (4) a government agency to handle low-asset bankruptcies and regulate private practitioners; (5) out-of-court mechanisms for restructuring corporate debt, which may be private or state-based or both; and (6) a profession capable of handling corporate liquidation and rehabilitation. See below, Halliday & Carruthers 2004b.

[3] This is a shorthand for developing and transitional economies that are disproportionately, although not entirely, concentrated south of the equator. It also encapsulates countries of Central and East Europe and Central Asia, among others.

1. NATIONAL MODELS FOR TRANSNATIONAL LEGAL ORDERING

The global frequently institutionalizes the local, argues Santos (2000). At its extreme, this argument holds that any global or transnational institutionalization of norms is the elevation of one country's particular norms to the transnational status of universals. In the case of corporate bankruptcy law, in fact, two major sets of national reforms had a double impact on global formulation and dissemination of new norms. In 1978, the United States initiated what would become a global movement by extensively revising its bankruptcy laws and orienting them around a central unifying concept – that failing businesses with some hope of rescue should be rehabilitated within the protections of a bankruptcy court. The 1986 English Insolvency Act cautiously followed the US path toward a business bankruptcy law that would increase the probability of reorganizing rather than liquidating troubled companies.

On the one hand, each country's reforms had extensive potential impact on other countries in close trading or geopolitical relationships. The outworking of the US reforms became increasingly influential on countries within the US orbit, especially after the fall of the Berlin Wall. Major law reforms by Britain likewise were variously ramified across national frontiers throughout the British Commonwealth.

On the other hand, in the case of the United States, in particular, the central tendency of the US reforms became a touchstone for all international financial institutions and IOs that sought to create global and regional transnational norms for corporate bankruptcy systems. Indeed, some of the variation between the US and British versions of a corporate reorganization regime helped shape debates in IOs across the world.[4] More broadly, elements of the Washington Consensus that would be exported to the developing world, particularly on privatization and downsizing of the state, drew on the Thatcherite underpinnings of the English Insolvency Act.

The 1978 US Bankruptcy Code and the English Insolvency Act 1986 involved extensive substantive and procedural legal changes. Less obvious, however, were the institutional underpinnings of the substantive law. Both bankruptcy laws involved (1) shifts of regulatory power between the market and the state, (2) elements of state restructuring and reallocation of functions, and (3) changes in the structures and functions of the market (Carruthers & Halliday 1998). I shall later show that each of these had ramifications for restructurings of the state in countries after the Asian Financial Crisis and throughout the developing world.

A. *Re-Drawing the Boundaries of the Market and State*

In broad terms, corporate reorganization can take place in three institutions. First, it may be controlled by the state and take place under the supervision of state

[4] This chapter draws on research projects undertaken with Bruce Carruthers, Susan Block-Lieb, and Sooguen Oh. See Block-Lieb & Halliday 2007a; Carruthers, Babb, & Halliday 2001; Carruthers & Halliday 2007; Halliday & Carruthers 2004a, 2007.

authorities. When corporate reorganization is the primary responsibility of a government department, then state officials representing state interests preside over mergers and acquisitions, reorganizations, and liquidations, which dispose of enterprises in distress. Second, reorganizations might be left entirely to market forces, where creditors, such as banks, seize assets of companies unable to pay their debts as they come due, where more financially robust firms take over weaker firms, or where owners and managers simply dissolve a business that is no longer viable. Third, reorganizations might take place primarily in the market, but under supervision or regulation of a state entity, most often a court, but sometimes a specialized agency of trustees.

Where the public-private boundary is drawn has significant consequences for all parties to bankruptcy. If it is vested in the state, it endows officials with significant powers and discretion, often at the expense of private creditors and debtors. If it is left to the market, it yields major benefits to private parties, but often at the expense of a public interest. But the drawing of the boundary between state and market control of bankruptcies has significance not only for bankruptcies per se, but also for the functioning of the market as a whole.

It was precisely this fault line between market and state that defined a key aspect of Mrs. Thatcher's policy to dismantle the residues of Keynesianism in English market regulation and to reinvigorate the market. Her insolvency reforms pursued this aim on two tracks. One was to downsize the state. Consistent with its policy to privatize governmental functions wherever possible, the Department of Trade and Industry in 1979 advised the government's insolvency reform committee that it intended to engage in radical privatization, shifting as much bankruptcy work into the private sector as could be managed.[5] Its Green Paper in 1982 proposed moving the bulk of personal bankruptcy work away from the Official Receiver to private practitioners. Government agencies would focus instead on regulation of business bankruptcies that were more consequential. Although the government essentially lost this battle, it did move forward on another track, namely, to transfer frontline regulation of company directors of ailing firms from government officials to private insolvency practitioners (Halliday & Carruthers 1996). This it proposed and institutionalized by the creation of an insolvency profession that was specifically charged to report on the behavior of directors. Government officials would supervise the supervisors, thus removing the state from hands-on regulatory responsibilities (Carruthers & Halliday 1998).

Ironically, in the politics of US bankruptcy reforms, an opposite movement was proposed. Rather than relying on judges and lawyers to collude over the administration of bankruptcies, a practice that had led to corruption and the running down of corporate assets, a Brookings Institute Report, and later, the US Bankruptcy Commission, proposed establishment of a new state agency, the US Bankruptcy Administration (Stanley & Girth 1971; US Bankruptcy Commission 1973). Replacement of

[5] *Minutes of the Cork Committee*, September 19, 1979, paras. 6–7.

the "receiver-trustee-lawyer cartel" with disinterested expertise would remove some 70–80 percent of routine bankruptcy cases from the private market for professional services and deal with them administratively. "Nationalization" generated a strong backlash from lawyers and judges and ultimately died on the drafting tables of Congressional committees, not least because the mood of the Carter Presidency had little tolerance for more government when Carter was bent on reducing it (Carruthers & Halliday 1998).

The significance of these proposals lies not in their implementation. Both were rejected. Rather, they signify that the politics of bankruptcy reform put on the policy reform agenda the prospect that a state may divest itself of certain powers or arrogate to itself powers previously outside its direct control. This recognition of the mutability of the state–market boundary heralded a variety of institutional designs for developing countries where the public–private boundary would be shifted in one direction or the other.

B. *Restructuring the State*

The struggle over the US Bankruptcy Administration was not only about moving work from private lawyers to public officials. It also proposed a new state agency that would vest control not in the judiciary, where it traditionally belonged, or in the executive, where it would naturally reside, but under the control of Congress. The struggle this generated points to prospects for restructuring of the state around governance of failing corporations.

In Britain this took a modest form. The Cork Committee, set up by the government in Britain to advise on bankruptcy reforms, proposed that all insolvency cases be vested in a new insolvency court that would be expert, efficient, and rationalized, a not so subtle contrast with the current "ridiculous jurisdictional situation" that was "absolutely crazy," said a member of the Committee. A hierarchy of courts from the county level to the High Court would "adhere from top to bottom." Some work would also be moved out of the courts and onto the Insolvency Service. But it came to naught, as the Thatcher government could not tolerate added administration and cost at a time it was reducing the size and cost of the civil service (Carruthers & Halliday 1998: 456–70).

The proposal by reformers to upgrade radically bankruptcy courts in the United States had a different fate. The United States already had a specialized bankruptcy court, but it had been impugned by the Brookings Institution as "a dreary, costly, slow, and unproductive process" that was "shabby and indifferent," with the result that major corporations and banks wanted little to do with it. Spurred substantially by the bankruptcy judges and the financial community, the Commission proposed upgrading bankruptcy courts to the elevated status of "Article III" federal courts. Judges would be appointed by the President and serve for fifteen years. They would be specialists far removed from corruption. In short, they would deliver efficient, neutral, and competent justice. Although this proposal sparked vigorous resistance from the prestigious federal judiciary, in its broad outline it was signed into law on November 6, 1978 (Halliday & Carruthers 1998).

Although not anticipated in 1978, the significance of this innovation spilled far beyond the borders of the United States. The World Bank and IMF both assimilated the concept of specialized bankruptcy courts into their global norms and pressed the concept vigorously in their country-by-country reform packets (International Monetary Fund [IMF] 1999; Oh & Halliday, forthcoming; World Bank 2001a). This initiative, in turn, generated lively political infighting within court systems and between judiciaries and executives across the world.

C. *Restructuring the Market*

Bankruptcy systems require specialists. Because corporate failure involves cash flow and balance sheets, accounting expertise is essential. Because reorganization requires new capital, financial sophistication is integral to turnarounds. Because liquidation or reorganization of companies usually involves legal regulation, legal advice is usually critical. But the history of bankruptcy practice across countries demonstrates that the division of labor can be highly variable.

The model in Britain before 1986 had similarities to many parts of the developing world. Because insolvency practitioners did not require licenses and were not regulated by any government or professional association, the British insolvency domain bred a small class of workers who were variously labeled as "cowboy liquidators" or "company vultures." Because most practitioners were qualified accountants, they were among the professionals who seized the opening for reform to professionalize insolvency practice. The English Insolvency Act, therefore, is notable for its institutionalization of a specialized private industry of professionals who would qualify to preside over corporate liquidations and reorganizations. Parliament vested several professional bodies with powers of self-regulation so long as they had a code of ethical conduct, strict accounting rules, entry examinations, disciplinary powers, renewal requirements, and insurance coverage (Halliday & Carruthers 1996). The insolvency profession could now embrace lawyers, accountants, and possibly even surveyors. Most importantly, however, by delegating self-regulatory powers to private bodies, the government itself was able to minimize its regulatory responsibilities and interference – yet another mechanism for shifting work out of the state and into the market.

The impact of reforms for professions in the United States took a different form, but one not inconsequential for later transnational norms. Lawyers conventionally have monopolized bankruptcy work in the United States, but until 1978 this work was largely derogated within the legal profession and marginalized in boutique law firms. In part, its marginality derived from the limited challenges in the work; in part, they followed from a fee structure that gave few incentives for the most sophisticated lawyers to enter the field. The Bankruptcy Code changed this in a seemingly inconsequential change in fees that had extraordinary effects on recruitment to this subspecialty. On the one hand, the 1978 Code made it possible, indeed highly desirable, for large firms even before they were technically bankrupt to use the law as a shelter from creditors and a staging ground for restructuring a company so as to re-enter the market in more competitive mode. On the other hand, the new challenges this legally enabled prospect for creative reorganizations opened up attracted the best and brightest in the bar because it was accompanied by a change in fee structure. The Bankruptcy Code now permitted fees to be calculated in part by the size of the bankruptcy estate (all the assets of the corporate debtor) and the value brought to the reorganizing enterprise. No longer restrained by hourly billing, lawyers who retrieved millions or billions of dollars for the bankruptcy estate, and, therefore, gave restructuring a greater chance of success, could now benefit proportionately. It was a concept not so dissimilar to lucrative mergers and acquisition work. It had the effect of bringing top-flight lawyers into the field, thereby upgrading in the private professional market a quality of service that paralleled the upgrading of judicial sophistication and authority in the courts (Carruthers & Halliday 1998: 441–9).

The startling success of this innovation in the quality of bankruptcy practice was not ignored by IOs as they began to develop global and transnational norms. A sophisticated private profession functioned in two ways amenable to wider ideologies of transnational norm making. It permitted the state to retract its interventions into the market because it could delegate with confidence to private professionals so long as they were ultimately accountable, usually to courts. Even more, it demonstrated that the scope of corporate restructuring by professionals might be greater than hitherto imagined for state-owned enterprises in transitions from command economies, and of massive unwieldy conglomerates in state development economies. Yet again, precedents from advanced economies fed into sets of global norms that would radiate across the world, restructuring states, markets, and the boundaries between them.

2. GLOBAL AND TRANSNATIONAL DESIGNS FOR LEGAL ORDERING

Three sets of events propelled IOs into the construction of national bankruptcy regimes in developing and transitional countries: the fall of the Berlin Wall; the debt crises in pivotal developing and transitional economies, such as Mexico and Russia; and the Asian Financial Crisis.

After the fall of the Soviet Union, the newly emancipated command economies were impelled to institute bankruptcy systems as a condition of a market economy. New opportunities opened up for state restructuring, but now requiring substitutes for the ideologically discredited state-centered models. In the search for new models, those advocating an apparently coherent neoliberal orientation could fill the vacuum. Bankruptcy regimes that celebrated market solutions to failing companies, albeit solutions constrained and enabled by law, had immediate appeal. Not only the European Union, but also the European Bank for Reconstruction and Development (EBRD), the OECD, the World Bank, and IMF, among transnational organizations, hired consultants and contributed advice on an ad hoc basis to aid in reforms. This occurred without any coherent template or consensus among the IOs about substantive law or institutions, but they all involved both substantive and institutional reforms and they generally tended toward a relaxation of hard liquidation provisions that might prematurely kill businesses that had some hope of rehabilitation.

In the debt crises of Mexico and Ecuador, and even more radically, in the interventions of IFIs in Thailand, Indonesia, and Korea during the Asian Financial Crisis, an array of institutional and structural proposals became embedded in agreements between national governments and their multilateral bankers of last resort. These already began to show signs of convergence. It also became clear to IOs acting as "repeat players" that the repetition of *ad hoc* approaches squandered the cumulative experience of the IFIs and provided too little normative guidance for countries that sought to immunize themselves from prospective crises.

A. *Designers*

As a result of these three sets of events, a variety of global and transnational norms were formulated through the deliberations of five classes of actors, all responding from different perspectives to the same sets of events, progressively, in convergent ways (Halliday & Carruthers 2007). First, global clubs of nations, most notably the G-7 and G-22, charged IOs to develop norms and create regulatory frameworks, including debtor-creditor regimes, that would forestall financial risk and stimulate economic development (G-22 1998a). Second, global financial institutions, led by the IMF and World Bank, and regional financial institutions, particularly the Asian Development Bank (ADB) and EBRD, each developed transnational norms, whether standards (Asian Development Bank 2000), conclusions (International Monetary Fund [IMF] 1999), principles (World Bank 1999; World Bank/UNCITRAL 2005), or diagnoses (European Bank for Reconstruction and Development [EBRD] 1999). Third, these efforts were infused by expertise from international professional associations, the most prominent among them being the International Association of Restructuring, Insolvency & Bankruptcy Professionals (INSOL) and the International Bar Association (IBA). Fourth, a global consensus on bankruptcy norm making was forged by the United Nations Commission on International Trade Law (UNCITRAL), which drew all of the other interested IOs into its deliberations, as well as sixty representative state delegations (United Nations Commission on International Trade Law [UNCITRAL] 2004), building from its greater legitimacy as a representative UN organization (Halliday & Carruthers 2009). Fifth, several advanced economies, of which the United States was by far the most influential, exercised influence directly onto IFIs during national bailouts and directly through

UNCITRAL as a vocal delegation. The OECD, another club of nations, facilitated norm development and diffusion, principally through its annual regional forums in Asia, where the debt crisis had threatened to destabilize the entire world economy.

These transnational initiatives of global norm making drew on three sources. One was experiences of advanced economies, most particularly Britain and the United States, in their own domestic lawmaking efforts to create bankruptcy systems that would rescue troubled businesses if that were possible, preserve whatever value still remained in companies that were headed to liquidation, and protect creditors, workers, and the public interest. The other was from the experiences of IFIs themselves in their repeated efforts to create bankruptcy systems where none had previously existed or to reform bankruptcy systems in developing countries where their pathologies had led, so it was concluded, to national financial crises.

A more diffuse and third source derived from economic ideologies, some of which had already infused reforms in advanced countries, such as Thatcherism in Britain, and others of which would inform economic development in poor countries. For the latter, a paradigm of the second wave of law and development (Salacuse 2000) derived from the Washington Consensus and the Post-Washington Consensus. Where the former emphasized privatization, the latter acknowledged institutions, and legal institutions among them, as critical regulatory structures for developing economies (Easterly 2007). By the later 1990s, new doctrines of law and finance, sometimes fortified with suspect data (La Porta et al. 1997), coupled with institutional economics (North 1990), animated the legal departments of IFIs to engage in institution-building. Because this also enabled IFI lawyers to emerge from their subsidiary service role to economists, doctrines that emphasized legal foundations of viable markets gave IFI lawyers precisely the justification they required to insist that legal reconstruction must exist alongside economic reconstruction.

The Report of the Working Group on International Financial Crises of the G-22 opened with the assertion that "the international financial crisis that began in Asia, and has now spread to other continents, lends urgency to efforts to strengthen the architecture of the international financial system."[6] Among its key observations was "the critical importance of strong insolvency and debtor-creditor regimes to crisis prevention, crisis mitigation and crisis resolution."[7] Such regimes must provide a "predictable legal framework" for dealing with troubled firms, a regime that is "fair and predictable."

In this, the G-22 specified with respect to insolvency a basic premise of law and finance: "a comprehensive and effective legal and regulatory framework is a fundamental prerequisite for economic development."[8] The mantra repeatedly stated

[6] G-22. 1998a.
[7] Id., p. 5.
[8] Asian Development Bank 2000.

by all IFIs integrated this ADB premise into a theory of law and markets: good law increases investment, which in turn stimulates economic growth (and, for some organizations, reduces poverty). Good insolvency law, said the ADB, required "certainty and predictability," "commercial stability and order," "commercial efficiency," and "fair commercial or equitable treatment," as well as "transparency."[9] For the World Bank, "transparency, accountability and predictability are fundamental to sound credit relationships."[10] The World Bank well summarizes the viewpoint of the IMF, UNCITRAL, ADB, and other IOs that "strong institutions and regulations are crucial to an effective insolvency system." States UNCITRAL's Legislative Guide at the outset: the institutions of an insolvency system must provide "the most efficient, timely and fair outcome to those for whose benefit an insolvency regime exists."[11] An elaborate rhetoric sought to legitimate the norms in terms of their "modernity" and "universality" and inevitability (Halliday, Block-Lieb, & Carruthers 2009).

B. *Designs*

Global norms converged on the nine key objectives of bankruptcy systems promulgated in UNCITRAL's Legislative Guide on Insolvency (2004). In fact, these bore a close resemblance to those already appended to the G-22's 1997 report on the global financial architecture, a set of norms generally incorporated into most IO formulations. The UNCITRAL objectives are readily summarized by recommendations that express their principal heads:

> In order to establish and develop an effective insolvency law, the following key objectives should be considered:
>
> (a) Provide certainty in the market to promote economic stability and growth;
> (b) Maximize value of assets;
> (c) Strike a balance between liquidation and reorganization;
> (d) Ensure equitable treatment of similarly situated creditors;
> (e) Provide for timely, efficient and impartial resolution of insolvency;
> (f) Preserve the insolvency estate to allow equitable distribution to creditors;
> (g) Ensure a transparent and predictable insolvency law that contains incentives for gathering and dispensing information; and
> (h) Recognize existing creditors rights and establish clear rules for ranking of priority claims.[12]

9 Id.
10 World Bank/UNCITRAL 2005.
11 United Nations Commission on International Trade Law (UNCITRAL) 2004.
12 Ibid.

The underlying principle that animated all these objectives was an imperative that, whenever possible, a failing business should have the option and means to be reorganized rather than simply liquidated (Block-Lieb & Halliday 2006). This became a rallying cry not only for professionals, who benefitted from the intensive care that rehabilitative ideals demanded, but also from policy-makers, who much preferred laws that softened hard budget constraints and keep workers gainfully employed (Carruthers, Babb, & Halliday 2001).

Global and transnational actors eventually settled on six institutional elements for any bankruptcy system to conform to the consensus. These became the matrix that the activist and interventionist IFIs applied to the respective countries that they diagnosed for institutional deficiencies and prescribed institutional remedies.

1. Substantive and Procedural Law

Bankruptcy systems require substantive and procedural bankruptcy law. Implicitly, this requires legislative action to put on the books one or more statutes by which commercial actors can regulate their behavior in the market. Often it also requires executive action to formulate specific procedures that will make the process predictable and orderly.

2. Courts

Bankruptcy systems require courts. Their functions may range widely. Most narrowly, they arbitrate disputes among parties that otherwise would have managed liquidations or reorganizations through market transactions; they can also bind authoritatively private agreements. More broadly they may serve as the arena in which a liquidation is authorized and as the neutral authority that provides oversight of company reorganizations. Repeatedly, in the norms developed by development banks for insolvency, it is said that courts must be the centerpiece of any insolvency regime (International Monetary Fund [IMF] 1999; World Bank 1999, 2001a). Even if most liquidations or restructurings are not done in courts, at least the prospect that courts might intervene casts a shadow over all out-of-court negotiations and thereby anchors it (United Nations Commission on International Trade Law [UNCITRAL] 2004). But, as IFI officials and consultants repeatedly state, the impact of courts on the vast majority of out-of-court restructurings only works when debtors and creditors alike know that failure outside the courts will bring certain liquidation or other actions not entirely at the volition of the parties.

3. Out-of-Court Agencies

Bankruptcy regimes sometimes work most effectively when there are out-of-court agencies that can aid companies to restructure without the cost and delay of court proceedings. The Bank of England has produced its London Rules to facilitate workouts that are brokered by the Bank (Meyerman 2000). INSOL has Workout Principles for debtors and creditors to renegotiate loans outside of court.

4. Government Agency

Many countries have a government agency or ministry that handles bankruptcies less as a mediation service and more as an imperative organization. These range from the rare agency that is the principal locus of liquidation and reorganization rather than the courts (e.g., Colombia) to agencies that handle minor bankruptcies where the assets are not sufficient to compensate private practitioners (e.g., England's Insolvency Service). Government agencies frequently have a regulatory role over private practitioners and trustees that are appointed as fiduciary agents of the state. IFIs have installed several variants of out-of-court agencies in Latin America and Asia (Mako 2001, 2003). If out-of-court agencies do not work, then companies have recourse to courts.

5. Professions

Finally, bankruptcy systems require expert professions. Although it is conceivable to imagine an entirely government-staffed insolvency system, it occurs nowhere in advanced countries. If part of the predictability and fairness purported to be necessary for handling ailing corporations resides in courts, the other part resides in the private market for professional services. In various permutations, corporate failures usually require some combination of lawyers or accountants or specialist insolvency practitioners who may be licensed originally as lawyers and accountants. An effective insolvency system, therefore, requires the expansion of the private market for professional services, a market that can be stimulated and constrained by state actions, ranging from incentives to regulation (Asian Development Bank [ADB] 1999; International Monetary Fund [IMF] 1999; World Bank 2001b, 2005).

These six elements of a bankruptcy system have institutional corollaries. If, for instance, a bankruptcy system has not been operating in a developing market, the introduction of a powerful court injects an actor into commercial practice that interposes a state institution into negotiations hitherto conducted among private actors. If a state has been accustomed to administrative decisions over which major corporations will survive or which will be merged or liquidated, then a privatization of companies and of bankruptcy practice removes from the state a capacity to intervene directly into the affairs of business enterprises. These two examples point to a more general phenomenon. Almost any application of comprehensive insolvency norms to a developing or transitional nation will demand some restructuring of the state and hence a redistribution of power inside and outside the state.

3. STATE RESTRUCTURING

Empirical research on China, Indonesia, and Korea in the 1990s to 2007 demonstrates that state restructuring manifests itself in three main clusters: new functions for the state, a shift in functions and power within the state, and a displacement of functions from the state.

New functions for the state. In East Asia, all reform efforts sought to strengthen courts by giving them more power, by improving the quality and probity of judges, and by inserting courts more centrally into restructurings of debt incurred in the market. Occasionally, as in Indonesia, states were prevailed on by IFIs to create a new agency to relieve pressures on courts. This out-of-court agency injected the state into the mediation business – providing an arena, supposedly neutral ground between creditors and debtors, where financial restructuring of a company could occur without need to involve courts.

Shifts in functions within the state. Construction or reconstruction of bankruptcy systems invariably leads to a reshuffling of functions – and powers among state institutions. Within the court system, for instance, IFIs have regularly recommended the creation of a special court, sometimes with particular powers, enhanced rewards for judges, and greater public exposure – all of which can heighten the visibility and impact of this usually underprivileged branch of Asian states. But if judges are to have heightened powers to render judgments on matters of great economic consequences, they themselves require regulation and that, in part, has energized IOs to press for new regulatory structures institutionalized to scrutinize the finances of public officials and to forestall corruption, a ubiquitous corrosive of state authority in corporate bankruptcy cases. In state-led development economies, such as Indonesia, Korea, and China, the IFI formulas effectively also shifted regulatory control away from state agencies to the courts. This occurred in Korea, from the Ministry of Finance and Economy to the courts, and it is presumed to occur in China, away from the State Enterprise and Trade Commission, and its successor, the State Asset Supervisory Administration Commission (SASAC), to the courts, a shift that is partial and uncertain several years after implementation of the 2006 Enterprise Bankruptcy Law.

In addition, in each of China, Indonesia, and Korea, the imperative to create an effective bankruptcy system concomitantly empowered legislatures at the expense of executives. In place of arbitrary or regularized rulemaking and rehabilitation by civil servants, China, Indonesia, and Korea each drafted and passed major statutes to govern corporate reorganization. In China and Indonesia, this ostensibly moved the locus of decision-making power away from technocratic bureaucracies and into elective arenas – an entirely different locus of state authority with significantly different power configurations and governance accountability. I shall review below one main instance of this shift of power within the state: the retraction of Korean bureaucratic interventions into the restructuring of major market players and the expansion of court authority.

TABLE 4.1. *Sites of state restructuring by functions of state*

Functions	Structures	States: China	Indonesia	Korea
New functions *for* state	Empower courts	X	X	X
	Create new state or quasi-state agencies		X	
Shift in functions *within* the state	Move powers from executive to courts	X	X	X
	Create specialized courts		X	X
	Control of judges	X	X	X
	Limit illicit activities of state officials		X	
	Empower legislatures	X	X	X
Displacement of functions *from* the state	Create, empower market professions	X	X	X
	Empower creditors and debtors to initiate bankruptcy	X	X	X

Displacement of functions from the state. Openings widened in the 1990s for state functions to be displaced to markets or "intermediary organizations," as they are styled by the Chinese. This shift correlated with the discrediting of the state as an economic manager of command or state-development economies, and the overwhelming of the state by the magnitude of its ambitions. In reconstituted bankruptcy regimes, the state restructuring pressed by IOs took two principal forms. One required the creation of an insolvency profession, or the reconstruction of accounting, legal, and other professions, in order to provide an adequate supply of competent technical services for corporate turnarounds. In effect, this took the form of creating regulatory systems for professional service markets. Another required a new sense of responsibility and capacity of private market actors – debtors and creditors – to monitor and adjust to changing financial conditions of companies. Bankruptcy systems thus lowered direct oversight responsibilities of government officials and heightened incentives for market actors to maintain vigilance over the financial condition of debtors and to take readily available steps to remedy situations where credit and firms were at risk. I review below one notable case in point: China's effort to retract direct administrative control over state-owned enterprises and to energize market solutions.

Table 4.1 summarizes several types of state restructuring that occurred in the three countries. The remainder of Section 3 analyzes one notable example of struggles over state restructuring from each country that illustrates a particular category of state change.

A. *Displacement of Functions from the State: China*[13]

In command economies, all decisions for enterprises were made by government officials. The fall of command economies in the former Soviet Union, and the diminution of command economies in East Asia (e.g., Vietnam, China), involved simultaneously the release of the private market to grow at its own pace and the restructuring of the state-owned sector, among other things, to push state-owned enterprises (SOEs) out of the comfortable cocoon of state protection and into competitive markets.

In the years following Deng Xiaopeng's opening of China's economy to market forces in the late 1970s, an array of commercial laws were introduced to the National People's Congress (NPC) (Peerenboom 2002). China's first bankruptcy law since the Republican Period, the Enterprise Bankruptcy Law (1986 EBL), was affirmed by the Standing Committee of the NPC in December, 1986 (Cao 1998a, 1998b; Zheng 1986). This draft law applied only to SOEs, but it had two crucial provisions: an enterprise could be liquidated if it were declared bankrupt; and, if an enterprise showed some prospect of becoming economically viable, it could be restructured in its finance and operations (Peng 1987). In these two provisions, the law stepped outside the parameters of a command economy that hitherto had not contemplated that enterprises could be closed and workers laid off. It also anticipated what would become a central theme of government policy in coming decades – the preference to restructure rather than dissolve enterprises.

China's State Economic and Trade Commission (SETC) had principal administrative responsibility for managing the SOE sector. In 1994, it took the first of a series of administrative measures to compensate for the almost complete failure of the 1986 Enterprise Bankruptcy Law to liquidate or restructure companies.[14] It pressed for reorganizations inside the state-owned sector rather than liquidations. Alongside this initiative, the Central Bank in 1994 instituted its Capital Structure Optimization Program (CSOP), whereby banks could write off a certain number of loans by allowing weak enterprises to be liquidated. This experiment began in 1994–5 with eighteen large cities and some seven billion yuan in prospective write-offs, expanded to fifty-six cities in 1996, and, by 1998, had reached 118 cities with write-off quotas at forty billion yuan. In all cases, complained foreign specialists, the heavy hand of the state guided permissions for bankruptcy, merger, acquisition, and reorganization (World Bank 2000: 3–4). The net result, however, was simultaneously to strengthen the financial viability of the best firms, so eventually most could compete in a market, while eliminating most firms that required state subsidiaries and would never earn their way.

[13] For an extended analysis of this case, see Halliday & Carruthers (2009), chapter 7.

[14] Asian Development Bank (ADB) 1996: 32.

Despite the use of bankruptcy courts for failed companies, it became increasingly clear that China's fast-growing market sector was ill-served by the primitive state of its bankruptcy system (ADB 1996). The Enterprise Bankruptcy Law (EBL) applied only to SOEs. Most enterprises in China were neither within the jurisdiction of the 1986 EBL or the object of close attention by state authorities. China regulated corporate failure with a multiplicity of regimes: (1) for SOEs in general, the 1986 EBL; (2) for SOEs in selected cities and industries, the regulatory regime erected by the SETC; (3) for other "legal persons" (i.e., non–state-owned companies), there are some limited bankruptcy provisions in the Civil Procedure Law and Commercial Law; (4) for companies in special economic zones, such as Shenzhen, there are special laws; and (5) for joint ventures with foreign companies, the Ministry of Foreign Trade and Economic Cooperation (MOFTEC) had special regulations.

Beginning in 1994, the government opened up a second track of reforms, this time legislative. The NPC Committee on Finance and Economy established a drafting team with the charge to create a comprehensive bankruptcy law that would encompass all enterprises in China, state-owned and private, legal person and non-legal person, wherever they were located. To inform its deliberations, the People's Republic of China (PRC) sought technical assistance from the ABD. In a series of studies and reports,[15] the Bank called for a comprehensive, consistent bankruptcy law for all trading entities with legal and natural person status. It proposed the establishment of a complete insolvency system: specialized courts with trained judges and officials, competent professionals, and a regulatory agency within the government. At the same time, it also sought structural changes that would differentiate bankruptcy practice from administrative interventions in order to "establish a very clear demarcation line between the involvement of the executive arm of government and the judicial arm in the administration of the new law." Yet it also recommended the creation of new state agencies – a central clearinghouse to handle bank vulnerabilities and the huge amount of debt owed between state enterprises, as well as a "powerful, independent, specialized" state agency to handle bankruptcies of SOEs that could never survive in a competitive market.[16] Its principal substantive thrust was an emphasis on enterprise reorganization.

The ADB's analysis and prescription coincided closely with the judgment of the World Bank four years later.[17] While the Bank advocated a comprehensive

[15] R38–95 (1995), Report to ADB Directors; TA 2271-PRC (1996), Final Report on State Enterprise Insolvency Reform; TA 2748-PRC (1997), Draft Final Report on Restructuring of Insolvent State Enterprises.

[16] ADB 1996: 6.

[17] The Bank mounted a more expansive and systematic evaluative exercise, which included analysis of SETC and court bankruptcy data, interviews in five cities (Shanghai, Shenyang, Changsha, Wuhu, and Loudi), a statistical analysis of 195 completed bankruptcies in four cities, and fifteen case studies (World Bank Draft Report September, 2000: i).

bankruptcy law for all enterprises, including natural person enterprises, it recommended phasing in SOEs in order to mitigate potential social effects.[18]

In 1996, the NPC technical drafting committee produced a draft that sought to hold in tension features found in most capitalist countries and those with a distinctive Chinese character.[19] The draft law proposed the usual provisions for liquidating companies, but it strongly emphasized a capacity for reorganizing companies. Unlike the 1986 EBL, it reflected an increasing awareness of bankruptcy systems in advanced countries, and particularly Germany and Australia. It marked a significant shift toward a court-controlled process that is driven principally by creditors and relies heavily on specialized trustees and practitioners. Nonetheless, the powerful Legal Work Committee of the NPC called the process to a halt in 1996. For four years, members of the drafting team visited various parts of the world, broadened their exposure to foreign systems, and prepared to resume their deliberations, which they obtained permission to do in 2000.

From 2000 to 2005, the NPC drafting team produced a succession of drafts, all of which gave failing firms three options: to be liquidated, to go through conciliation (a sort of debtor-creditor negotiation for smaller companies), or to be reorganized under court protection. Various entities of the NPC brought in consultants from the World Bank and ADB. Most importantly, the German aid organization Deutsche Gesellschaft für Technische Zusammenarbeit (GTZ) hosted a series of conferences on successive drafts to which it brought leading international specialists to comment on potential refinements of the law.[20] In 2006, the OECD hosted another large conference in Beijing to spur reforms in a direction consistent with international standards (OECD 2008). Later that year, the new Enterprise Bankruptcy Law (2006 EBL) was adopted by the NPC Standing Committee, to come into force on June 1, 2007.

Passage of the law had two significant consequences for the structure of the state. On the one hand, it purported to remove the state almost entirely from direct administrative control of all enterprises. The principal exceptions were a special category of 2,167 SOEs that were carved out of the bankruptcy regime, at least for a time, to be administered by the powerful State Asset Supervisory Administration Commission (SASAC). State regulatory agencies also retained some discretion to keep the reorganization of substantially state-owned enterprises out of the courts. The 2006 Enterprise Bankruptcy Law signaled one more major retraction of the state from direct economic administration. On the other hand, this shift to market forces, managerial discretion, and market professions significantly enhanced the potential power of courts. Although much of bankruptcy practice would now rely

[18] Because the World Bank believed that government fears over social instability were particularly acute for SOEs, this is a tactical move to remove a barrier to immediate passage of the law.

[19] We refer here to the Bankruptcy Law of the People's Republic of China (draft), hereafter cited as Draft Law, dated April 26, 2001.

[20] Cf. GTZ, "Brief on Recent Developments in Chinese Bankruptcy Law" 2004. Internal Report.

on private professionals, the state reinserted itself as a forum of last resort, although now as an arena for debtor-creditor negotiations.

China's construction of a bankruptcy system, and the correlative reconstruction of state involvement in corporate restructurings, did not result from the imposition of transnational norms on a weak financial and political system. The engagement of the IFIs and bilateral aid organizations occurred on China's terms, as the reforms very much followed China's timetable. Nevertheless, the final result shows a striking convergence toward the global norms enunciated by the World Bank and UNCITRAL. Thus, the secular change in China's social market economy demanded legal mechanisms to handle market failures. China put these in place carefully, experimentally, and incrementally. China set the terms of IFI and donor involvement. In the final event, however, the successive engagements of transnational organizations in China's reforms, and the reformers' increasing awareness of other national practices, led to the enactment of a law that adheres broadly to the governing principles of global insolvency norms. Whether this shift in formal law would be matched by law-in-practice, however, has remained a much more uncertain outcome (Halliday 2007).

B. *Shifting Powers inside the State: South Korea*

The case study of Korea illustrates how transnational pressures shift the allocation of power among state institutions. The architecture of state institutions came into sharp focus in the Korean bankruptcy reforms, not least because the Asian Financial Crisis spurred the concentration of a large number of reforms into an express package negotiated between the government of Korea and multilateral institutions in 1998. Korea's remarkable rise from a third-world to first-world economy in three decades followed the classic state development model of economic growth, where powerful government agencies not only set macroeconomic policy, but also intervened deeply into the microeconomy. Industrial policy was directed by Korea's powerful Ministry of Finance and Economic Planning Board, and agencies that channeled credit decided which industries would be prioritized and how tariff protections would shelter nascent industries until they were ready to compete on the world market (Cumings 1997; Woo-Cumings 1999; Woo 1991). Government ministries intervened directly into the affairs of major companies, essentially determining which would obtain financing, which should be restructured, and which might be liquidated. Corporate restructuring, therefore, rested substantially in the hands not of market actors, but of state agents, a proposition as true for the industrial as well as for the finance sectors.

Where the fates of companies substantially reside in the hands of officials, little recourse is made to bankruptcy law. Between 1990 and 1996, an average of less than 100 cases used Corporate Reorganization, Composition, or Bankruptcy Laws to cope with financial distress (Nam & Oh 2000; Oh 2001). Few judges had ever handled a bankruptcy case. Any financial weakness of consequence in a company brought an administrative response, but the structural issue far exceeded bankruptcy proceedings. The powerful finance agencies of the state doubted the capacity of the courts to handle major economic cases. Although judges were among the most highly qualified law graduates and their position carried high status, their training and proclivity gave them limited mastery over certain types of commercial cases. For government ministries to retreat from direction of the economy, as the prescient Booz-Allen Report recommended in 1997, a sharp change of course involving a paradigmatic change of economic governance was required (Booz-Allen & Hamilton 1997).

When the financial crisis in late 1997 impelled the Korean government to seek a financial bailout, the IFIs imported their institutional template for macroeconomic change, prescriptions which included legal regimes for market regulation. Bankruptcy reforms and corporate restructuring regimes featured prominently in the IFI's mandate for change (Mako 2001, 2002a, 2002b; Oh 1999). The most notable, in effect, was to limit severely the intrusiveness of the Ministry of Finance and Economy (MOFE) into microeconomic decision making, not least the extension and direction of credit. Banks and debtor corporations would make market-based decisions, including those about reorganization and liquidation. The treatment of failing companies that could not be managed in the private market would now be conveyed to the courts. In a word, the World Bank and IMF envisaged a renovated court-based bankruptcy system that would effectively transfer the microeconomic powers from MOFE to market actors and the courts. Laws, not administrative discretion, would create the new governance regime for corporations in financial difficulty.

The IFIs recognized that, at the height of the crisis, decisive administrative action could not be avoided. The government announced a series of "Big Deals" in October 1998, which compelled major Korean conglomerates to merge, principally it has been thought, to maintain their financial viability and improve their balance sheets (Nam & Oh 2000). In partnership with the new Financial Supervisory Service, MOFE compelled domestic banks to sign a Workout Accord in which they committed to develop a set of out-of-court practices to monitor more effectively the financial situation of their borrowers. If companies became financially distressed, banks were expected to compel financial restructurings, all of which were intended to keep companies out of bankruptcy – and away from courts (Iskander et al. 1999; Meyerman 2000; Oh 2005). MOFE continued to expand these out-of-court expedients in subsequent years, with a 2001 Workout Amendment, and, later that year, enactment of the Corporate Promotion Restructuring Act, measures which ironically sought the powers of courts to make binding Memorandums of Understanding that hitherto had lacked the force of law (Mako 2002a; Ministry of Finance and Economy, Korea 2001, 2002; Oh 2002).

In the best of circumstances, the implementation of out-of-court measures by banks would have attenuated direct administrative interventions into the affairs of firms by government agencies. In fact, because several of Korea's most prominent banks themselves had required an infusion of government money, government regulators often were integrally involved in day-to-day decision making. Much more importantly, however, alongside the retraction of MOFE from micromanagement of firms, the World Bank and IMF legal departments pressed the government of Korea to push courts far deeper into commercial life, upgrade the commercial expertise of judges, and strengthen the competency of courts. They proposed a plan to establish in Korea a specialized bankruptcy court to accomplish these aims.

The concept of a specialized court sprang directly from the US Bankruptcy Code and had made its way into the norms of the Washington-based IFIs. Consistent with the debate in the US Congress during passage of the 1978 Code, IFIs supposed that a specialist, highly competent, experienced judiciary with clear jurisdiction and extensive powers could be entrusted with the most sophisticated of company restructurings. Months earlier the IMF had proposed a specialized Commercial Court in Indonesia, a proposal that the government of Indonesia accepted. Because Korea already had an Administrative Court and Patent Court, it seemed a short step to adopt one for a function critically important for market stability.

Fierce opposition sprung up from within the legal complex. Although specialized courts did exist, judges stayed there only for the duration of their normal rotation. A specialized court would require a redesign of judicial careers and a retreat from the model of the generalist judge. The Supreme Court was uncertain that the flow of cases would warrant a dedicated court, but it was the fiscal implications of a special court that finally persuaded the Supreme Court that such could not be afforded (Oh 2001).

Nevertheless, the Supreme Court did concede that there was value in specialization for complex cases. It adopted a practice whereby a court could appoint a Bankruptcy Committee of business experts to assist judges in complex cases, a practice that worked well.[21] More consistent with IFI preferences, it also created a functional equivalent of a specialized bankruptcy court: a specialized chamber in the Seoul District Court and some other major centers in the country. It appointed outstanding judges to these courts, and built up a bankruptcy jurisprudence of opinions, a practice manual, workshops, and training (Oh 2001). The results vindicated the expectations of the IFIs. Filings substantially increased. Judges became increasingly confident in their ability to handle sophisticated cases. Creditors and debtors, in their turn, began to see the courts as a viable arena for restructuring, certainly to be preferred to arbitrary government interference. Almost a decade later, the intended empowerment of the courts appears to be realized in everyday practice.

[21] Interviews 2298, 2280.

C. Vesting New Powers in the State: Indonesia[22]

The case study of Indonesia illustrates how global and transnational pressures, with the leverage offered by a financial crisis, spur the creation of new laws and the vesting of new powers in the state with the intention of enhancing its institutional capacity. In February 1998, the IMF was called into Indonesia because of a massive financial crisis, worsened by a host of problems in the restructuring of external debt and the reorganization of banks and companies within the country (Lane et al. 1999; Pincus & Ramli 1998). The crisis in 1998 galvanized the IMF and World Bank, among other multilateral institutions, to consider instant and drastic reform of bankruptcy law and the institutional apparatus administering it. The IFIs sought immediate triage for the companies unable to pay anywhere from US$30 billion to US$80 billion of foreign debt, not to mention mountains of debt denominated in rupiahs. More ambitiously, the IFIs sought to lay a foundation for a longer-term solution that would provide orderly mechanisms for dealing with corporate debt in ways that would forestall future crises.[23]

The fully defined version of IFI interventions in Indonesia would eventually include substantive and procedural statutory reforms, the creation of a new Commercial Court that would be responsible for corporate bankruptcies, the setting up of an out-of-court agency for negotiations between debtors and creditors, and the formation of a new insolvency profession. The IMF took responsibility for working with a team of domestic Indonesian reformers on the courts. The World Bank's private restructuring group took the lead for setting up an out-of-court mechanism for restructuring debt.[24]

At the beginning of the crisis, the government acknowledged that Indonesian corporations owed US$120 billion, of which US$60 billion was distressed. This debt needed to be restructured through a variety of mechanisms, such as forgiving debt, converting debt to equity, and extending payment terms or changing interest rates. Led by the World Bank restructuring specialist, and drawing on experiments and practices as far removed as Mexico, Venezuela, Thailand, and Britain, the IFIs agreed with the government of Indonesia to institute in November 1998 the Jakarta Initiative Task Force (JITF) – a quasi-independent government agency that would offer expert negotiation services to companies and their lenders.[25] The service itself purported to be neutral, favoring neither debtors nor creditors. Its purpose was to bring major creditors and debtor corporations to the

[22] For a detailed account of the politics surrounding Indonesian bankruptcy reforms, see Halliday & Carruthers 2009: chapter 5.

[23] Interviews 2256, 2305.

[24] Interviews 2351, 2252, 2268, 2318, 2356, 3002.

[25] GOI, Letter of Intent, October 19, 1998 (http://www.imf.org/external/np/loi/101998.htm, last accessed June 8, 2007).

table[26] in order to forge voluntary agreements about how to restructure a company's debts without recourse to the courts. Foreign experts would provide short-term assistance. If the out-of-court negotiations did not work, then creditors could take a company to bankruptcy court.[27]

Indeed, the JITF was designed to place a structure somewhere between the courts and everyday market bargaining. An organization that could resolve debtor-creditor disputes without recourse to the judiciary had much to recommend it. IFIs believed that too many cases before the new Commercial Court might overwhelm it and thereby destroy a fragile institution at its genesis. Nevertheless, the courts, in their turn, were designed to act as a "hammer" for corporate debtors on the assumption of IFIs that the credible threat of likely liquidation of a company in a court would predispose debtors to negotiate in good faith within the JITF.[28] Yet the creation of this negotiation arena within the Ministry of Finance, although rather independent of it, signified a far more active state intervention into the domain of debtor-creditor relations than had previously existed in Indonesia. Creditor banks complained that, in the private market, they had no capacity to enforce their loans or to compel debtors to renegotiate nonperforming loans in ways that would resolve the debt overhangs that threatened bank stability. State intervention offered a practical remedy.

The Jakarta Initiative appears to have an affinity with the supposed preference of Indonesians for nonconfrontational methods of dispute resolution (Bappenas 1998). However, the bank's approach owed less to cultural fit than to practices it had instituted in similar and quite dissimilar cultural contexts. In fact, it can be argued that the partial failure of JITF occurred because the IFI institutional designers were not able to get political support for key elements of the regime. They had argued that an effective out-of-court agency that would bring debtors to the table and produce tangible agreements required a balance of positive and negative incentives. Positive provisions included tax breaks, banking and capital incentives, the removal of adverse tax consequences in debt-to-equity swaps, and protections so companies would not be delisted on the Jakarta Stock Exchange. But these provisions were not sufficient. The IFIs, therefore, pushed for penalties, which included threats that companies could lose their licenses, the Attorney General could push recalcitrant companies into the Bankruptcy Court, the names of debtors who negotiated in poor faith would be openly published and thereby shamed, and ultimately that companies would face certain liquidation in a bankruptcy court. The government resisted the negative incentives, either by refusing to adopt them, or by adopting but failing to implement them. Moreover, coupled with the failure of the Commercial Court to "discipline" debtors effectively, the absence of negative incentives removed

26 Major parties would include the business (debtor), creditors, such as banks, and often the Indonesian Bank Restructuring Agency (IBRA), which had substantial financial interests in many companies after banks transferred their bad debts or problem loans to IBRA.

27 Interview 2253.

28 Interview 227.

any powerful sanctions to force companies to reach realistic agreements with their banks.[29]

The results of this structural innovation were both symbolic and precedential. The JITF completed its work in December 2003. In its final report, it could claim that it had restructured some ninety-six corporations with a total debt of US$20.5 billion, approximately a third of the corporate distressed debt outstanding at the onset of the crisis.[30] Yet critics of the Jakarta Initiative maintain that this was more symbolic than real. With few negative sanctions, creditors had little leverage to compel real financial restructuring. Instead, they were compelled to take enormous "haircuts," up to 90 percent of outstanding debt, stretched over many years, in order to conclude Memoranda of Understanding.[31] How much of this debt was repaid remains unknown. Nonetheless, even if symbolic, the JITF did set a precedent – the potential value of an out-of-court, state-based institution to facilitate negotiations when market mechanisms failed. When JITF was dissolved in 2003, the government set up a new institution, the National Mediation Center, which compels any corporations in civil disputes to submit themselves to mediation before going to court. That some core officials of this new Center were recruited from JITF indicates that even a flawed model can provide a basis for subsequent domestic reforms.

4. RECURSIVITY AND SETTLING ON STATE RESTRUCTURING

I have shown selected examples of reforms in three Asian countries where the prospects for transformations of the state over the past decade have been very substantial. In Indonesia, the reform movement since the fall of Suharto can be construed as the emancipation of a state captive to "crony capitalism" and a reconstruction of that authoritarian state in ways that comport with core ideals of global norms on good governance, market regulation, separation of state powers, and the establishment of some measure of the rule of law. In China, thirty years of change methodically displaced a command economy with a burgeoning "socialist market economy," accompanied by the legal apparatus that IOs avow is necessary for a stable financial system. In Korea, the aftermath of the Asian Financial Crisis can be seen as a dismantling, or at least reconfiguring, of the developmental state, a state where the macro- and leading elements of the microeconomy took their direction from the Ministry of Finance and other agencies of the state.

Although a highly technical area of law and finance, bankruptcy reforms have been integral to each of these transformations. They offer a particular frame through

29 Interviews 2277, 2251.

30 Jakarta Initiative Task Force. "Successful Completion of the Jakarta Initiative Task Force." Press release, December 18, 2003. www.indonesia-oslo-no/pr-10.htm, accessed October 19, 2004.

31 Interviews 2260, 2277, 2251.

which to appraise state restructurings, not least because it is possible to capture with clarity global norms on the one side and observe closely their differential institutionalization in countries exposed to those norms on the other.

I have established that IFI's so-called technical lawmaking in fact involves substantial shifts in regulatory functions and the restructuring of the state and its relationship to the market. The case studies indicate that the implementation of reforms varies significantly and that an implementation gap almost invariably opens up between intentions and outcomes. Theoretic development, however, requires two further steps. The first is to identify dynamics that are more or less conducive to a settling on new configurations of state structures. The second is to connect these findings with research on institutional change and legal transplants that seek to specify conditions under which global and transnational architects of the state will actually make an impact on state structure; in short, what are the conditions of efficacy by global architects of change? I treat these in turn.

Research on major legal change has established that it has a recursive character (Halliday & Carruthers 2007). An episode of activity on behalf of major legal change invariably begins with a build-up of domestic or international pressures and gains momentum, sometimes explosively, with a trigger or crisis. An episode of legal change usually ends when, at a high threshold, institutions and behaviors settle at a new equilibrium of activity, or at a low threshold, the parties and pressures for change dissipate whether through exhaustion, defeat, or distraction, among others. The phenomenon of settling, therefore, becomes a crucial indicator of legal change, and no less so in the reconstruction of institutions by architects of the state (Grattet, Jenness, & Curry 1998; Jenness & Grattet 2001).

In a global context, it has been shown that legal change involves three principal cycles: (1) among global norm-making institutions, as they negotiate over competing or consensual global norms (Halliday 2009); (2) through domestic legal cycles, as law-on-the-books encounters law-in-action, an encounter that frequently leads to further rounds of reform in courts, legislatures, and executive agencies (Liu & Halliday 2009); and (3) cycles of negotiation or reciprocal reference between domestic lawmakers and global norm-making institutions (Halliday & Carruthers 2007, 2009).

Whether and how long it takes for these cycles to lead to a settlement of institutions and practices at a new equilibrium rests on solutions to four recurring problems that potentially bedevil actual changes in behavior: (1) actor mismatch (where domestic lawmakers or global norm-makers do not reflect the full panoply of interests in legal change, especially those capable of nullifying formal legal change in practice); (2) diagnostic struggles (where various interests for or against reform seek to establish their particular definition of the problems to be remedied by law reforms in the minds of lawmakers); (3) contradictions (where a failure to obtain effective political settlements among competing global actors or domestic interest groups has the effect of drawing those tensions inside the law reforms and rendering them unstable);

and (4) indeterminacy (where gaps, ambiguities, inconsistencies, tensions in global norms or the law or reform institutions generate subsequent efforts to fill gaps, remove ambiguities, and resolve tensions).

If these obstacles to settling on a reform potentially bedevil any legal change, they are intensified when the change also involves the significant shifts of power that occur in transformations of the state or market and relationships between them. Failures to effect reforms in practice, to erect functioning institutions based on IFI designs, and to realize structures that emerge from the drawing boards of global architects, are crystallized in ubiquitous implementation gaps that are readily acknowledged by IFIs. Four examples from corporate bankruptcy reforms underline the point that the probability of restructuring in practice that is, a settling on a new equilibrium of behavior and a reduction of the implementation gap, requires empirical attention by scholars and practical attention by designers and lawmakers to the mechanisms that drive repeated cycles of reform until some settlement occurs.

The substantial failure of Indonesia's effort to empower significantly the courts in corporate restructuring follows from an *actor mismatch* in the politics of legal change. Neither IFIs nor Indonesian politics took sufficient note of the interests of debtor corporations. Ignored in lawmaking, some of the most powerful corporations permitted, perhaps authorized, their legal counsel to subvert the judicial process when actual cases reached the Bankruptcy Court. The Court became a debtors' haven in part because a set of measures over which they had little control were instituted without consultation or effective political settlement. They reacted by undermining the Jakarta Initiative and bribing judges, so much so that creditors lost confidence in the courts and effectively abandoned them. It is essential to recognize that this was a power struggle centered on whether a hitherto weak institution, the courts, would wield power previously controlled by the executive, often in close association with Indonesia's largest corporate groups.

In the earliest cycles of law reforms following the Asian Financial Crisis, lawyers and economists essentially engaged in a *diagnostic struggle* over their respective perceptions of why courts did not efficiently deal with corporate liquidations and restructurings (Halliday & Carruthers 2004a). Economists insisted that the problem lay with too much judicial discretion and pressed through reforms that compelled judges to rule quickly based on a strict financial calculus. Lawyers retorted that the law required discretion and substantial judicial powers because corporations and their accountants could distort numbers and, in any event, the strict financial calculus could lead to devastating practical results, as the Dong Ah case dramatically illustrated.[32]

The status of commercial courts in China illustrates the *contradictions* that bedevil much Chinese lawmaking and institution-building in the development of the private

[32] In this case, a huge corporation was liquidated prematurely, many thought, when a more flexible approach could have preserved the viable part of the corporation and saved many jobs.

market. To overstylize the contrast, a strong current of opinion within the Chinese Communist Party insists that courts should not be given too much autonomy from local or national political control when major business cases might have consequences for social stability. This emphasis on a *socialist* market economy can be juxtaposed with advocates' emphasis on increased court autonomy from politics on the grounds that a socialist *market* economy must be seen by investors and market players to be above arbitrary interventions and uncertain application of rules. Not infrequently, this divide is reflected in the tension between formal laws that appear to vindicate the latter ideology and everyday practice that reverts to the former ideology.

Actor mismatch, diagnostic struggles, and contradictions frequently lead to formal law that is *indeterminate* and ambiguous, and to law in practice that is *inconsistent*, as functions are often allocated among rival bureaucratic agencies that tend to interpret law in ways consistent with their competing institutional interests. In Indonesia, for instance, the attack on the Bankruptcy Court by corporate leaders disaffected by their exclusion from lawmaking began with a legalistic maneuver that threw into doubt the meaning of one of bankruptcy law's most fundamental, and presumably clear, concepts – that of "debt." Hence began a steady erosion of the Court's potential power, thereby forestalling the prospect of a new center of power in a state restructured to enable a more efficient, predictable, and transparent system of debtor-creditor relationships.

5. EFFICACY OF STATE RESTRUCTURING

If the dynamics of recursivity drive global norm making and restructurings of the state around those norms, when are the global architects of the state likely to be more effective? What determines their efficacy? What explains the level of equilibrium at which settling will occur? How wide will be the implementation gap between global intent and domestic action?

The responses of China, Indonesia, and Korea to their domestic crises and international pressures can be observed closely in the corporate bankruptcy reforms with which each state engaged. From these struggles emerge a set of propositions that intersect with the rich literature on institutionalization and legal transplants. From both, I propose that the efficacy of transnational pressures for state restructuring turn on the following: (1) the clarity of the global and transnational norms, (2) the power of the IOs, (3) the weakness of nation-states, (4) the extent of local demand and mobilization, (5) the continuity of exogenously encouraged reforms with domestic trajectories for change, (6) the situations in which global designs come to be placed on national policy agendas, and (7) the magnitude of the shift in power required by a state to conform to global designs. These may be clustered in four sets of factors.

A. *Clarity of Global and Transnational Norms*

Normative and temporal contexts for state restructuring vary a great deal. At one moment in time, there may be transnational normative anarchy, where legions of conflicting and partial norms offer no clarity and maximum choice for adopting states. At another historical moment, there can be global or transnational normative convergence, where states confront change with a coherent script for restructuring.

At the time of the Asian Financial Crisis, IFIs had been developing an ad hoc set of prescriptions on corporate bankruptcy regimes for command economies moving to market economies and for countries that had confronted debt crises in the 1990s (Block-Lieb & Halliday 2007a; G-22 1998a; Halliday, Block-Lieb, & Carruthers 2009; International Monetary Fund [IMF] 1999). At the point of the crisis in 1997, these had not yet been codified, certainly within any international deliberative forum. Thus, part of Indonesia's domestic struggle over restructuring from 1997 to 2000 turned on competing domestic groups that appealed to conflicting international norms (Halliday & Carruthers, 2009).

By the early 2000s, however, several IFIs had published norms that were highly convergent, and in 2004, UNCITRAL completed its Legislative Guide for Insolvency Law, which purported to be a global consensus on the authorized alternatives for a bankruptcy system, building from the greater legitimacy of UNCITRAL as a representative institution, especially compared to the international financial institutions (Block-Lieb & Halliday 2007b). These had a belated but confirmatory impact on Indonesia, whose legislature finally passed a large packet of bankruptcy amendments in 2005. Korea's reforms did reflect the global consensus, not only for the retraction of state intervention in everyday market decisions, but also in the construction of a bankruptcy regime that greatly strengthened courts and rolled Korea's three bankruptcy laws into a single unified act (Oh & Halliday 2009). Furthermore, China's marathon reform effort, begun in 1994 and completed in 2007, similarly moved ostensibly toward the coherent norms articulated by UNCITRAL, the World Bank, and some core foreign states.

Hence, the quick cycles of norm-making by IOs led to rapid convergence between 1997 and 2004. From global normative incoherence emerged a codified set of norms that were conducive to settling on legislative enactments quickly thereafter and on affirmation of institutional reforms already in place. But global normative convergence is not enough, as variation in response to transnational architects clearly demonstrates.

B. *Asymmetries of Power between International Organizations and Nation-States*

Variations in asymmetries of power between global actors and nation-states existed among China, Indonesia, and Korea before the Asian Financial Crisis (Carruthers &

Halliday 2006). Indonesia was most vulnerable and Korea least so. This generic difference, however, was altered by the crisis itself. The financial emergency impelled by critical losses of foreign reserves and collapse of national currencies suddenly gave IFIs enormous sway over national political authorities.

Indonesia confronted international financial institutions on the weak side of an extreme asymmetry of power. IFIs controlled capital vital to forestall a collapse of Indonesia's financial system. Indonesia had little option but to comply with exogenous demands for major institutional reforms related to corporate restructuring, most notably, the establishment of a new Commercial Court and the formation of an out-of-court restructuring facility. In Korea, the timing and some of the direction in the Korean legal and institutional reforms emerged when IFIs, as bankers of last resort in 1998, insisted on immediate reforms (Oh 2003). The government had very little choice but to abandon much of its state-driven model of corporate restructuring for a new model based on increasingly unified global norms in this domain.

Because China remained substantially immune from the Asian Financial Crisis, the extreme asymmetry of power that set the terms for relations between IFIs and the nation-states of Indonesia and Korea was less evident with China. Yet China saw lessons in the crisis that impelled it to institute reforms. A succession of experts from IOs and advanced economies reacted to successive Chinese drafts for legal and institutional reform and sought to press China toward the global consensus that by 2004 was now codified within the UNCITRAL Model Law and Legislative Guide. Not least, the final decision to pass the law was a response to strong pressure from the European Union, which insisted that investment and European business activity in China would stall if a predictable bankruptcy regime were not put in place.

Variations in asymmetries of power were expressed through differences in the mechanisms that IFIs had available to press for national conformity to global norms. The economic coercion used by the IMF and World Bank against Indonesia and Korea could not be wielded against China, where IFIs had to rely mostly on persuasion (Carruthers & Halliday 2006). Even in Korea, which repaid its debt quickly and had close technical relationships with the IMF and World Bank, the IFIs quickly shifted to suasion and moral appeals for Korea to deliver on promises made at the height of the crisis.

Moreover, apparent differences in asymmetries of power may be more apparent than real. Although IFIs in emergency situations have maximum leverage to insist on restructuring, the power of the weak to foil the strong cannot be minimized, particularly at the stage of implementation (Halliday & Carruthers 2009). In the process of negotiating national commercial law regimes, the structure of the state also becomes an implicit object of negotiation between transnational and national bodies. The degree of asymmetry, therefore, does not by itself determine the efficacy of change in practice, although it influences the mechanisms in global-local encounters and the numbers of cycles before there is political settlement between global and local elites.

C. *Domestic Demand and Social Mobilization*

If ostensibly weak states do have far more power to foil IOs than is commonly supposed, then the probability of effective restructuring turns most decisively on two domestic conditions. One concerns the degree of supposed or actual continuity of exogenously encouraged reforms with domestic institutions, traditions, and trajectories for change. In Indonesia, for instance, whatever modest success the Jakarta Initiative could claim for restructuring of corporate debt in a new quasi-state, out-of-court agency derived partly from the IFI's bricolage in marrying a transnational model to a cultural preference (Campbell 2004). The Jakarta Initiative could be construed concomitantly as an emanation of Indonesian norms for dispute resolution and as an imported institution that had proved itself in other crisis situations.

Effective restructuring also turns on the extent of local demand and mobilization (Campbell 2004; Carruthers & Halliday 2006; Pistor et al. 2002). The partial failure of the Jakarta Initiative, for instance, stemmed from a deep divide between the parties to the JITF: Indonesian bankers and IFIs joined forces for workouts on terms that Indonesian corporate leaders resisted. This quasi-state agency thus sought to recalibrate market power from a situation where debtors could resist creditor demands with impunity to a situation where debtors were induced by positive and negative incentives to restructure debts in ways that would stabilize and normalize banking. Demand, therefore, was sectional and divided. The state reached into the market to assert a public interest where previously market actors had been left to their respective market powers. Hence, the equivocal outcomes of the Jakarta Initiative reflect, on the one side, a balance of power in which IFIs could demand, with some cultural legitimacy, the formal establishment of a new agency, whereas on the other side, major corporations could stunt its impact in the phase of implementation.

China had embarked on a program of domestic reform clearly mindful of market economies outside its borders, but nevertheless followed its own course at its own pace. On its own terms, China progressively familiarized itself with the designs for bankruptcy systems championed by IFIs, regional and global. It accepted technical assistance, always comparing and contrasting draft provisions for a comprehensive bankruptcy system with foreign norms, but never deviating from China's characteristic cautious and experimental approach to downsize an administrative state and vest powers in hitherto underdeveloped courts.

But domestic demand itself is highly political: transnational architects trigger competing interest groups. In all three countries, there was some domestic constituency for change. In Indonesia, domestic reformers obtained some cosmetic changes in law and institutions, but much less in practice. In Korea, academics and policymakers responded to international pressures, but without enthusiasm – one reason that cycles of domestic reforms continued for a decade. In China, global norms strengthened the hands of legal academic reformers and commercial interests concerned to maintain the flow of foreign capital. Yet, domestic interest groups favoring a higher threshold of change confronted others seeking to minimize the threshold of change. The effects of domestic demand expressed themselves more in national actors with the power to resist than in those with the intent to adopt.

D. *Scope of Restructuring*

Ultimately, the probability of settling change at a more consequential level of restructuring turns also on the magnitude of the shift in power required by a state to conform to global or transnational designs. IFI architects of the state deal principally with vested national elites for that is where political power currently lies. Restructuring of the state almost invariably means a redistribution of power. And to obtain the latter requires, at the very least, negotiation with those who currently hold the power to effect change. Therein lies a paradox because actor mismatch in law reform implies that many actors with interests and often with power in practice are excluded from negotiations around restructuring of the state. The degree of state restructuring, therefore, will be a partial function of the scope of power lost by those who currently hold it and the prospects for power gained by those currently without it. It can be anticipated that, the higher the losses or gains, the deeper the struggles and hence the more cycles of attempted reforms before they settle.

The intervention of global and regional institutions opens a wedge for peripheral or insurgent domestic constituencies to obtain a powerful international ally. If domestic reformers are currently kept at arm's length from state power, in a form of managed "actor-mismatch," then they have two avenues for the pursuit of power: either displace the office-holders in the state as it is presently structured, or restructure the state to create openings for them and their cause.

In Korea, the magnitude of the shift in power, from a restraint of MOFE to an empowerment of the courts, helps explain why cycles of reforms succeeded each other, almost annually, and why the shift advanced with uncertainty, as MOFE tried to limit recourse to the courts at every step. In Indonesia, the shift from executive control of the heights of the corporate sector to empowered courts was a sea-change in state power. For decades, courts and judges had been derogated and powerless. The notion that they might quickly become arbiters between a nation's most powerful economic players disrupted radically the long-standing ascendancy of the executive and the bargains it had manifestly and tacitly struck with leaders of industry. In China, above all, empowered courts potentially threaten both Party control of the entire state apparatus and intermeshed but covert economic relations between local political authorities and economic interests. For both reasons, the probability that this aspect of state restructuring will quickly eventuate is doubtful indeed.

Hence, the greater the scope of structural changes broached by IOs, the greater the threat to entrenched power-holders and the greater the opportunity for actors excluded from power. The implications are clear: more extensive structural changes demanded by IFIs will likely generate more vigorous domestic struggles, which in turn will lead to repeated cycles of domestic lawmaking and international efforts to guide it. The probability of an implementation gap increases where the power stakes are higher. Yet it is also possible that more extensive demands by IFIs, if accompanied by support from domestic allies, will lead to settled structural changes, even if these fall short of the aspirations of IFIs or go further than the fears of entrenched elites.

6. CONCLUSION

This analysis of transnational legal ordering has shown how the institution-building enterprise of IOs and IFIs repeatedly fails because policy entrepreneurs in the Global North[33] either do not admit, or fail to articulate fully, what it is really about – restructuring the state itself. This restructuring occurs not only through ostensible constitutional or governance programs, but also through such technical areas of trade regulation as corporate bankruptcy law. In the latter case, state restructuring often proceeds invisibly, well below the horizons of political observers. This chapter has shown that fully institutionalizing a corporate bankruptcy system, not to mention a central bank or anticorruption commission, involves shifts of power in unprecedented directions. It involves a redistribution of power toward institutions hitherto marginal in the power structures of society (e.g., courts) (Santos 2000). It imagines the empowerment of occupations hitherto thought to be second or third rate by national elites (e.g., judges) (Dezalay & Garth 2002b). It requires that dominant actors and entrenched institutions agree to forgo powers in favor of derogated or nascent actors. Hence, putatively legal reforms in fact present ruling classes, power elites, and one-party systems with high stakes. Not surprisingly, the threat to an entrenched power structure by exogenous and insurgent interests can trigger extraordinary resistance.

Close empirical analysis of corporate bankruptcy reforms after the Asian Financial Crisis reveals that efforts to restructure states by global architects have a recursive quality, where repeated efforts of domestic and international actors to induce reforms confront the ever-present difficulties of diagnostic struggles, actor mismatch, contradictions, and indeterminacy. Hence, nothing inevitable or inexorable about interventions by architects of the state exists. Episodes of induced change may lead to settled reconfigurations of the state that are minimal (Indonesia), modest (Korea), or potentially far-reaching (China). The level at which settlements occur, the degree of state restructuring, and hence the efficacy of IFIs can arguably be attributed to

[33] As the counterpart to the Global South, this term denotes those countries with advanced economies and at the center of the global geopolitical order, and the international institutions they disproportionately influence, such as the IMF, World Bank, regional development banks, among others.

the interplay of four main sets of factors: the coherence of global norms, the relative power of global versus state actors, domestic demand and mobilization for restructuring, and the extent of state restructuring that reforms will induce.

Research on transnational legal ordering, therefore, requires that occasions for state restructuring be revealed not only in manifest appeals to "downsizing the state" or "privatizing public functions," but also in complex domains of commercial law where the supposed neutrality and technicality of the subject matter too readily disguise fundamental IFI efforts to redesign states and reconfigure power. To discover the varieties of such interventions by IFIs elaborates the repertoires of global agents for state reconstruction. To reveal the fates of those interventions acknowledges the magnitude of IFI ambitions and demands theory that explains the limits of their efficacy.

5

Neoliberalism, Transnational Education Norms, and Education Spending in the Developing World, 1983–2004

Minzee Kim and Elizabeth Heger Boyle

In some ways, the spread of education policies around the world closely follows the pattern predicted by world polity theory, which stresses the embeddedness of nation-states in a wider world culture (Meyer et al. 1997). World polity theory contends that ideas and structures spread throughout many countries in short time periods despite the vast differences across those countries. From the world polity perspective, countries adopt education policies because this marks them as legitimate participants in global society; more pragmatically, it can also increase the amount of funding they receive from international sources (see Barrett & Tsui 1999). Transnational legal processes can be seen as an expression of global society, and they shape state change. Over the past century, the state's obligation to provide free education became taken for granted, as global civil society promoted the obligation and international law mandated it (Meyer 1980). Today, 90 percent of the countries in the world have laws making primary education compulsory (Benavot & Resnick 2006). In other ways, the issue of education funding reveals some gaps in world polity theory's explanations. Although institutionalized, the idea of free education was subject to powerful challenges from international financial institutions (IFIs) in the 1980s and 1990s. Neither its maintenance nor its implementation was assured.

In its current form, world polity theory has little to say about the process through which institutionalized ideas are maintained or the impact of disagreements on the perpetuation of institutionalized ideas. According to world polity theorists, key players in global civil society are transnational organizations, including international governmental organizations (IGOs) and international nongovernmental organizations (INGOs)[1] (Meyer et al. 1997). These organizations have special

[1] Although we use the term "INGOs," the highly transnational character of these organizations is apparent, as highlighted in this book. The increasing number and influence of INGOs suggests a

legitimacy to set policy standards because they are seen as acting in the interest of others rather than in their own self-interests (Boli & Thomas 1999). INGOs, in particular, work with grassroots activists to translate the principles of international law into a local vernacular (compare Merry 2006) and use networks to share advocacy strategies (compare Smith 1995). This does not mean, however, that all of these organizations advance the same ideas. This raises the question of the role different organizations play in the development and implementation of particular perspectives.

In addition, world polity theorists to date have not focused much on IFIs (for a recent exception, see Boyle & Kim 2009). The case of global norms concerning the financing of compulsory education illustrates a contradiction between IFIs and human rights–oriented IGOs and INGOs. Until recently, the former had advocated user fees to cover some of the cost of education, whereas the latter had consistently argued that children have a right to free, publicly funded education. In general, IFIs are thought to exercise power through the promise of resources, whereas other IGOs and INGOs are thought to exercise power more because their claims have special legitimacy.[2] Examining IFIs as well as international human rights organizations opens up consideration of how both material and symbolic resources can be used to bolster particular perspectives. We argue that this requires moving beyond a simple dichotomy – that IFIs have legitimacy concerns as well as material interests, and INGOs can generate financial support while claiming to represent the moral high ground.

Finally, this analysis advances world polity theory and transnational legal process theory (Koh 2006; Shaffer, Chapter 1) by considering the perpetuation and implementation of institutionalized ideas as separate processes. According to world polity theorists, the ways in which norms gain legitimacy within global civil society are almost identical to the ways in which global models, once dominant, produce change in national policies and outcomes (Meyer 2007). Once norms are institutionalized, they are simply taken for granted at both the global and the national level. Nation-states are committed to the valued principles, although it may take more or less time

coherent and vocal global civil society that carries a world culture (Boli & Thomas 1999). This global civil society is highly transnational, in that nonstate actors are brought together across state borders to elaborate discourses and practices (e.g., human rights, environmental protection, and social and economic development). Furthermore, these discourses and practices have impacts beyond national boundaries. INGOs are the key site in which the transnational organization of nonstate actors is enabled and legitimized (Keck & Sikkink 1998; Smith, Chatfield, & Pagnucco 1997). Previous globalization literature adopted the term "INGOs" to describe this type of organization, and we use "INGOs" to be consistent with our prior work and this literature with which we have engaged. The term was adopted before "transnationalism" was commonly in use.

2 Legitimacy is a complex concept. We apply a broad and general meaning of legitimacy as the perceived rightfulness attached to certain actors, actions, and ideas. For a more detailed discussion of the concept, refer to Shaffer (Chapter 1).

to translate that commitment into actual outcomes. In the case of education funding, however, actors and organizations with opposing ideas about government education funding and enforcement tools have been involved in development and education. Further, state implementation of global norms that involve state funding is particularly likely to be influenced by each state's global economic position and capacity (see Halliday & Carruthers 2009). Thus, the affirmation and perpetuation of ideas at the global level is relevant to implementation, but implementation operates somewhat independently of idea development. We consider both processes in our analysis.

Our analysis extends world polity theory to address these gaps. Specifically, we explain how policies gain and retain authority when international actors disagree. We explicitly consider the role of different types of international actors, including IFIs, in both the maintenance and the implementation of international education funding policies. Finally, we analyze norm development and implementation separately. Our findings suggest that, in the long run, neoliberal discourses on education promoted by economic actors were no match for discourses carried broadly in global civil society by child-rights INGOs.

1. EDUCATION AS A GLOBAL CONCERN: THE CONSTRUCTION OF TRANSNATIONAL LEGAL NORMS

In this section, we discuss back-and-forth debates over education funding at the international level. The norm of free universal primary education became institutionalized in international law in the immediate post–World War II era, and United Nations Educational, Scientific and Cultural Organization (UNESCO) was a key factor in spreading support for the law. There was a period in the 1980s, however, when IFIs, such as the World Bank, suggested that users should share the cost of public services, including education, potentially undermining this norm. Although the user-fee idea gained traction with national governments, it also coincided with counter-mobilization by INGOs. Ultimately, in the early part of the twenty-first century, even IFIs were rejecting cost sharing in the education context. History reveals that the financial clout of IFIs was insufficient to permanently undermine the institutionalized idea that primary education should be free.

Article 26 of the 1949 Universal Declaration of Human Rights (UDHR) asserts, "Everyone has the right to education. Education shall be free, at least in the elementary and fundamental stages. Elementary education shall be compulsory." The UDHR is a statement of countries' commitment to human rights, but it is not binding law. It was followed in the 1960s by two binding rights covenants. The 1966 International Covenant on Economic, Social, and Cultural Rights (ICESCR) codifies the right to education, stating in Section 13 that primary education "shall be compulsory and available free to all" and that secondary education "shall be made generally available and accessible to all by every appropriate means, and in particular by the progressive introduction of free education." The Covenant goes on to make provisions for higher education and for the construction of school systems. These international laws formalized a global commitment to state-provided education.

The 1950s and 1960s were the heyday of global organizing around the issue of education (Benavot & Resnick 2006), and the UNESCO, created in 1946, was the premier global organization dealing with the issue (Jones with Coleman 2005). UNESCO framed education as a global issue (Benavot & Riddle 1988), promoting the idea that education led to development and marked the path to modernity for newly independent nation-states (Chabbott 1999). The organization also took responsibility for training INGO personnel to implement education policies (Mundy 1998). Overall, during these decades, UNESCO was central to the institutionalization of a cohesive set of ideas concerning education.[3] These ideas, enshrined in international law, included the obligation of all states to provide free universal primary education to children within their borders and to move toward providing free secondary education.

In the 1970s, attention to education at the global level waned, and many wealthy countries cut their aid to education programs (Mundy 1998). A third-world bloc emerged to influence the United Nations' structure and policies (Mundy 1998). This bloc emphasized the ideas of dependency theory, that is, that the source of underdevelopment in the Global South was attributable to unequal economic power relations among countries. UNESCO tried but failed to bridge the demands emerging from developing countries with the liberal developmentalist ideologies of its wealthier members (Mundy 1998). Exacerbating problems at UNESCO, US President Reagan revoked US membership in the organization in 1984, citing its communist leanings (Jones 2007).[4] Britain and Singapore followed suit in 1985. Without these dues-paying members, UNESCO's budget, which was already very lean, plummeted by a quarter (Mundy 1998). This ensured that UNESCO's leadership role in education reform, and thus the expansion of education systems and the funding UNESCO advocated, was interrupted. Other multilateral organizations began to overshadow UNESCO's role in the education field. At the same time, IFIs began to emphasize neoliberal economic principles, such as cost sharing, as the solution to poor countries' problems.

The idea of making IFI's loans conditional on the implementation of neoliberal economic policies gained traction in the early 1980s. By agreeing to implement policy reforms, developing countries were able to acquire much-needed funds from international financial institutions (Babb 2005). Loan conditionalities were enshrined in "structural adjustment agreements" (SAAs) that emphasized the free market

[3] IFIs played a minimal role in constructing education policy at the global level at this time (Jones with Coleman 2005). The World Bank made a few education-related loans in the 1960s, for which UNESCO provided the technical support (Jones 2007).

[4] The United States did not rejoin UNESCO until 2002.

principles of restricted state spending, balanced budgets, market solutions to problems, deregulation, environments conducive to investment, privatization, and trade openness (Sadasivam 1997; Babb 2005). These reforms were to increase total wealth in the global system, which would benefit everyone in the long run.

The new discourse was a departure from earlier ideas. While UNESCO since the 1950s had promoted free primary education, the World Bank in the 1980s was promoting limited public spending on, and fee-for-service systems in, education, health care, and the provision of other public goods. It was not that IFIs were no longer supporting educational development; rather, they were minimizing the importance of government educational funding, which is critical in institutionalizing free education. The World Bank did not explicitly support tuition fees, but it supported various other types of fees in primary education, such as textbook fees (Kattan & Burnett 2004). It must also be noted that the World Bank suggested supplementing these cost-sharing reforms with programs to offset or waive the fees for the poor and other target groups, such as girls (Kattan & Burnett 2004). Overall, however, IFIs stressed austerity in public spending, which implied a reduction in public spending across the board, including for education (Tilak 1992).

By the end of the 1980s, SAAs had become defining documents for shaping education systems in less developed countries (Benavot & Resnick 2006). The language within the IFI loan agreements was kept vague, whereas supplemental policy guidelines and compliance evaluations provided specifics. Through structural adjustment loan conditionalities, IFIs advocated for a diversification of education finance through the adoption of increased cost sharing for public education and through privatization (World Bank 1987).

In summary, the 1980s encompassed two conflicting transnational legal orders, one advocating neoliberal policies of cost sharing and the other mandating government guarantees of the legal right to free primary education. By 2000, seventy-seven of seventy-nine countries studied in a World Bank report had adopted some type of user fee for primary education (Kattan & Burnett 2004).[5] Thirty-eight percent of countries had tuition fees for education; these and the others also sometimes had fees for textbooks, compulsory uniforms, parent-teacher associations, and/or activities. With the imposition of fees for primary education, there was a move away from the requirements of international law that UNESCO had worked to institutionalize. Since the UDHR was not binding law and the United States (the World Bank and the International Monetary Fund [IMF's] largest investor) had not ratified the ICESCR, the World Bank was not strictly bound by these provisions.

Paradoxically, however, the rise of neoliberal approaches to state education policies coincided with the growth of stronger INGO networks advocating more expansive education policies (Mundy 1998; see also Boyle & Kim 2009). Unlike IGOs,

[5] We cannot know if these user fees were caused directly by IFIs' education policies. Scholars have noted that IFI policies led to a decrease in international aid for education (Mundy 1998).

INGOs do not sit on the General Assembly of the United Nations and they do not have a direct voice in the construction of international law (Merry 2006). Nevertheless, they play a central role in global civil society (Smith, Chatfield, & Pagnucco 1997). During the 1980s, an "increasingly coherent and influential" group of INGOs emerged to champion the cause of providing educational opportunities for children (Schafer 1999: 69). Generally, these organizations were committed to increasing the quality of, and equality within, education. They were also concerned that enrollment rates, which had risen from 33 percent in 1960 to 66 percent in 1980, were beginning to stagnate (Schafer 1999).

The cases of the Global Campaign for Education and the World Education Forum illustrate the transnational character of discourse and action in the campaign for comprehensive education for children. In these campaigns, INGOs concerned with children's education (e.g., Oxfam, Education International, and Action Aid) moved beyond their role as service providers and formed a global alliance to advocate for free, publicly provided education for all children (Mundy & Murphy 2001). To realize their demands, they worked at both international and local grassroots levels. At the international level, their coalitions with UNESCO and the United Nations Children's Fund (UNICEF) bolstered those IGOs' efforts to expand comprehensive education norms. INGOs also generated international support to alter IFIs' resource allocations and assistance practices. At the grassroots level, they built strong coalitions with domestic NGOs and civil society actors to make demands on the governments of developing countries (Mundy & Murphy 2001). INGOs could both raise money and provide network support for educational reforms.

This collective organizing at the global level carried forward the world commitment to free education and encouraged resistance to the neoliberal regime. In 1989, the General Assembly of the United Nations adopted the Convention on the Rights of the Child (CRC), which reaffirmed the obligations of states to provide free primary education to their youngest citizens. The CRC has been ratified by every country in the world, save two. Many believe the CRC was a first step toward re-establishing economic, social, and cultural rights (Fernando 2001). The presence of an increasingly vocal and organized civil society at the global level explains, at least in part, why the World Bank was willing to work with UNESCO, UNICEF, and the United Nations Development Fund (UNDP) at the "World Conference on Education For All" in Jomtien, Thailand in 1990. However, the Jomtien Declaration took a step back from the CRC and other international law obligations, for example, calling for public-private partnerships (Tomaševski 2003). Thus, the World Bank maintained its emphasis on limited government spending for social services and the implementation of user fees.

By 1995, a growing chorus of criticisms over World Bank policies could no longer be ignored (Gertler & Glewwe 1992; Harrigan & Mosley 1991; Ogbu & Gallagher 1991; Sadasivam 1997; Sen 1999; World Bank 1994). Studies suggested a detrimental impact of World Bank education policies on the lives of children (Vavrus 2005).

INGOs used the language of rights and played a critical role in highlighting the negative impact of SAAs on the achievement of universal primary education (Mundy 2006).

Partly in response to this increasing criticism, the World Bank experienced a change in top management in 1995. The new officers expressed a commitment to focus more on alleviating poverty and less on economic growth *per se*. In the developing world, per child spending began to increase and primary enrollment rates began to creep up slowly. Nevertheless, the World Bank remained committed to its free market ideology and continued to make loans conditional on the implementation of neoliberal economic reforms. For example, in its *World Development Report 2000/2001*, the World Bank (2000) expanded the goals of economic growth, especially to include poverty reduction, but maintained its view that neoliberal strategies were the best mechanisms to achieve those goals.

Pressure from INGOs persisted and, in a striking turnaround in 2001, the World Bank actually changed its policies to be consistent with the goal of achieving free universal primary education worldwide by 2015. In 2001, the World Bank quietly indicated to countries that it did not support user fees for education (Makene 2007). In a 2004 report, the World Bank claimed that it had never suggested countries impose user fees for primary education and that it renounced user fees in that situation (Kattan & Burnett 2004). The need for this announcement highlights both that education user fees were perceived as illegitimate and that World Bank officials began to care about the legitimacy of their policies.

By 2006, the World Bank was considered the leading global advocate for greater public spending on education (Mundy 2006), although it was not committing large amounts of its own funds to that goal. In developing countries, only 2 percent of educational funds come from international aid, whereas governments fund 63 percent of educational costs and 35 percent is privately funded (UNESCO 2003). Government funding remains much lower in developing countries than in OECD countries, where 82 percent of compulsory education is financed by governments (OECD 2004). As a recent advocate of public education spending, the World Bank is now working with UNESCO and other IGOs to facilitate the provision of quality education by states.

This brief history shows the rising and falling fortunes of international policies. Initially, education was viewed as the path to economic development as well the best way to reduce inequality between the Global North and South. Beginning in the late 1970s, UNESCO and the World Bank began to promote opposing approaches to education. Most importantly, they disagreed on the role of the state in funding education. IFIs promoted the ideas of limited state spending and fee-for-user systems. They had the upper hand at this point, both because they had a unified vision of reform while UNESCO did not, and because the United States and other wealthy countries used the power of the purse to undercut UNESCO's authority.

However, this move toward neoliberal economics and away from the terms of international law reciprocally coincided with and may have helped fuel cooperation among UNESCO and INGOs and greater state commitments to education. In the 1980s, INGOs formed dense networks to construct and promote a more unified voice on education. By the turn of the new century, a human rights–based approach to education had won out over neoliberal approaches to education, as evidenced by the World Bank's formally distancing itself from user-fee requirements for education. The history of the transnational construction of global education principles illustrates how legitimacy lends power to ideas even when opposing views have strong financial backing. The principles laid out in international law continued to hold immense authority. These principles were legitimate because they emerged from processes that involved all countries, not merely wealthy countries (compare with Halliday & Carruthers 2009). In addition, collaboration among IGOs and INGOs created powerful civil society support at the global level, enhancing the legitimacy of any initiatives proposed by these global actors in education.

Although the principle of free primary education as a right is currently dominant within global civil society, the relative impact of this global consensus on state budgetary allocations for education is still an empirical question. Do formal state endorsements of international law or global activism result in greater state commitment to funding education? Did SAAs and their promotion of less government spending on education impose downward pressure on state government spending for education in developing countries? In the next section, we discuss the impact of these global contests and agreements on national education policies during the period 1983–2004.

2. STATE RESPONSES TO GLOBAL LAWS AND POLICIES: EDUCATION SPENDING

In the last section, we detailed how particular transnational actors promoted ideas about education funding. In this section, we consider how the opposing ideas of education funding at the global level played out locally, if at all. When national governments are pressured to maintain fiscal austerity by cutting expenditures and increasing debt service payments, governments may be forced to cut education spending and privatize the sector through user fees. International law supporting free primary education should operate against this pressure, however.

We know that neoliberal approaches to economic reforms have influenced nation-states' education funding during the period studied. For example, Avelino, Brown, and Hunter (2005) found that trade openness positively affected social security and education spending. In contrast, Mutangadura, Blau, and Lamb (2002) found a negative effect of IFI loan balances on educational outcomes in sub-Saharan Africa. Makene's (2007) case study of education in Tanzania discovered that, because of fees, some parents would enroll only a portion of their children in school. Deficit reduction, a central component of loan conditionalities, can also have an impact on education (Goldman 2005; Mahdavi 2004; Mosley, Harrigan, & Toye 1991). Reducing central government expenditure was mandated in 91 percent of structural adjustment programs in 1986, and reducing the budget deficit as a share of gross domestic product (GDP) was required in 83 percent (Cornia 1987). Although some studies have taken the important step of considering the impact of economic globalization on education in particular countries, they have not yet looked at educational commitments across a broad range of countries over time.

With respect to the impact of the norm for free and compulsory education, studies suggest that international laws, in the form of declarations and conventions, are an important way to make states formally commit themselves to certain policies. Initially, these domestic policies may be more statements of aspiration than enforceable realities (Boyle, Smith, & Guenther 2006), but they can have a real impact over time. For example, the disjuncture between domestic legal statutes making education compulsory and the reality of children attending school has been significantly reduced over time (Benavot & Resnick 2006). The same is true in other areas, such as human rights (Hafner-Burton & Tsutsui 2005), women's rights (Berkovitch 1999), and environmentalism (Hironaka & Schofer 2002). Transnational advocacy networks, which consist of a variety of individuals and organizations, encourage this process by shaming countries that are not adequately enforcing their policies (Keck & Sikkink 1998). However, the effect of international legal frameworks can be slow, diffuse, and difficult to track, and this is likely exacerbated in the case of education funding, where contradictory ideas were promoted by different international actors.

A. *Hypotheses for Statistical Analyses*

We have shown that several treaties and policies promoted by international organizations affected global education policy. The impact of these laws and policies on domestic education systems, and which laws and policies take precedence when contradictions emerge, are empirical questions. We provide preliminary answers to those questions in a statistical analysis of poor- and middle-income countries' educational expenditures from 1983 to 2004.

We look at two dimensions of nations' commitment to education: (1) the amount a country spends per child for education and (2) the percentage of government expenditures devoted to education. The former is most closely linked to children's actual experiences.[6] Our other measure, the percentage of total government expenditures devoted to education, reflects a state's relative commitment to education. Although

[6] We find that per-child spending is highly correlated (in bivariate tests) with completion rates for primary school, enrollment levels at the secondary and tertiary levels, and youth literacy rates. These bivariate statistics must be interpreted cautiously, however, because the measures are also all highly correlated with countries' wealth.

less clearly tied to educational quality variables, such as primary school completion rates, it has the advantage of being uncorrelated with countries' wealth and being closely linked to a country's relative prioritization of education in all areas of government spending. By considering both of these variables, we get a fuller picture of how states are transformed, and how their citizens are affected, by transnational processes.

Although we acknowledge that local factors, such as the proportion of children in the population, form of government, and so forth are likely to be influential in affecting government spending decisions, we think it is a mistake to treat nation-states as purely autonomous decision-makers. We expect factors in the global environment, including international conventions, integrated markets, and agreements with international financial institutions, to influence governments' decisions concerning education funding as well. The effect of "globalization," however, is not straightforward. As described above, the globalization of education policies is a complex set of processes, and various aspects of it are likely to influence national education spending differently.

Turning to our specific hypotheses, we begin with the likely effects of neoliberal economic policies. In the year that an SAA is entered, the country may already be taking steps to demonstrate its fiscal responsibility (Abouharb & Cingranelli 2006). For example, cost sharing and budget efficiencies can make a state look like a more promising loan candidate to the IFIs. Thus, we predict:

> *Hypothesis 1A. Entry into a structural adjustment agreement by a country will be associated with lower levels of per-child spending on education.*

Once countries are subject to SAAs, typical provisions include making debt repayment a top priority, which should have a direct negative effect on the relative amount of funds devoted to education spending:

> *Hypothesis 1B. The implementation of a structural adjustment agreement by a country will be associated with a lower proportion of its budget spent on education and lower levels of per-child spending on education.*

In sum, we expect countries to trim their overall budgets in preparation for entering into an SAA, while the implementation of the SAA will reduce the relative spending on public services, such as education.

It is important to note, however, that SAAs are adopted and operate in a broader context. In a previous article (Boyle & Kim 2009), we found that the implementation of SAAs prompted an increase in child-rights INGOs within countries, which in turn drove up primary and secondary school enrollments. Thus, structural adjustment policies may recursively lead to counter-hegemonic organizing, attracting INGOs that wish to mitigate the perceived deleterious effects of SAAs. If this occurs in the sphere of education spending, we may see less of a negative effect of SAAs on per-pupil spending. The reasons, nature of resistance to, and recursive implications of interventions by IFIs encompass an important area of study, taken up by others as well (Halliday 2007).

As our historical analysis demonstrated, global economic integration and SAAs do not encompass the entire process of globalization. Child-rights IGOs, such as UNESCO, support the ratification of international treaties and monitor their implementation. States that ratify key international treaties are likely to be the most committed to education:

Hypothesis 2. Countries that ratify more child-related treaties will spend greater proportions of their budgets on education and will have greater levels of per-child spending on education.

The relationship we propose is associational rather than causal – the countries that most vigorously support international law concerning education are also the most likely to make education a national priority.

In the related area of human rights, research has shown that countries with poor human rights records are somewhat *more* likely than other countries to ratify human rights treaties (Hafner-Burton & Tsutsui 2005). This is because ratification provides them with a veneer of respectability even if they do not intend to comply with the treaties. Perhaps government officials in these countries believe ratifying treaties will take attention away from their violations. The same pattern may hold for countries with minimal commitment to education. If countries sign on to education-friendly treaties only as a formality, Hypothesis 2 will not be supported.

The presence of INGOs can promote the global norm of universal education in local contexts. Empirical work has shown that INGO linkages are critical for prompting states to follow up on their commitments (Hafner-Burton & Tsutsui 2005), in line with world polity theory:

Hypothesis 3. The greater the child-rights INGO linkage within a country, the greater the proportion of the country's budget devoted to education and the greater per-child spending on education.

United Nations agencies and INGOs do not have as many resources as IFIs, and therefore, they generally cannot offer financial motivations for compliance with international laws concerning education. At the same time, they hold special legitimacy because they are not motivated by profit and they do not represent the interests of just one nation-state. World polity theory will be supported if these nonfinancial factors are influential in education spending.

B. *Statistical Research Design*

The goals of our analysis are to determine the impact of global education-related laws and policies, and of transnational mobilization on states' allocation of resources for education. The core arguments to be examined are that neoliberal economic reforms have led state governments to reduce their role in financing education, and that global discourse and organizing around child rights have pressured state governments to strengthen their financial commitment to education. To evaluate these arguments about the evolution and impact of the neoliberal economic and child-rights regimes, we utilize cross-national longitudinal data at yearly intervals for poor- and middle-income countries between 1983 and 2004. Appendix A provides details on measurement and sources for the data used in this analysis.

1. Dependent Variables: Education Spending

As noted, several different ways exist to measure educational expenditures. First, we could look at actual levels of spending in constant US dollars. The problem with this measure is that it is one that cannot be appropriately compared across countries. Countries such as China and India, with huge populations and large productive capacities, will naturally spend more money on education than tiny countries like Vanuatu or Equatorial Guinea. Even a fixed-effects statistical model that controls for initial levels of spending cannot fully correct for this because raw dollar increases in spending, although they happen over time, are determined to a large extent by the initial level of expenditures. The question, then, is the appropriate metric to "relativize" educational expenditures across countries. Several possibilities exist, and each has somewhat different implications.

We choose two methods of standardization – one that focuses on the *demand* for education and the other that focuses on a state's ability to *supply* education. In terms of demand, the number of children who could potentially be in school in each country represents the country's need for education. To reflect this need, we create a measure of spending per potential student. This measure is operationalized as educational spending per person younger than 14 in each country. (We choose 14 as the cut-off age because there is comparative data available for the size of this demographic group.) Figure 5.1 shows the trend for educational spending per person younger than 14 for the countries in our sample. In our analysis, the variable is logged to reduce skewness.

In terms of each country's ability to supply education, we standardize across each country's productive capacity as represented by the percentage of state expenditures devoted to education in an equation that controls for the overall size of government as a percentage of GDP (Kaufman & Segura-Ubiergo 2001; Rudra & Haggard 2005).[7]

[7] An alternative standardizing tool is measuring education expenditure relative to gross domestic product (GDP). This metric, however, would conflate the size of the country's economy with the size of its government. For example, the analysis would not distinguish between countries with large government sectors that devote relatively few state resources to education from countries with small government sectors that devote relatively large levels of state resources to education. We also ran separate analysis using this measure and found similar patterns of results to the ones using education spending as a percentage of state spending.

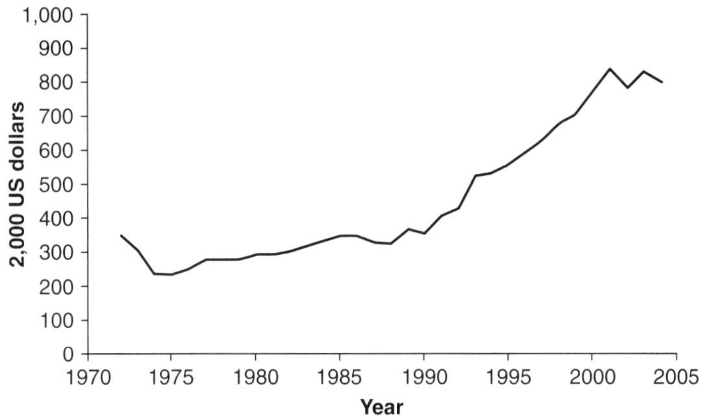

FIGURE 5.1. Government Education Spending per Child under Age 14 Years in Non-OECD Countries from 1972 to 2004.

Figure 5.2 shows the percentage of state expenditures devoted to education for the countries in our sample. We obtained our figures from the annual IMF *Government Finance Statistics*. Ultimately, with these two dependent variables, we are able to capture both capacity (educational expenditure as a percent of total government expenditures) and need (educational expenditures per potential student).

One issue with measuring national levels of education spending is that in federal systems, local governments may contribute funds to education that are not captured in the national measure. Although it would be optimal to include total government education spending, annual data are available only for central government expenditures. Fortunately, prior analyses report that central governments retain responsibility for most social services even after decentralization (Kaufman

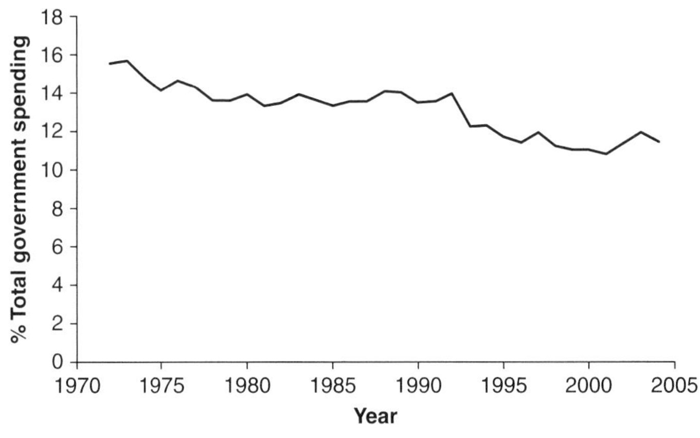

FIGURE 5.2. Share of Education Spending in Total Government Spending in Non-OECD Countries from 1972 to 2004.

& Segura-Ubiergo 2001). Supporting this conclusion, we ran our analysis excluding Eastern European nations, which tend to be decentralized, and found no important differences in the results. It is important to note that the country with the greatest levels of decentralized spending – the United States – is not included in our analysis because it is not a poor- or middle-income country.

2. Independent Variables

The Proportion of Child-Rights Treaties Ratified by Each Country. Our analysis utilizes measures of the penetration of global norms concerning education since 1983. We consider, first, the ratification of five major child-rights treaties and the related International Covenant on Economic, Social, and Cultural Rights by each country. The five child-rights treaties include the International Labour Organization (ILO) Minimum Age Convention (1973), UN Convention on the Rights of the Child (1989), ILO Worst Forms of Child Labor Convention (1999), the UN Optional Protocol on Child Soldiers (2000c), and the UN Optional Protocol on Child Prostitution (2000b). Treaty ratification is operationalized as the proportion of treaties signed out of treaties that could be signed by each country in a given year. We expect variances in the proportion (0 percent to 100 percent) between countries and across time. Our hypothesis is that a stronger commitment to treaty ratifications should be associated with increased government education spending.

Child Rights-INGO-Domestic Civil Society Linkage. The second measure of child-rights mobilization is the number of INGOs to which citizens or organizations of a country belong. INGO linkage captures the extent of a state's participation in world society, in this case, in the sphere of child rights (Boli & Thomas 1999). Membership data comes from the *Yearbook of International Organizations* (Union of International Associations various years), which reports country memberships annually from 1982. Using the 2007 version, the most current version available, we identified ninety-three child-rights INGOs operating in the world. An INGO is regarded as a child-rights INGO if its purposes include the promotion of child rights, the promotion of education, eliminating child labor, eliminating child trafficking, eliminating corporal punishment, or similar goals or activities.[8] INGO linkage is operationalized as the proportion of existing child-rights INGOs within each country. This INGO measure has the advantage of being independent of the overall increase in INGOs over time.

Structural Adjustment Agreements and Implementation. Some analyses have suggested that conditionalities placed on nation-states wishing to borrow money from

[8] We coded country membership information in child-rights NGOs using 1981, 1985, 1990, 1995, 2000, and 2005 data and interpolated the values among those years. Because NGO data are highly serially autocorrelated, interpolation of NGO data is an appropriate way to handle missing data (Boli & Thomas 1999; Boyle & Kim 2009; Meyer et al. 1997).

the World Bank or the IMF have hurt the most vulnerable members of societies, including children (Evans 2002; Tomaševski 2005). These studies tend to be based on single-case studies or on policy documents of the World Bank or the IMF. These studies are essential for showing detailed processes working on the ground or the nature and transformation of the education-related policies of the World Bank or the IMF. However, it is unknown whether, and to what extent, these claims can be generalized across many countries over different time periods. To assess these claims across countries and over time, our analysis utilizes information on World Bank structural adjustment agreements. Each year a country enters an SAA counts as a 1; all other years are coded as 0. We separately construct a measure of SAA implementation. We assume that the effect of SAA implementation does not occur immediately, but rather takes some time. Consistent with the literature (Abouharb & Cingranelli 2006), our data indicate that, on average, SAAs last for three years. Thus, it appears reasonable to assume that most direct changes associated with the implementation of SAAs should appear in the three years following an SAA (compare Zack-Williams 2000).[9] We code the three years following the adoption of an SAA as 1.

Percentage of Population under 14 Years of Age. Once a country has committed to universal schooling, we might expect public investments in schooling to rise or fall, depending on the sheer size of the school-aged cohort. Because of efficiencies, each additional child in a country probably increases expenditures on education at a decreasing rate. Thus, we expect that the greater the percentage of individuals under age 14 in a country, the lower the per child rate of education spending. We also control for another important demographic factor: total population. Data for these variables come from the World Bank *World Development Indicators* (2006).

3. Control Variables

Democracy. Another local factor we consider is the nature of the government. Democratic and autocratic systems undoubtedly treat education differently. Although both are concerned with training young people to fill jobs, authorities in democratic systems may be more interested in using education to foster individual initiative, whereas authorities in autocracies are more likely to use education to inculcate a mindset supportive of the government. It is difficult to say how this will play out in overall expenditures on education, but it could be influential. This indicator is derived from the institutionalized polity score created by Marshall and Jaggers (2002). The indicator ranges from −10 (full autocracy) to +10 (full democracy). The polity score is updated on a yearly basis, and we use the 2004 version of it, which covers the period 1993 to 2004. (We use only the data relating to our time period.)

9 Although it would be useful to consider even longer-term effect of SAAs, it is impracticable in this analysis.

This indicator is included to evaluate how the effects of cultural and economic globalization may be influenced by the presence of a more autocratic or democratic government.

Gross Domestic Product (GDP) per Capita. In order to account for a country's general level of economic development, we include GDP per capita. When GDP increases, spending in all areas, including education may increase. However, this does not necessarily reflect an increased relative commitment to education. The GDP per capita measure comes from the World Bank *World Development Indicators* (2006) and is logged to reduce skew.

Foreign Direct Investment (FDI) and Trade. Our measure of trade follows the standard practice in the literature, which is to consider the sum of exports and imports as a share of GDP. FDI is measured as net inflows of FDI as a percentage of GDP. Both measures are from the World Bank *World Development Indicators* (2006).

Lagged Dependent Variable. Education spending and our independent variable indicators are changing only incrementally over time, so our time-series models will exhibit high levels of serial autocorrelation (Baltagi 1995; Kennedy 1998; Ostrom 1990). We address this by including a three-year lagged term. As our analysis covers the period 1983 to 2004, lagged terms include values from 1979 to 2000. Using a lagged dependent variable is appropriate in our analysis for two reasons. First, the most serious consequence of this method is to discount the importance of variables that are actually influential (Achen 2000). Nevertheless, the results, while more conservative, will still be unbiased. Second, substantively, this research focuses on factors influencing changes in the levels of educational expenditures over time rather than differences across countries; thus, controlling for previous levels of educational expenditures is crucial for the analysis.

C. *Statistical Analysis*

We investigate the effects of transnational neoliberal orders and global, free, universal education norms on education spending with a pooled time-series analysis in which the unit of analysis is country-year. The data file includes 22 years for most of the countries. Pooled time-series analysis is an appropriate and accessible method for measuring dynamic historical trends, such as the increase in globalization and its effects on education spending across many different states. The period 1983 to 2004 covers the most critical years for the intensification of neoliberal approaches to education promoted by IFIs (particularly through SAAs) and the expansion of global child-rights discourse. In addition, the time period incorporates considerable variation in national economic and political circumstances.

In a pooled time-series regression, variation occurs across two dimensions: space and time. Variation across space is the differences observed across countries.

Even excluding developed countries from the analyses, these variations are huge. Countries differ in terms of population size, land mass, productive capacity, level of inequality, and along hundreds of other dimensions. Variation across time, by comparison, relates to changes in each country's characteristics over a designated period of time. In general, this variation is much smaller than variation across countries. For example, even if Bangladesh were miraculously to double its gross domestic product, it would still be much poorer than South Korea or Chile. Any cross-national statistical analysis must consider which dimension of variation – space, time, or some combination of both – is relevant to its core questions.

In the current analysis, we are most interested in variation over time because we want to know how particular interventions in countries at particular times have affected educational expenditures in those countries. For the reasons just noted, we have to take care to keep our over-time analyses from being overwhelmed by cross-country (spatial) differences. A fixed-effects model with lagged dependent variables allows us to do this (see Halaby 2004).[10] Such a model focuses on over-time change while controlling for variations across countries (by including a "dummy" variable for each country in the analysis). For example, using a fixed-effects analysis, we can consider how changes in one country's population from year *x* to year *y* are related to changes in educational expenditures across the same time period, while controlling for the national differences in population size.[11]

Using this general structure, we specify our model as follows:

$$\begin{aligned}\text{Education spending}_{it} = {} & \alpha + \beta_1 \text{past level}_{it-3} + \beta_2 \text{SAA approval}_{it} \\ & + \beta_3 \text{SAA implementation}_{it} + \beta_4 \text{treaty}_{it} + \beta_5 \text{INGO}_{it} \\ & + \beta_6 \text{pop14}_{it} + \Sigma(\beta_k \text{controls})_{it} + \varepsilon_{it}\end{aligned}$$

[10] Another alternative is a random-effects model, but Hausman's chi-square test indicated that fixed effects were preferable for our models. A key advantage of fixed effects models for longitudinal data is that they allow the fixed, unobserved factor to be correlated with the independent variables, whereas random effects models assume independence (Halaby 2004). This is a clear advantage for the purpose of this analysis, where it is almost impossible to specify all the factors affecting the dependent variables and where such unobservable factors are likely to be correlated with specified independent variables. The fixed effects model takes the general form:

$$Y_{it} = \Sigma(\alpha_i D_i) + \beta_{it} X_{it} + \varepsilon_{it}$$

where Y_{it} represents the dependent variables in state i in year t, and D_i represents a vector of state-specific indicator variables with individual-specific constants α_i. X_{it} represents a vector of independent variables with coefficients β_{it}. ε_{it} represents the error term.

[11] The downside of this analysis is that we cannot control for time-invariant measures, such as regional effects and ethnolinguistic fractionalization. We separately ran random effects analysis with these additional controls (results not shown) and found no significant change in the magnitude and direction of our key time-varying measures.

"Education spending $_{it}$" represents our two dependent variables, educational spending per child and the share of central government education spending allocated to education, respectively, in state *i* in year *t*. SAA variables are World Bank loan approvals and implementation. The globalization of child-rights variables are the proportion of child-rights treaties ratified and the proportion of child-rights INGOs linked to a country. The proportion of children under age 14 in the population measures the relative size of educational need. Controls include general economic globalization (foreign direct investment [net inflow] and trade), and country-specific political (democracy versus autocracy), economic (GDP per capita), and demographic (population) variables. By controlling the political, economic, and demographic factors most commonly expected to affect education spending, we hope to understand the effects of cultural and economic globalization above and beyond these factors.[12] We utilize two-tailed tests for each hypothesis in an attempt to take opposing arguments offered in the literature into account.

D. *Statistical Analysis Results*

Figures 5.1 and 5.2 show the trends for government education spending for the developing countries in our sample when no other variables are considered. Educational spending per young person held fairly constant until 1990, when it began to increase steadily (Figure 5.1).[13] During the same period, the share of education spending as a percent of total government spending remained fairly constant at around 14 percent until the early 1990s, when it showed an over-time decrease to about 12 percent (Figure 5.2). The raw trends are difficult to interpret. They may reflect demographic shifts – fewer young people could mean more spending per child even if education budgets are stable or declining. Alternatively, higher enrollment

[12] We tested our analytical model with additional controls, including primary and secondary enrollment rates and interactions between key independent variables (results not shown), but these additional variables did not have significant independent effects on either measure of education spending or influence the direction or significance of our key independent variables.

[13] Since the 1990s, primary enrollment rates began once again to increase and, on average, per-child spending began to see slow but steady increases. Note that this is different from per *pupil* spending, for which data are not available. Per-pupil spending may well have gone down in the same period. Some argue, however, that IFIs continue to be obstacles to realizing children's rights to education and government funding for education (Tomaševski 2006). From this perspective, the world ought to be moving more quickly toward high-quality primary education for all than it is. Although the IFIs celebrate increased primary enrollment, they continue to suggest ceilings on state education funding. For example, Uganda under the World Bank's SAAs doubled primary enrollment between 1996 and 1999 (World Bank 2002a). However, this increase was accompanied by a dramatic decline in quality, collapsing test scores (e.g., the number of third-grade pupils achieving a "satisfactory score" on English oral test fell from 92 percent to 56 percent), and increased numbers of students per teacher (from 35.2 to 60.1) (Clemens 2004; World Bank 2002a). This was because Uganda doubled enrollments without adopting a corresponding increase in education funding.

rates resulting from the retraction of user fees may require states to invest more in education. This could explain increasing education outlays per child in countries. Figure 5.2 would then indicate that, even as education spending increases, other budget items increase more. The figures, in combination, strongly suggest that overall government spending did not decrease very much, if at all, during the height of neoliberalism. Beyond that, they mostly indicate the necessity of a multivariate analysis – simple averages over time are not teasing out the impact of different globalizations.

Turning to our multivariate analysis, the three models in Table 5.1 focus on government education spending per child in the population for the periods 1983 to 2004. Model 1 includes control variables only. SAA variables are added in Model 2. Last, measures of the penetration of global norms concerning education are added in Model 3. Looking at Table 5.1, it is clear that state policy was not directly affected by the ratification of treaties or by SAAs, but rather by the more indirect and diffuse forces of international child-rights INGOs and global financial flows that may respond to these treaties and agreements.

With respect to structural adjustment loans (in Models 2 and 3), we found no support for Hypotheses 1A and 1B. Neither entering into an SAA nor the implementation of SAAs was associated with per-child education spending. However, considering that increasing exports is a core strategy endorsed by IFIs, our findings suggest that loan conditionalities may indirectly decrease per-child education funding. One of the main goals sought through World Bank loan conditionalities – increasing trade – was in fact negatively associated with education spending.

In terms of laws and INGO influence, we found mixed results. States' formal commitment to IGOs' ideas of free and compulsory education, as operationalized through the ratification of child-oriented treaties, did not directly translate into more state funding for education.[14] Thus, Hypothesis 2 was not supported. However, nation-states embedded in the global child-rights regime through stronger linkages to child-rights INGOs were significantly more likely to increase the level of education spending per child, lending credence to Hypothesis 3. INGOs appear to operate as key intermediaries for the conveyance of norms through transnational processes. Education spending per child increases 8 percent for each 10 percentage point increase in the proportion of child-rights INGOs linkage. Consistent with the findings of Hafner-Burton and Tsutsui (2005) and Boyle and Kim (2009), this suggests that mobilization based on international laws has more substantial power than the international laws themselves.

[14] We tested if more general human-rights laws rather than more limited child-rights treaties are relevant to education spending using an alternative treaty measure consisting of the entire set of human-rights treaties (12), but this alternative measure did not have a significant effect on education spending either (results not shown).

TABLE 5.1. *Unstandardized coefficients from the fixed-effects regression of various indicators on education expenditure per child under age 14 years in population, 1983–2004*

	Education expenditure per child under age 14 years in population		
	Model 1	Model 2	Model 3
Percent Population Under Age 14 Years	− 0.030***	− 0.029***	− 0.028***
	(0.005)	(0.005)	(0.006)
Democracy	0.006*	0.006*	0.005*
	(0.003)	(0.003)	(0.003)
Gross Domestic Product (GDP) per Capita (logged)	0.829***	0.835***	0.802***
	(0.071)	(0.071)	(0.071)
Total Population (logged)	0.019	0.023	0.020
	(0.033)	(0.034)	(0.033)
Foreign Direct Investment (percent GDP, 1 year lagged)	0.015**	0.015**	0.011*
	(0.005)	(0.005)	(0.005)
Trade (percent GDP, 1 year lagged)	− 0.002**	− 0.002**	− 0.002**
	(0.001)	(0.001)	(0.001)
Loan Agreement		0.023	0.020
		(0.024)	(0.024)
Loan Implementation		0.012	0.004
		(0.020)	(0.020)
Child-Rights Treaty Ratification			0.000
			(0.000)
Child-Rights International Nongovernmental Organizations (INGO) Membership			0.008***
			(0.002)
3 Year Lagged Education Expenditure per Student	0.189***	0.190***	0.179***
	(0.028)	(0.029)	(0.028)
Constant	− 1.130	− 1.263†	− 1.260
	(0.761)	(0.770)	(0.760)
Observations	614	614	614
Number of Countries	71	71	71
R-squared	0.602	0.603	0.617

Note: Standard errors in parentheses. † < 0.10 * $p < 0.05$ ** $p < 0.01$ *** $p < 0.001$ (two-tailed test).

Child-rights INGOs are not the only types of INGOs relevant to state education spending. In fact, in a separate analysis, we found that women's rights INGO linkages (Paxton, Hughes, & Green 2006) had the same positive effects on both education spending measures. However, child-rights INGOs do not appear to represent general transnational civil society activity in a country. In another separate analysis, we did not find significant effects on education spending of more general human rights INGO linkages (Tsutsui & Wotipka 2004) or total INGO linkages.

The combined findings for treaty ratification and INGO linkages provide an important insight into how the cultural aspects of globalization transform state's financial decisions. In a previous article, Boyle and Kim (2009) found a positive, significant effect of child-rights treaty ratification on the number of country memberships in child-rights INGOs. It appears that child-rights treaty ratification, while purely symbolic on the surface, legitimizes child-rights discourse in global civil society, which in turn facilitates the diffusion of child-rights INGOs into national civil society and empowers domestic mobilization around child rights (Boyle & Kim 2009; Hafner-Burton & Tsutsui 2005; Liu & Boyle 2001). Transnational mobilization of child rights and linkages to national civil society strongly affect governments' financial commitment to primary education. This suggests a concrete way in which transnational efforts transform the state in the education sphere.[15]

Turning to the control variables, we find, as expected, that the greater the percentage of individuals under age 14 in a country, the lower per-child education spending. GDP per capita is positively associated with per-child education spending. This confirms previous research findings that relatively affluent countries are capable of spending more on education. Democracy was positively associated with per-child education spending. Overall, our findings suggest that state economic capacity and the relative proportion of children in the total population, which constitutes the supply and demand sides of states' capacity to fund education, matter in determining raw level of state funding for education.

In Model 1, we find mixed effects for FDI and trade on raw education spending per child. Foreign direct investment was positively associated with the level of state education funding per child. Higher levels of foreign investment may drive up the need (or perceived need) for skilled labor, leading to a greater investment in education. Trade had the opposite effect on education spending, indicating that more exports and imports (relative to the size of their economies) are associated with relatively less money for education. These opposite trends need to be explored in greater depth in future work. It may be that higher trade in a developing country is associated with agriculture and the extraction of raw materials and expansion of the manufacturing sector where imported materials are processed to export. All of these tend to require low-skilled labor, which reduces the incentive to invest in skills and education (Grootaert & Kanbur 1995). Another explanation for this finding is that open trade places countries in a "race to bottom" in which governments retrench social programs in the name of competitiveness and austerity (Huber & Stephens 2001; Palley 2002). Foreign investors, in contrast, may be less interested in

[15] Interestingly, we find (in an analysis not shown) the influence of child INGOs is not stronger as a country ratifies more treaties. While international laws about universal, free education may provide tools for civil actors' mobilization at the global and national levels, the strength of child-rights INGOs' influence on state education spending in a specific developing country is not a simple function of the number of treaties the country ratified.

exploiting cheap labor and more closely linked to economic growth, which will have an indirect effect on governments' ability to invest in education (De Soysa & Oneal 1999). Foreign investors may be under higher scrutiny by the media and human rights and other activist groups and connected with child-rights INGOs and IGOs (McClintock 1999; Spar 1998).

Table 5.2 summarizes models of our other measure of states' education spending: the share of education spending in total government spending. The analysis is for the same period as our per-child analysis: 1983–2004. Child-rights treaty ratification had a positive effect on the share of education spending, but not on per-child education spending. Otherwise, the effects of the penetration of global norms for comprehensive education were similar for relative education spending and per-child spending. Child-rights INGO linkages had a strong positive effect on both aspects of education spending. This suggests that the global norm of comprehensive education affected both absolute and relative state commitment to education in the same way.[16] Given the downward trend in the share of education spending in total government spending in the developing world over the last several decades, a robust positive effect of child-rights INGO linkage on the share of education spending suggests that the presence of child-rights INGOs in a particular country increases the government's education spending.

In other ways, the two analyses differ. First, the effects of foreign investment on the share of education spending was different from those on per-child education spending, whereas the effects of entering into SAAs (not associated) and trade (negatively associated) were the same as those on per-child education spending. SAA implementation had a negative effect on the share of education spending (the statistical significance of this effect was marginal). Trade openness was also negatively associated with the share of education spending. Foreign investment had no significant effect on the share of education spending. Second, economic capacity and demographic demand factors, which were statistically significantly associated with raw

[16] To test the robustness of our results, we first considered outliers and influential cases. We used a number of diagnostic procedures, including partial plots and Cook's D, to identify these cases. We identified a number of Eastern Europe countries having a different pattern. The removal of these Eastern Europe countries individually or the entire group of Eastern Europe countries had no substantial effect on the key variables in the models in terms of the sign, significance, and main conclusions. In addition to it, we ran all models using random effects and found the results on the key variables – child-rights treaty ratification, child-rights NGO linkage, loan agreement, and loan implementation – are consistent with those in the fixed effect models (results not reported here). We also performed various sensitivity tests on the models. From scatterplots of the residuals, we did not find substantial problems of heteroskedasticity or nonnormality. Although there is a modest level of multicollinearity for our main model (Model 3 in Tables 5.1 and 5.2), correlations among independent variables were less than 0.39. Furthermore, the overall stability of the sign and significance across models with different specifications supports the robustness of the results presented here.

TABLE 5.2. *Unstandardized coefficients from the fixed-effects regression of various indicators on share of education expenditure in total government expenditure, 1983–2004*

	Share of education expenditure in total government expenditure		
	Model 1	Model 2	Model 3
Percent Population Under Age 14 Years	− 0.012 (0.056)	− 0.022 (0.057)	0.002 (0.057)
Democracy	0.036 (0.031)	0.038 (0.031)	0.027 (0.031)
Gross Domestic Product (GDP) per Capita (logged)	2.048** (0.787)	1.935* (0.790)	1.274 (0.797)
Total Population (logged)	0.150 (0.291)	0.057 (0.297)	0.046 (0.293)
Foreign Direct Investment (percent GDP, 1 year lagged)	0.038 (0.044)	0.042 (0.044)	0.010 (0.045)
Trade (percent GDP, 1 year lagged)	− 0.017* (0.008)	− 0.017* (0.008)	− 0.018* (0.008)
Loan Agreement		− 0.257 (0.265)	− 0.279 (0.263)
Loan Implementation		− 0.306 (0.228)	− 0.419† (0.227)
Child-Rights Treaty Ratification			0.009† (0.005)
Child-Rights International Nongovernmental Organizations (INGO) Membership			0.076*** (0.021)
3-Year Lagged Share of Education Expenditure in Total Government Expenditure	0.236*** (0.035)	0.235*** (0.035)	0.226*** (0.035)
Constant	− 5.875 (8.339)	− 3.399 (8.462)	− 1.934 (8.386)
Observations	797	797	797
Number of Countries	85	85	85
R-squared	0.091	0.095	0.117

Note: Standard errors in parentheses. † < 0.10 * p < 0.05 ** p < 0.01 *** p < 0.001 (two-tailed test).

levels of per-child spending on education, were largely insignificant in determining the share of education spending in total government spending. In other words, the percent of a country's budget spent on education is not determined by the number of young people in that country, GDP per capita, or levels of democracy. These factors are not critically important in predicting the relative priority states assign to education over other areas.

3. CONCLUSION

This chapter demonstrates the persistence of institutionalized principles at the global level, even when they become the object of controversy and disagreement. Despite tensions between two transnational legal orders – one advocating a universal right to free primary education and the other invoking neoliberal approaches to smaller government, such as cost sharing for education – the institutionalized idea of strong state support for primary education maintained its dominance in the global system. This was true at the level of both global policy development and national policy implementation. While the World Bank initially proposed user fees for public services in the early 1980s, it explicitly carved out an exception for primary education by the early 2000s. Meanwhile, nation-states generally did not heed its call for smaller government in education – at least not directly. In our statistical analysis, contrary to our predictions, SAAs had little effect on spending for education. This is consistent with the idea of Killick (1996) that SAAs are not strongly enforced. However, global economic integration in the form of imports and exports did exert downward pressure on such spending. Because a goal of IFIs is to increase global trade, this suggests some indirect negative effects of their policies on education spending. Overall, the inconsistent effects of SAAs, trade, and FDI suggest that states were able to resist the full implementation of neoliberal policies despite the material resources attached to their policies.

In contrast, we find strong and consistent evidence that INGOs played an important role in maintaining state support for education during the time period studied. Their impact was stronger and more consistent than the impact of the ratification of international child-rights treaties or SAAs. Our historical analysis suggests that their networks of members brought material as well as normative resources to bear to support free universal education and minimize the impact of user fees. Our results highlight the key role of transnational civil society acting as an intermediary for the transnational construction, conveyance, and implementation of legal norms for primary education.

Future analyses will want to consider precisely why and how this INGO effect occurs. One possibility is that child-rights INGOs actively mobilized and strengthened the legitimacy of free universal education norms. Another is that they created more "ports of entry" for free universal education norms. These, in turn, may have prompted more domestic civil society mobilization around child-rights laws, and buffered states from conflicting messages. It is also possible that INGOs merely signify states' openness to global civil society – countries that allow/encourage lots of INGOs may also be open to ideas generated by the United Nations and UNESCO. One thing that INGOs are not doing, according to our analysis, is merely replacing resources that states would ordinarily spend on education. This is inconsistent with our finding that the presence of INGOs consistently increased governments' education spending.

Our findings suggest that legitimacy is important in constructing, conveying, and implementing transnational legal norms. Advocates promoting children's rights to free compulsory primary education had greater legitimacy over neoliberal approaches to education funding because the former ideas had been enshrined in international law and were promoted successfully for decades by UNESCO. Ultimately, the promotion of user fees for education threatened the legitimacy of the World Bank, and it was forced to change its position. At the same time, material resources also matter. The user-fee idea gained traction in part because UNESCO lost a substantial amount of its funding at a critical moment. Furthermore, INGOs provide resources as well as legitimacy to countries. By incorporating IFIs into our historical and statistical analyses, we avoid an overly simplified dichotomization between material resources and legitimacy.

Ultimately, our analysis sheds light on the future of education funding around the globe. Although global civil society successfully buffers downward pressure on education spending and contributes to an increase in both raw and relative terms, the extent of the increase may be inadequate. As discussed earlier, since the 1990s, primary enrollment rates have increased sharply in many developing countries (World Bank 2002a). State budgetary allocations are not keeping up. These trends are worrisome. Under these conditions, the rapid growth in primary enrollment is often accompanied by a deterioration in school conditions and education quality in terms of teachers, class time, classrooms, and other educational facilities (Clemens 2004; Duraisamy et al. 1997). An important next step is to study whether and how these conditions become a basis for transforming transnational education norms (Shaffer, Chapter 2).

APPENDIX A. *Operationalization of variables and summary statistics (87 countries analyzed)*

			Descriptive statistics		
	Operationalization	Source	Observation	Mean	Standard deviation
Dependent Variable					
Education Expenditure per Child	Logged education spending per person under 14 years of age (consolidated central governments)	IMF: GFS Yearbooks	682	4.96	1.57
Share of Education Expenditure	Percent total expenditure (consolidated central governments)	IMF: GFS Yearbooks	797	12.64	6.01
Independent Variables					
Demand for Education					
Population under 14	Percent population under 14 years	World Bank: WDI	797	34.12	9.58
Global Child-Rights Discourse					
CR Treaty Ratification	Proportion of CR treaties ratified out of CR treaties available (0–100%)	UN and ILO	797	52.50	31.90
CR NGO Membership	Proportion of CR INGOs to which a country has a linkage out of CR INGOs available (0–100%)	UIA Yearbooks	797	34.74	14.98
	Coded in years 1980, 1985, 1990, 1995, 2000, and 2001				
	Missing values interpolated				
World Bank Structural Adjustment Agreement (SAA)					
World Bank SAA	Dichotomous "1" if SAA received; "0" if not	Correspondence with World Bank	797	0.14	0.34

World Bank SAA Implementation	Dichotomous "1" for the 3 years following SAA receipt and "0" otherwise	Correspondence with World Bank	797	0.28	0.45
Control Variables					
Political					
Autocracy/democracy	Democracy-autocracy measure (−10–10)	Polity IV dataset	797	2.63	7.19
Economic					
GDP per Capita	Logged GDP per capita (US$2000 value)	World Bank: WDI	797	7.40	1.14
Demographic					
Total Population	Logged total population	World Bank: WDI	797	12.71	0.70
Economic Globalization					
Foreign Direct Investment, 1 year lagged	Foreign direct investment net inflow (% of GDP)	World Bank: WDI	797	2.04	2.97
Trade, 1 year lagged	Trade (% of GDP)	World Bank: WDI	797	74.76	42.07
Lagged Term					
Lagged Term for Education Expenditure per student	Logged education expenditure per person under 14 years of age, 3 years before (consolidated central governments)	IMF: GFS Yearbooks	689	4.87	1.53
Lagged Term for Share of Education Expenditure	Education expenditure as % total government expenditure, 3 years before (consolidated central governments)	IMF: GFS Yearbooks	797	12.47	5.92

Abbreviations: CR, child rights; GDP, gross domestic product; GFS, Government Finance Statistics; ILO, International Labour Organization; IMF, International Monetary Fund; INGO, international nongovernmental organizations; NGO, nongovernmental organizations; SAA, structural adjustment agreements; UIA, Union of International Associations; UN, United Nations; WDI, World Development Indicators.

6

Access to Medicines and the Transformation of the South African State

Heinz Klug

From India, Brazil, Thailand, and the Middle East to Kenya and South Africa, access to essential medicines remains a highly contested issue internationally and nationally. Most recently, the transnational nongovernmental organization Medecins Sans Frontieres (MSF) has campaigned against attempts by the European Union to put pressure on the Indian government during trade negotiations to make changes to that country's intellectual property laws to limit the production of "generic" medicines. Describing India as the "pharmacy of the developing world" through which many developing countries are able to gain access to affordable essential medicines, MSF has welcomed the Indian Patent Office's rejection of some patent applications of major multinational drug companies on the grounds that the drugs do not meet the standards required to issue a new patent under Indian patent laws. MSF has called on the Indian government to stand firm against demands to increase the level of intellectual property protection above the requirements of the World Trade Organization (WTO) agreement on Trade Related Aspects of Intellectual Property (TRIPS) (Medecins Sans Frontrieres[MSF] 2011). In Kenya, there are complaints that the anticounterfeiting law adopted in 2008 is being used to block generic drugs (Kwamboka 2011), and in South Africa, the government was congratulated by the Treatment Action Campaign (TAC) for a successful antiretroviral tender dramatically reducing the cost of these drugs in the public sector and raising hopes that more people needing treatment may be served (Section 27 2011).

While the complex international debate over access to medicines, the economics of drug discovery, and intellectual property continues, the problem of access to essential medicines also provides an extraordinary context in which to explore the interaction of transnational legal norms and the transformation of domestic law and institutions in different countries (Shaffer, Chapter 1). On a global plane, John Braithwaite and Peter Drahos have presented "globalization as a contest of principles" (Braithwaite & Drahos 2000: 7) and argue that "regulatory globalization is a process in which different types of actors use various mechanisms to push for or against principles" (Braithwaite & Drahos 2000: 9). This process sped up in the mid 1980s and led, Peter O'Brien argues, to the emergence by the mid 1990s of a "world economy marked by the establishment of international norms and competitive standards in all fields." Focusing on medicines, he notes that "within the industrial sector, pharmaceuticals is the branch which provides the outstanding example of success for international producer associations" (Drahos 2002; O'Brien 1998: 77). In another study focusing on the globalization of intellectual property rights, Susan Sell adopted an analytical framework of "structured agency" to explain the role of private interests in the emergence of the TRIPS agreement. She explains how the "global campaign for access to essential medicines has emerged to protest US trade policy in intellectual property and the TRIPS tradeoff in favor of commercial interests over public health concerns" (Sell 2003: 146).

The challenge of a globalized regime of pharmaceutical discovery, supply, and regulation has produced a range of theoretic responses and studies. On the one hand, there has been a revival of the debate over public goods in which the importance of recognizing global public goods has been advocated as a means to manage globalization (Kaul et al. 2003), especially in the realm of public health (Woodward & Smith 2003). On the other hand, Adriana Petryna and Arthur Kleinman argue that the globalization of pharmaceuticals is a "multiscaled movement with political, economic, and ethical dimensions" that together "constitute a 'pharmaceutical nexus'" (Petryna & Kleinman 2006: 20). They contend that the "idea of a nexus is meant to capture a broad set of political and social transitions that fall under and to some extent happen through the globalization of pharmaceuticals" (Petryna & Kleinman 2006: 21). I have argued that the global HIV/AIDS pandemic and the absolute necessity of providing access to antiretroviral medicines as a means to address this scourge requires the introduction of a human rights approach as a way to rebalance claims for the protection of intellectual property and public health (Klug 2010a). In different ways these studies and the analytical frameworks they bring to bear seek to address in one specific realm the challenge to governance that globalization represents more broadly.

While debates over globalization and governance have tended to focus on the limits of national authority in the context of globalized economic relationships (Guehenno 1995; Ohmae 1990), others have focused, on the one hand, on the interaction between territorial authority based on political and military authority, and on the other hand, on interdependence based on global competition and production (Cox 1994) or on the possibilities of establishing new forms of governance to regulate globalization (Ruggie 2003). More recently, David Held has made a concerted attempt to envision how global processes may be regulated by focusing in part on the changing role of law in providing the basis for a "rule-bound multilateral order" (Held 2004: 119). Boaventura de Sousa Santos and Cesar Rodriguez have explored the role of counter-hegemonic globalization in the creation of a "cosmopolitan legality" (Santos & Rodriguez 2005). In my own work, I have also explored the role of social movements in the construction of a global response to HIV/AIDS (Klug 2005) as well as the ways in which global and local legal regimes shape the rules that govern access to essential medicines in developing countries (Klug 2008). Common in much of this work is an assumption that globalization in whatever form is, in effect, transforming the world in which we live. While Ronald Rogowski had earlier explored how domestic political alignments are shaped by different patterns of cross-border trade (Rogowski 1989), the "transformationist thesis" led to the construction of an analytical framework that sought to map "global flows, networks and relations" in terms of "their fundamental spatiotemporal dimensions: extensity, intensity, velocity and impact propensity" (Held et al. 1999: 21). Using these analytical tools, the authors of this approach turned their attention to the nation-state and discussed the impact of globalization on state power and democratic politics. From this analysis, they concluded that "contemporary patterns of globalization also generate significant institutional impacts in so far as they reconfigure institutional agendas and invite institutional innovation" (Held et al. 1999: 440). Their lens, however, was turned outward to the global. Although they recognized that, at the political level, these impacts "required the development of new modes of national policy coordination and bureaucratic organization to manage the internationalization of policy decision-making," there was less focus on the impacts that globalization or transnational law and policy might have on the structure of the state itself and on the processes of policymaking that occur within the state.

To explore these dynamics, we need to focus more directly on the internal workings of the state itself. Although states are in constant evolution, the pace of change may vary dramatically, as governmental institutions operate within a continuing process of reconstruction, responding to different events, opportunities, and constraints both from within and across their geographical boundaries. South Africa's transition to democracy happens to have marked a spectacular moment of change as apartheid gave way to a new constitution and a democratically elected government committed to transforming the society (Klug 2000). High on the agenda of the ruling party, the African National Congress (ANC), was the transformation of the state. Despite its commitment to address the legacies of apartheid and its own relative strength and political will, the ANC would have to pursue its goals within the framework of the negotiated constitution, inherited state institutions, and the global environment. Within this interconnected landscape of national and transnational arenas, institutions, and political engagements exists a political, economic, and policy environment to which the state must constantly seek a coordinated response. At the same time, different institutions, policymakers, social movements, and civil society more generally are also constantly jostling to encourage the state to pursue one or other of the available options. As the state responds to this shifting set of opportunities and constraints, whether real or perceived, impetus is given to different policies and competing political and economic factions, enabling particular institutions and rules to be embraced, created, reshaped, or simply foregone.

The story of the struggle over HIV/AIDS policy in South Africa, from a pattern of denial at the highest levels of government (Gevisser 2007; Govender 2007; Nattrass 2007) to the decision of the Constitutional Court to grant a court order requiring government to provide nevirapine to help prevent mother-to-child transmission of HIV (Klug 2010b; Sachs 2009), has been told many times. Also frequently told has been the story of activists and social movements from the streets of South Africa to the halls of international diplomacy, a campaign that brought together local activists, transnational nongovernmental organizations (NGOs), government, and international policymakers to secure eventually the adoption by the WTO Ministerial meeting in November 2001 of the Doha Declaration on the TRIPS Agreement and Public Health (t'Hoen 2009). There is also the story of litigation in multiple forums and the policy breakthroughs that led the government of South Africa to formally adopt a program to provide antiretroviral (ARV) treatment in the public health system (AIDS Law Project 2003; Geffen 2010; Kapczynski 2009). There is no end to these stories so long as the pandemic continues. This chapter retells these stories for the purpose of exploring the interaction between an emerging transnational legal order for intellectual property, an exploding health crisis, and the restructuring of the state as the country emerged from apartheid. Relying on personal experience in debates over access to medicines, both in South Africa and internationally, informal interviews and discussions with government officials, policymakers, and activists, as well as an extensive review of documents and secondary sources, this chapter explores these "transformations" (Shaffer, Chapter 1) as products of the interaction between global opportunities and constraints as well as the agency of different participants in the debates and struggles over access to essential medicines in South Africa.

In setting the stage for exploring the process of "transformations" of the state, this chapter begins with an overview of the transnational and local context. Following this overview, the chapter examines three distinct areas of law and policy formation in the new South Africa – trade, health, and competition – which together form the legal and policy background in which any attempt to improve access to essential medicines is located. In each of these sections, the chapter considers the existence of both transnational and local constraints and opportunities that shape the changing process of policy formation and law. With these different arenas outlined, the chapter then specifically considers the question of access to essential medicines as a realm in which to identify the interaction and effects of these different policy and legal changes. Finally, the chapter argues that mapping the repeated transformations of the state by focusing simultaneously on the constitutive elements of each policy area as well as the complex environment of "structured agency" that provides the space in which participants are able to achieve institutional and policy innovations enables us to understand how the allocation of important resources, such as essential medicines, may be reconfigured both nationally and transnationally.

1. GLOBAL AND LOCAL CONTEXT

South Africa's democratic transition formally began in early 1990 with the unbanning of the liberation movements and the release of Nelson Mandela from prison. Coinciding with, and in many ways facilitated by, the end of the Cold War, the new government, ushered in with the first democratic election four years later, faced an international environment in which alternatives to a free market economy seemed nearly unimaginable (Saul 2002). Although the ANC imagined a state in which the government would be an active participant in restructuring the economy and transforming society, the nature of the negotiated transition placed significant constraints on the new government. First, the new government would inherit the former bureaucracy, the members of which were guaranteed their positions for the first five years. Second, the government would have to operate within the context of a new "interim" constitution and government of national unity while working simultaneously to produce a "final" constitution within two years and to implement its own election promises of reconstruction and development. Finally, these constraints coexisted with an atmosphere of high elation and seemingly boundless possibility as the country managed to weather the tensions of what was at times a violent democratic transition while the world was captivated by the sight of lines of voters peacefully casting their ballots for a new democratic order.

Although the new democratic government was determined to address the legacy of apartheid – stark racial inequality and extreme poverty – through its Reconstruction and Development Programme (RDP) (African National Congress [ANC] 1994a), it soon discovered that the state was in fiscal crisis and its capacity limited. This was the result of the combined effect of international sanctions, especially the impact of high interest rates on sovereign debt, and the fiscal expenditures of the former government, which had tried desperately to buy legitimacy in its final years. It was in this climate, a local context of domestic stress with limited alternatives due to international myopia, that the ANC found itself casting around for a feasible macroeconomic strategy. At the same time, the old apartheid government was arguing for an end to South Africa's international isolation. It began to negotiate the terms of South Africa's reentry into the world economy and to participate in the negotiations to form the World Trade Organization (WTO). The old government continued to embrace the "developed country" status that South Africa held in the former trade regime, formed by the General Agreement on Tariffs and Trade (GATT). While there were some in the ANC who argued for negotiating a change of status to "developing country," the pressures to end international isolation without delay meant that this option was foregone.[1] The only alternative open increasingly seemed to be a policy aimed at generating

[1] By retaining its developed country status, South Africa would be required to implement all its WTO obligations, including the heightened intellectual property standards contained in the TRIPS agreement by the beginning of 1995, as compared to developing countries – including India and Brazil – which only had to embrace these obligations by the beginning of 2005.

economic growth through a rapid reintegration of the country into the international economy so that both the state and society would have the resources required for the process of transformation that the country needed. It was this impetus that had led the ANC to join the old government in traveling to Marrakesh in April 1994. South Africa thus became a founding member of the new WTO even before the holding of the country's first democratic elections.

As the state began to be transformed, reorienting itself from a regime committed to upholding apartheid and protecting the interests of a small privileged section of its citizens to a new constitutional state formally committed to protecting the rights of all its citizens while addressing the legacies of the past, there would be enormous pressures and opportunities for institutional reform (Mhone & Edigheji 2003). Shifting policy imperatives changed the allocation of resources and allowed different sectors of the state the opportunity to reshape institutional structures and missions. Important parts of these processes were the opportunities and constraints offered by engaging with different international institutions, policymakers, and NGOs. This would lead to changes in both the institutional forms and legal regimes that addressed particular issues. Changes or transformations of the state were, however, not uniform in character. The extent and nature of change would, on the one hand, depend on the relative power of the transnational institution or model, whereas on the other hand, the opportunity to implement change would in many cases depend on the confluence of various local conditions and, at times, the tensions between different policy sectors or the social problems these sectors were trying to address. Transformation of the state in this sense, then, remained nonlinear and uneven.

Whether the product of long-term planning or the result of a more immediate shift in the macropolicy framework, different policies and the institutions associated with them gained more or less political weight and then capacity as the transformation of the state unfolded. Thus, within the broader process of transformation, it is possible to identify specific policy processes, legal reforms, implementation efforts, and institutional initiatives and to demonstrate how these particular parts of the state responded to, or were impacted by, the respective constraints and opportunities that arose over the first fifteen years of democratic government in South Africa. For present purposes, the focus will be on two different institutional clusters, trade and industry and health, and two specific bodies of law, intellectual property and competition law, and how these have interacted with the broader social struggle over access to essential medicines in the context of South Africa's continuing HIV/AIDS pandemic.

In the case of trade and industry, the engagement with government was at first concentrated in the area of macroeconomic policy and the implementation of policies aimed at addressing the overall commitments made by the country in the newly signed WTO agreements. At first, relatively few activists from the ANC were available to engage with government officials at the lower levels of the bureaucracy. Under these conditions, the old bureaucracy merely universalized its language, arguing that South Africa had been a founding member of the GATT and now, as a founding member of the WTO, should be a leader in implementing its commitments to reduce trade barriers,[2] including the extraordinarily high tariffs that protected most local industry during the apartheid period. As a subunit of trade and industry, the officials handling intellectual property issues merely asserted that South African law had long protected patents and other forms of intellectual property; therefore, they argued the TRIPS agreement held no significant consequences for the country.

The Health Department started in a very different position, as the health sector had an organized network of ANC-aligned activists and professionals who had worked together with the ANC to develop policies aimed at significantly transforming the sector. The ANC Health Department had also worked very closely with the World Health Organization (WHO) and UNICEF to produce a proposed National Health Plan for South Africa that was published in 1994 as part of the ANC's preparations to govern (ANC 1994b). Among the principles contained in the plan were commitments to state responsibility, community participation, and an intersectoral approach recognizing that "related sectors such as education, employment, water, sanitation and housing" are key determinants of health requiring closer collaboration between government departments (van Rensburg & Pelser 2004: 114). The ANC's Health Plan reflected international experience and influence in its adoption of a primary health care approach based on public funding in which "promotive and preventive services in the public sector were to be free, while free health care was to be introduced in the public health sector for specific patient groups" (van Rensburg & Pelser 2004: 114–15). As for the provision of drugs, the WHO seconded an official to work within the Health Department to help develop a new drugs policy that would promote access to essential medicines.

Competition law and policy did not at first receive significant attention, as it was neither the focus of local activists nor did it have a major international nexus. This was the case despite the new government's commitment, articulated in the ANC's election manifesto, to having an antitrust policy (ANC 1994a: s 4.4.6.2).[3] International engagement initially saw the ANC being warned against adopting "old-style" antitrust policies; the response was to knock competition policy off the front burner of policy formation in the early 1990s. It would only be later that questions of market failure and competition would rise to new prominence. When legal reform was finally embarked on in the second half of the 1990s, it encompassed both the adoption of a new competition law as well as the creation of new institutions to effectively implement the new policy direction. Although there are no international institutions such as the WTO, the WHO, or UNICEF in the field of antitrust and competition law, the newly emergent Competition Commission in South Africa soon became a

2 Author's interview with official in Department of Trade and Industry, Pretoria, 1999.

3 Stating that, "The RDP will introduce strict anti-trust legislation to create a more competitive and dynamic business environment."

founding member of the International Competition Network (ICN) that was formed in October 2001 by antitrust officials from fourteen jurisdictions. The goal was to enhance international antitrust enforcement. This engagement was highlighted in May 2006 when David Lewis of the South African Competition Tribunal welcomed "280 delegates from 64 countries, comprising competition authority officials and, non-governmental advisors ('NGAs') from the private bar, business organizations, multilateral organisation and academia" (Moodaliyar & Hartzenberg 2006: 1) to the ICN's 5th Annual Conference in Cape Town.

2. TRADE LAW AND POLICY: EMBRACING FREE TRADE AND REENTERING THE GLOBAL ECONOMY

On the day Nelson Mandela was released from prison in February 1990, he announced his continued allegiance to the Freedom Charter adopted by the Congress Alliance in 1955. He argued that "the nationalization of the mines, banks, and monopoly industry is the policy of the ANC, and a change or modification of our views in this regard is inconceivable" (Marais 2001; Ottaway 1993: 132). The negative response of the markets was instantaneous, a pattern that would be repeated on multiple occasions in response to any initiatives by the ANC or later the Mandela and Mbeki governments to question the basic structure or workings of the South African economy. As the value of the rand, South Africa's currency, jolted downward, and the value of stocks on the Johannesburg Stock Exchange plummeted, the ANC's economic policymakers found themselves caught in a riptide from which they had no immediate means of escape. In these early years after the collapse of state socialism in the early 1990s, there seemed to be no alternative to the market-oriented prescriptions being proffered by the International Monetary Fund (IMF) and the World Bank, or what was increasingly termed the "Washington Consensus." Even as the South African government adopted an economic strategy that has been described as constituting "a compelled accommodation of a global economic system capable of fiercely punishing any 'deviance'" (Marais 2002: 85) and which was heralded around the world for achieving "sound economic fundamentals," it would still face capital flight, instability in the value of the currency, and severe local market fluctuations at every move, whether it was the appointment of the first black Minister of Finance or global reaction to political and economic instability in neighboring Zimbabwe.

As economic policy evolved in the first years of the Mandela government, the core term embraced by the ANC was "growth through redistribution." Inherent in this notion, however, were two alternate possibilities. On the one hand, it could mean that macroeconomic policy should aim to "stimulat[e] demand through the redistribution of income" (Hirsch 2005: 51), an essentially Keynesian approach to the problem of entrenched inequality and poverty. On the other hand, it could also be what Alan Hirsch terms "more Asian in its approach," focusing on "increasing productivity to compete in export markets." This approach would achieve redistribution, argues Hirsch, "through the social wage in the form of education, health and other social services that could improve the capacity of existing and new industrial workers." This second idea of "redistribution through growth" would slowly gain ascendance within the ANC Government. While this government's first attempt to achieve growth through redistribution in the form of the RDP ran aground on the shoals of bureaucratic incapacity and intransigence, the shift in policy from the RDP to the GEAR (Growth, Employment, and Redistribution) would dramatically change the macroeconomic direction of policy and provide openings for greater internationalization as well as a range of new market-oriented initiatives. These ranged from Black Economic Empowerment, a policy and legal framework designed to integrate the economy racially, to the creation and consolidation of a new competition regime, attempting to address problems of collusion and market dominance as a means of attacking the high degree of monopoly power in the South African economy.

Joining the WTO trade regime would provide the new government with both opportunities and constraints. At times, the new government would embrace different options depending on the often unforeseeable and contradictory conditions that arose in relation to different policy initiatives, such as the Generalized Export Incentive Scheme (GEIS) that the old regime adopted to encourage manufactured goods exports as it attempted to break out of its international economic isolation at the beginning of the political transition in April 1990. Although this program would prove extraordinarily expensive, costing the state about US$5 billion (21 billion rands) over its seven-year history, even at times grabbing "the lion's share of the budget of the DTI [Department of Trade and Industry]" (Hirsch 2005: 132), the new government could not easily scrap it. To do so would send a negative message about the new government's commitment to a speedy reintegration into the global economy. Eventually, however, this immense fiscal burden imposed on government by the GEIS could be relieved and the demise of the GEIS blamed on the country's international commitments, as the state had agreed in the WTO to phase out export subsidies by 1997.

In another case, however, the state had, in its efforts to take advantage of both the global euphoria at the peaceful demise of apartheid and the benefit of being an early adopter, accepted the retention in the WTO of South Africa's status as a developed country in GATT. It thus failed to take advantage of the transitional arrangements available to developing countries in the new TRIPS agreement. The consequences of this decision became only too clear when, in 1997, the government attempted to adopt a domestic version of the WHO's essential medicines program, only to face enormous opposition from the pharmaceutical industry and its allies, including the United States. At the same time that the new government in Pretoria was trying to defend its new drug law, it was demonstrating its commitment to reducing trade barriers by shifting resources into the Department of Trade and Industry (DTI). The

DTI was the first government department in the new South Africa to have a brand new headquarters. From a facility designed in the form of a campus in downtown Pretoria, it had the goal of promoting its policies and programs by increasing public access and facilitating entrepreneurial activity through the provision of government services.

The emphasis on export-led economic growth was also encouraged by funding that the Japanese government provided to the World Bank and granted to South Africa's first Minister of Trade and Industry, Trevor Manual, to bring labor, business, and the government together to research and agree on means "to make South African industry more competitive" (Hirsch 2005: 133–4). The Japanese Grant Fund led to the introduction by the DTI of a range of measures that included a preshipment export finance guarantee, a skills development strategy, a restructured program for supporting industrial innovation, and a competitiveness fund. The latter fund included about US$250 million worth of discounted loans that, between 1995 and 1998, went to sectors, such as the textile industry, the competitiveness of which was impacted by the steady reduction of import tariffs. At the same time, the country continued to suffer during these early postapartheid years from limited local investment and extremely evasive foreign direct investment opportunities. With a relatively small and largely impoverished domestic market and a limited regional economy, investment remained tied to government initiatives, whereas an increasingly open market put direct pressure on local producers. In the end, the failure to use more interventionist methods to promote economic reform was blamed on WTO rules. As Alec Erwin, the second Minister of Trade and Industry in the Mandela government, argued in 1999, in reference to the history of state intervention in Asia: "[a] country such as South Africa, which started its economic reform in the 1990s, was prevented from using such interventionist methods by World Trade Organization rules" (Erwin 1999), affecting the use of industrial policy and thus the boundary of the state and the market.

3. HEALTH LAW AND POLICY: APARTHEID'S LEGACY, SOCIAL SERVICES, AND PUBLIC HEALTH

Unlike trade and industry in a free market economy, in which public policy forms a framework within which a myriad of private parties pursue their own goals, health care usually involves a significant amount of direct state delivery of public services. Although the extent and quality of state provision varies greatly even in systems classified as free-market medicine, such as the United States and South Africa (van Rensburg 2004: 14), there is a significant amount of state provision of health services (such as the Veterans Administration and county hospitals in the United States or the provincial hospitals in South Africa), which predominantly serve the poorer sections of the community. In addition to health services, the state continues to have ultimate responsibility for public health in the same way it has overall political responsibility for economic development. Not unlike economic conditions, the state response to public health is often more reactive than proactive; it responds to one health crisis after another rather than planning and executing strategies to address health care needs or to improve the existing health care system. The legal framework that provides for the health care system, which is dominated by science and medical professionals, is even less central to policy than in the economic realm, where at least it is understood that the legal framework often determines the structure of opportunities and constraints. Nevertheless, the legal regulation of health care has a long history in South Africa.

While the first legal regulation of health care began in the Cape colony in 1807 after the second British occupation, it was only in response to the 1883 smallpox epidemic that the colonial legislature passed a public health act creating "both the Colonial Public Health department and the post of a medical officer of health for the colony" (van Rensburg 2004: 57). It was yet another health crisis, the "disastrous influenza epidemic of 1918" (van Rensburg 2004: 72), that was the impetus for the adoption of the first national public health legislation in the Union of South Africa that was formed by the unification of four British-controlled colonies in 1910. The Public Health Act of 1919 created a three-tier system of health care management – national, provincial, and local – that has continued to frame authority over health care ever since, including postapartheid health care, despite the goal of creating a unified system of health care. Whereas the racial segregation of health care under apartheid merely formalized what had been practiced from the earliest of colonial times, the carving out of ten "black" homelands and the further division of the health care system into separate systems for colored, Indian, and white South Africans meant that the first democratic government inherited a completely fragmented health system. As Cedric de Beer concluded in his study of health care under apartheid, the rejection of earlier reform proposals in the 1950s "heralded a period when little thinking or action was taken to improve the health services available to the majority of the population" (De Beer 1984: 29). After forty years of fragmentation, the effort to rebuild South Africa's health care system would take place in the shadow of the country's worst ever health crisis, an exploding HIV/AIDS pandemic.

One of Nelson Mandela's first actions after coming to power in 1994 was to declare that free health services must be provided to all children under the age of six and to pregnant women. These administrative decisions were based on the ANC's National Health Plan for South Africa that viewed health from a developmental perspective and as an "integral part of the socio-economic development plan for South Africa" (ANC 1994b). With the adoption of the 1996 Constitution, these commitments to guarantee rights to basic nutrition, health, and social services, while limited by the state's ability to supply the necessary services, were constitutionally guaranteed. They were also embodied in the government's adoption of a health policy designed to provide free universal access to primary health care as well as to "ensure the universal availability of high quality, low cost essential drugs" (Department of Health 1997: 1.1.2

(c) iv). At the same time, the new government began the extremely difficult process of restructuring the health services. The process was made even more difficult by the fears and suspicions of different health workers and administrators who, after being kept in separate, highly unequal services, were now required to come together in a unified health system.

The restructuring of the health service provides a good example of the difficulty of state reconstruction that faced the postapartheid state. First, the administrative boundaries within the country were redrawn so that, instead of four provinces and ten "homelands," the country now has nine provinces. Second, within each province the apartheid health services that served different groups – whites, coloreds, and Indians – as well as the different layers of health services for the African majority, whether under the control of the national government or various "homeland" administrations, all had to be consolidated into a single system under a single management. Finally, the new system had to be structured to incorporate the new relationships between the national government and the provinces created in the 1996 Constitution, in which there was both concurrent legislative authority over health as well as a degree of exclusive authority over specific services. At the same time, health facilities across the country began to bear the strain of serving more and more patients because of both the opening of access to the formerly racially exclusive hospitals by the historically excluded majority as well as the consequence of the increasing burdens of the growing pandemic.

While the policy outlines of a future "single, unified health system" were laid out in the government's 1997 White Paper on the Transformation of the Health System in South Africa, the difficulty of reforming the health sector and the escalating health crisis was reflected in the fact that it took until 2003 before the proposed national health legislation became law. The White Paper set out detailed policies and goals and imagined a scheme in which "the three spheres of government, NGOs and the private sector [would] unite in the promotion of common goals" (Hassim, Heywood, & Berger 2007: 98). Despite recognizing that the national, provincial, and local levels of government would "play distinct and complementary roles," it also specified that the health system would "focus on districts as the major locus of implementation" and that an "integrated package of essential PHC [primary health care] services will be available to the entire population at the first point of contact." The White Paper was supplemented by a number of other policy documents and the 1999 Patients' Rights Charter, but it was only with the passage of the National Health Act 61 of 2003 that these policies became law. By this time, South Africa's standing in the global public health community had been severely damaged by the government's post-1999 "debate" over HIV/AIDS and its questioning of both the efficacy of the antiretroviral drug regimes that came on the market in 1996 as well as President Thabo Mbeki's debating the nature and provenance of the virus. Global incredulity reached its peak at the International AIDS Conference in Montreal, where the South African delegation presented garlic, beetroot, and other nutritional supplements as central ingredients in the fight against HIV/AIDS, but failed to include antiretroviral drugs in its display describing its public health response to the pandemic.

Not only has it taken years to achieve formal legal change, but debates over health reform and policy are often well ahead of the more painstaking process of institutional reform and implementation (Harrison 2009). In the late 1980s and the early 1990s, policy debates focused on the need for a single health system to facilitate cross-subsidization between the highly unequal branches of the existing system, but moves to implement a system of national health insurance were relegated to the back burner of the legislative and policy agenda with the adoption of the Growth Employment and Redistribution (GEAR) policy. Although the ANC's National Health Plan adopted in 1994 had promised that a Commission of Inquiry would be established to look into the health crisis and alternatives, such as National Health Insurance (ANC 1994b: section 5), it was not until the revolt against Thabo Mbeki at Polokwane in 2007 that the ANC formally placed the establishment of a National Health Insurance (NHI) system back on the political agenda (McLeod 2009). This most recent round of policy formulation eschewed the earlier proposals that would have established a system of social health insurance, thus maintaining a dual system of public and private medicine. The Polokwane decision instead "has created the space for a somewhat different vision of change in the South African health system – one that focuses from the outset on achieving universal coverage by promoting income and risk cross-subsidies in the overall health system" (Mooney & McIntyre 2008: 639). While promising to establish a system of health financing that facilitates the integration of health services into a single system, the implementation of this proposal remains contested. Despite a 2009 report by the ANC National Executive Committee's subcommittee on the implementation of a National Health Insurance Policy (ANC 2009) and the promotion of the policy at the ANC National General Council meeting in 2010 (ANC 2010: section 1), the debate over required legal changes continues.

4. COMPETITION LAW AND POLICY: ENFORCING COMPETITION AND TRANSFORMING THE ECONOMY

The RDP, the ANC's election manifesto in the first democratic election, identified the "excessive concentration of economic power in the hands of a tiny minority of the population" and the domination of production, distribution, and the financial sector by a "small number of very large conglomerates" as defining characteristics of the South African economy (ANC 1994a: para. 4.1.5). In response, the RDP suggested that the new government would "introduce strict anti-trust legislation to create a more competitive and dynamic business environment" (ANC 1994a: para. 4.4.6.2). The RDP also argued that "domination of business activities by white business and the exclusion of black people and women from the mainstream of economic activity" were major causes of concern. One of the central objectives of the RDP would be "to deracialise business ownership and control completely, through focused policies of black economic empowerment" (ANC 1994a: para. 4.4.6.3). This strong antitrust approach, however, was deemphasized within two years as the government shifted its macroeconomic policy to the GEAR. Although the GEAR did not explicitly address the problem of economic concentration, its emphasis on deregulation, privatization, and fiscal responsibility, as well as the government's concern to make the South African economy more competitive internationally and to attract greater amounts of foreign direct investment, all militated against policies of strong government intervention that were implied by the need to tackle the concentration of economic power identified as a central problem in the RDP.

Significantly, however, the very same neoliberal or pro–free-market ideology that critics of the GEAR bemoaned provided a policy space in which those concerned with economic concentration and monopoly power could raise questions of market failure and the need to create a more competitive environment. The dual role of competition law, providing opportunities to facilitate investment as well as discipline anticompetitive features of the economy and economic behavior, was emphasized in the debate over reforming the existing law when a member of Parliament pointed out that "one of the main perceived impediments to investing in South Africa was the view," held by potential US investors, "that the economy of this country was characterized by excessive concentration" (Hansard 1998: 22.9; Legh 2002: 87). Competition law in South Africa was based on judicial doctrine that evolved from conflicting principles of Roman-Dutch law, on the one hand, which held that contracts shall be honored even in the face of restraints of trade, and, on the other hand, the English common law notion that restraints on trade are prima facie unenforceable. The result was a judicially constructed compromise that restraints on trade were not per se illegal, but could be invalid as against public policy. The adoption of first the Regulation of Monopolistic Conditions Act in 1955 – which only regulated restrictive practices that were inimical to the public interest – and later the Maintenance and Promotion of Competition Act of 1979 – which followed the UK statute and extended the reach of the law to acquisitions and mergers – saw the emergence of a statute-based competition law. Under the 1979 statute, all conduct was lawful until declared unlawful by the Minister. In an attempt to quiet business uncertainty, the state issued a government notice in 1986 (GN 801 of 2 May, 1986) that pronounced a range of generically framed practices to be unlawful. These unlawful practices, however, were subject to criminal sanction, making the implementation of competition law reliant on the criminal justice system. There were no reported cases of successful prosecutions under the 1979 Act.

The weakness of the law in this period may be accounted for in part by the fact that the administering agency, the Board of Trade and Industry, had no enforcement powers of its own but could only advise the relevant Minister, subjecting the implementation of the law to political control. The result was that the law was used primarily against the restrictive practices of importers and had minimal impact on monopoly conditions in the domestic economy. The new 1998 statute addressed that issue by introducing the concept of "abuse of dominance" into the law and creating new institutions in the form of an independent agency and specialized courts – the Competition Commission, the Competition Tribunal, and the Competition Appeal Court – that would have a degree of independence in implementing the law. The new competition law not only addresses issues of economic concentration and abusive practices, such as collusion and price setting, but also seeks to provide greater access to the economy for those historically excluded. Introducing the second reading of the Bill in Parliament on September 22, 1998, the Minister of Trade and Industry identified "exceptionally high levels of concentration and monopolization, low levels of consumer choice and highly priced basic commodities, a poorly developed small-medium enterprise sector, ownership structures that benefit a handful at the expense of the majority, and finally, low levels of productivity that result from excessive rent-taking in the economic process" as targets of the new law. He went on to argue that "[t]he Bill seeks to encourage competition, not because we wish to adhere to some textbook ideal," but rather because in addition to addressing "important economic and social objectives . . . [w]e need to ensure efficiency and adaptability if we are to survive in the global economy" (Hansard 1998: 22.9.1998, 19:6830).

In the years since its establishment, the Competition Commission has publically tackled illegal anticompetitive practices in many of South Africa's major industries, including the automotive and pharmaceutical industries. Most recently, it has strengthened its reputation by "targeting crucial industries such as construction, food and healthcare, and mobilizing public support by targeting emotive markets such as basic foodstuffs, which heavily affect the poorest South Africans" (Mail & Guardian 2008). The Commission and the Tribunal – which hears cases involving illegal practice under the Act as well as appeals from the Commission – have also been highly creative in their strategies to make the law effective. For example, the Tribunal has exercised its power under the law to impose contractual terms as remedies for breaches of the law (*Association of Pharmaceutical Wholesalers & Others v Glaxo Wellcome [Pty] Ltd & Others* 2000) and approved a merger on the condition that the parties out-license specific products so as to maintain a competitive market (*Glaxo Wellcome plc v Smithkline Beecham plc* 2000). In its struggle over access to medical treatment in the context of South Africa's HIV/AIDS pandemic, the TAC, a nongovernment organization, brought a complaint against the pharmaceutical industry to the Commission. The Competition Commission reviewed the pricing of certain medicines and found evidence to support the complaint that, even when taking into account the costs of production, research, development, and an appropriate rate of profit, the prices charged could not be justified. When the case was referred to the Tribunal on three grounds, including excessive pricing, the pharmaceutical industry sought a settlement with the complainants. That led to an agreement requiring the companies to voluntary license certain of their antiretroviral patents to generic competitors (*Hazel Tau v GlaxoSmithKline & Boehringer* 2002).

Competition law in postapartheid South Africa has become a means to pursue many goals that were thought by some to have been precluded by the embrace of more liberal market-orientated policies after 1996. The new competition law is serving as a substitute for the more direct interventionist policies that the ANC government had imagined would be at its disposal before it took power in 1994. While the turn to the market and competition law as a means to regulate the market seems to support the claim that South Africa has embraced the imperatives of a globally dominant neoliberal economic agenda, it is also clear that the implementation of competition law in South Africa might serve a number of social and economic goals that are not necessarily part of the transnational neoliberal "consensus." The South African government clearly sees the "new legislation as an important instrument in industrial and social policy. It is not only intended to deal with pure competition issues but was also intended to be a mechanism to restructure industry in South Africa as well as to meet claims of previously disadvantaged communities, small business and Labour" (Legh 2002: 88). At the same time, there is tension within the government between those who argue that the imperatives of competition mean that all industries must be subject to competitive discipline and those who argue that the country's development needs and the struggle to reduce the country's high levels of unemployment require the government to show more flexibility and support for certain industries. While the new competition law in South Africa is in many ways modeled on European Union, United Kingdom, and Canadian statutes, and draws on legal concepts developed in the United States, it also represents a hybridization of transnational legal norms and institutional models designed to both accommodate international restraints and to take advantage of the opportunities these norms and models provide to pursue particularly national goals that are peculiar to the history and social context of South Africa.

5. IMPACT ON ACCESS TO MEDICINES

The year 1996 marks a pivotal moment in which four seemingly unrelated developments created the preconditions for confrontation over access to essential medicines in South Africa. First, it was in 1996 that the promise of antiretroviral treatment made it clear that HIV/AIDS could, in most cases, be treated as a chronic condition rather than as a terminal illness. Second, it was in that year that the Constitutional Assembly in South Africa enacted the "final" Constitution that includes a right to health care among the new constitutionally guaranteed socioeconomic rights. Third, in an attempt to take advantage of the global economic expansion, the South African government adopted GEAR, an economic program designed to attract foreign investment by implementing strict fiscal discipline and putting in place an export-led development strategy. Finally, after a long internal policy process, the government adopted a National Drug Policy aimed to guarantee access to essential medicines by regulating the pharmaceutical market to assure the supply of affordable drugs in both the public and private sectors. Despite all these developments and an exploding HIV/AIDS rate of infection, there was little public or policy discussion at this time of how these different developments and policy choices would either impact one another or even the ability of each to achieve the goals they represented.

A. *The Health System and Access to Essential Medicines*

The South African health care system reflected the legacy of apartheid. Although nearly 80 percent of the population did not have access to private health care, the private sector consumed 48.5 percent of total health care expenditure in 1992/3 (Department of Health 1996: 3). Similarly, the structure of South Africa's pharmaceutical industry, as well as the pharmaceutical supply system, reflected these patterns. While the industry was dominated by subsidiaries of the multinational pharmaceutical corporations, the market the industry was geared to serve reflected the apartheid divide. The private sector was responsible for 80 percent of the country's total expenditure on drugs in 1990, although 60–70 percent of the total volume of pharmaceuticals was consumed in the public sector. Although the highest value for the industry lay in supplying the small, predominately white middle class served by the private health system, the vast bulk of drugs produced and sold in South Africa were and still are distributed through the public health system. This latter segment, however, represents only a fraction of the industry's sales by value, because the government purchases in bulk and obtains substantial discounts from the manufacturers. Although pharmaceutical firms made only a small profit on the supply of drugs to the public system, they were thus able to sustain their profits by charging relatively high prices to private consumers.

Although the high cost of drugs in the private market could have been addressed by the introduction of generic medicines, the very structure of the South African market initially discouraged generic drug manufacturers from entering the market. Generic manufacturers were discouraged from entering the market because the brand manufacturers already provided, either directly to the private market or by providing the public sector at a discount close to generic prices, the bulk of the drugs consumed in the country. Although the bifurcated structure of the pharmaceutical market reflected the old apartheid system, in which those served by the public sector had little or no political power, the new government's goal of broadening access to health care by integrating the public and private health care systems changed this equation (Heywood 2005; Sanders & Chopra 2006).[4] Such is particularly the case

[4] After the 1994 elections and over the following eighteen months, there was a heated debate and legislative initiatives addressing the reform of the health system in South Africa. These initiatives then faltered.

in relation to the supply of medicines. The goal of improving standards through the creation of a greater public-private partnership tied to ideas of equalization and cross-subsidization through a Social Health Insurance program based on the goal of sharing costs – possibly including a more extensive system of co-payments – made the cost of medicines in the marketplace a central concern of the new government (McIntyre & Van Den Heever 2007; Government Notice 903, 11.11.2009, Government Gazette No. 32564).[5]

In response to this condition, the new government published a National Drug Policy in January 1996. As a way of attacking the comparatively high cost of drugs in the South African market, the new policy promoted the use of generic drugs and suggested several ways to reduce unacceptably high retail prices, including allowing the state to facilitate the availability of affordable drugs in the private sector. It was that policy imperative that led to the passage of the Medicines and Related Substances Control Amendment Act in December 1997 (Act 90 of 1997) with the aim of bringing down the cost of medicines. Although the new medicines law was designed to fundamentally change the distribution practices of the pharmaceutical manufacturers – prohibiting, for example, industry employees from serving on the Medicines Control Council and blocking manufacturers and wholesalers from providing bonuses, rebates, or other incentives to doctors – the key feature of the Amendment was the "measures to ensure supply of more affordable medicines." These measures included empowering the Minister of Health "to prescribe conditions for the supply of more affordable medicines . . . so as to protect the health of the public . . . notwithstanding anything to the contrary in the Patents Act"; and to "prescribe the conditions on which any medicine which is identical in composition, meets the same quality standard and is intended to have the same propriety name as that of another medicine already registered in the Republic." The effect of these provisions would have been to allow the parallel importation of medicines, generic substitution without the consent of the prescriber, and even compulsory licensing.

The pharmaceutical market in South Africa was valued at over US$2 billion in 2008, but is expected to grow to more than US$3 billion by 2012 (Business Insights 2010). Growth is premised on both a continuing health crises as well as government policy changes, including the decision to raise the CD4 count criteria, which determines when HIV-positive patients are treated with ARVs, from less than 200 to less than 350 cells per cubic millimeter, which will extend the provision of ARVs to nearly 80 percent of HIV-positive individuals; the establishment of a national health insurance scheme that will provide greater access to medicines; and regulatory developments that are predicted to speed up product approvals, bringing

[5] Although these promises of legal change in the broader health system are yet to come to fruition, indications are that the debate remains alive and that the government is now moving toward the creation of a national health insurance scheme. The government has since established a National Health Insurance Advisory Committee to the Minister of Health in terms of Government Notice 903, Government Gazette No. 32564, September 11, 2009.

more medicines into the market. Today the public sector accounts for approximately 21 percent of consumption by value, more than 80 percent of which is comprised of generic medicines, whereas the private sector consumes about 79 percent by value of which 70 percent is prescription medicines, representing approximately 55 percent of the value of the market (Maloney & Segal 2007: 28–9). Of these private prescriptions, only 22 percent, or 12 percent by value, are generic medicines (Maloney & Segal 2007: 29–30). The private over-the-counter market represents a further 24 percent of the market by value (Maloney & Myburgh 2007: 30). Of even greater significance is that "around 75 percent of this demand is met by imports" (Kgara & Barsel 2010: 50). The overall picture thus remains the same as before: The country remains dependent on imports (particularly for active ingredients), the bulk of medicines are consumed in the public sector, yet demand in the private sector determines the real value of the market.

Over a decade since the adoption of a new drug policy, the structure of supply and demand in the medicines market (in which roughly 70 percent of demand by volume comes from the public sector, whereas 70 percent of value derives from the sale of pharmaceutical products in the private sector) thus remains largely unchanged. The structure of the market is no longer defined by the formal racial divisions of apartheid, but the division between public and private markets in health care and pharmaceutical sales reflects a class divide that continues to have significant racial dimensions (Mooney & McIntyre 2008). Important also is the impact of government policy on reducing the price of medicines in both the public and private sectors; there has been growth in the production of generic medicines but not growth in the value of the market, contributing to decisions by the multinational corporations to close factories and to reduce their productive capacity in the country. While these decisions were driven as much by global developments in the pharmaceutical industry as by opportunities in the local market, ANC resolutions and some policymakers demand that government tenders be linked to the development of a local pharmaceutical industry, including even the possibility of creating a state-owned pharmaceutical company that links questions of market structure and productive capacity. At the same time, the very nature of pharmaceutical production – requiring skilled personnel, the refinement of fine chemicals, and massive economies of scale to drive down costs – places constraints on the scope of interventions available to the South African government even if it were to embrace the notion of a developmental state.

B. *Local Law and Global Reaction*

Simultaneous developments in the mid 1990s, including changes in economic policy and law as well as the exploding HIV/AIDS epidemic, set the stage for a protracted confrontation about access to medicines in South Africa, with ramifications in both the domestic and international arenas. The amendments to the Medicines Act were initially viewed as a simple adoption of the WHO-recommended measures to improve access to essential medicines, but the changing health conditions as well as the growing international conflict over the implementation of TRIPS and the expanded protection of patent rights suddenly placed these reforms under the spotlight of international concern. At the same time, the new government's economic policies, changing from a domestic focus on reconstruction to a focus on global reengagement, including a full embrace of the WTO and TRIPS, heightened the sensitivity of the government to external pressure. This was particularly so when these pressures seemed to threaten directly the policy of attracting multinational capital and increasing industrial capacity domestically as a means of supplying the regional or even continental market.

South Africa's attempt to improve access to essential medicines by creating a more competitive market through considering parallel importation and even compulsory licensing soon attracted the attention of the international pharmaceutical industry and the US government in particular. In fact, the US government was active in the debate very early on. The United States Trade Representative (USTR) wrote a letter to South Africa's United Nations representative in April 1997 querying South Africa's implementation of TRIPS and raising questions about compulsory licensing. By the time the Amendment Bill was before Parliament, US opposition was already evident. The US Embassy in Pretoria presented the US government's views at a parliamentary hearing on the proposed amendments, and the US ambassador to South Africa made frequent public and private statements against the legalization of parallel imports. Within two months of the Amendment's adoption, the Pharmaceutical Research and Manufacturers of America (PhRMA) requested the USTR to designate South Africa a priority country under section 301 of US trade law because "South Africa has become a 'test case' for those who oppose the US government's long-standing commitment to improve the terms of protection for all forms of American intellectual property, including pharmaceutical patents" (Consumer Project on Technology 1999).

Bristol-Myers Squibb specifically complained about South Africa's decision to permit registration of a generic form of the cancer drug paclitaxel (BMS brand name Taxol), an issue that the USTR took up directly during a WTO Trade Policy review a year later in Geneva. One month later, on May 1, 1998, the USTR put South Africa on the Special 301 Watch list. In June 1998, the White House announced that four items for which South Africa had requested preferential tariff treatment under the Generalized System of Preferences program would be put on hold until adequate progress was achieved in the protection of intellectual property rights in South Africa. At the end of October, Congress passed an omnibus appropriations bill containing provisions cutting off US aid to the South African government pending a Department of State report outlining its efforts to "negotiate the repeal, suspension, or termination of section 15(c) of South Africa's Medicines and Related Substances Control Amendment Act No. 90 of 1997."

The local response to the Medicines Act was led by the Pharmaceutical Manufacturers' Association of South Africa, which, on behalf of forty-two parties, including local companies, subsidiaries of transnational corporations, and the multinational corporations themselves, filed suit challenging the constitutionality of the 1997 amendment to the Medicines Act. They made a number of constitutional claims but argued most specifically that the Act's provisions that empower the government to determine the extent to which rights granted under a patent in South Africa shall apply and which allow the government to prescribe conditions for the supply of more affordable generic medicines together deprive owners of intellectual property in the affected pharmaceutical products and thus of their constitutionally protected property rights. Significantly, the domestic litigation initiated in this case, facilitated by the financial resources of the multinational corporations, took on a form unique in the South African context. The plaintiffs engaged a major private law firm, and state attorneys soon found themselves completely snowed under with the volume of filings and alternative lines of attack (interview, 1999).[2] Not only did the plaintiffs initiate the litigation with a request for an interim interdict preventing the law from being implemented, they soon followed with a series of claims in alternative forums – to the public protector and the Competition Board, respectively. The claims challenged government statements about the cost of drugs and called for an inquiry into an alleged anticompetitive attempt by pharmaceutical distributors to create a joint company to engage in the parallel importation allowed under the Act.

In a notice of motion filed in the High Court of South Africa (Transvaal Provincial Division) in Pretoria on February 18, 1998, the plaintiffs articulated an extraordinary array of claims against the Act's validity. In addition to asserting that the Act violated their patent rights as well as South Africa's legally incorporated international obligations under TRIPS, the plaintiffs claimed that the powers granted the Minister of Health amounted to an unconstitutional delegation of legislative authority to the executive because it failed to set out policy considerations or guidelines that would limit the Minister's power, but instead merely empowered the Minister to discriminate unconstitutionally against local manufacturers in favor of imported medicines. Plaintiffs also charged that various sections of the Amendment were unconstitutional because they violated the basic values and principles governing public administration included in s195 of the Constitution. As if this was not enough, the claimants then argued in the alternative that the Act conflicted with the legislature's constitutional obligations to take into consideration the recommendations made to the Portfolio Committee on Health and the Select Committee on Social Services in the National Council of Provinces – South Africa's second chamber. The claimants requested that the legislature transmit to the Constitutional Court a transcript of all the proceedings on the Bill that preceded the passage of the Act. In her founding affidavit, M. T. Deeb, Chief Executive Officer of the Pharmaceutical Manufacturers Association, argued that s15C is in conflict with the TRIPS Agreement; Deeb went so far as to claim that "Parliament ought not to have made a law which is in conflict with South Africa's international obligations" (Deeb 1998a: para. 10.2.5). Linking of the domestic constitutional claim with international trade issues continued when, in a supplementary affidavit to the plaintiff's amended particulars of claim filed on July 23, 1998, Deeb argued that the USTR's placing of South Africa on the 301 Watch list "demonstrates that the provisions in the Amended Act which affect intellectual property are seen to be at least potentially in conflict with South Africa's international obligations and hence I submit that it cannot be regarded as being in the public interest as it may lead to the imposition of sanctions against this country and will before that in fact may already have led to an undermining of investor confidence in South Africa" (Deeb 1998b: para. 20.6).

This threat of wider economic repercussions highlights the conflict between the domestic initiative to reduce drug prices and the global environment in which the policy was developed. It is also important to recognize that, even at the international level, there are often tensions between the approaches taken by different government departments in their pursuit of different policies. While the 1997 amendment put South Africa into a direct bilateral trade conflict with the United States, these tensions were not confined to the trade arena, but also surfaced at the World Health Assembly (WHA), the governing body of the WHO, where South Africa was active in trying to reshape the debate over patent protection for pharmaceuticals. At the same time, South Africa's leadership in the World Health Assembly was in stark contrast to the government's unilateral decision not to implement the law – pending further legal proceedings – and the growing policy conflict over the government's response to HIV/AIDS, which included questioning the very biomedical basis of the epidemic. Here the law may be seen to be simultaneously facilitating, delaying, and providing a space for different players to achieve a variety of goals in their struggles to gain access to affordable medicines, to further particular economic policies, or to protect their property interests.

At the end of April 1999, the USTR scheduled an "out-of-cycle" review for South Africa under Special 301. It argued that South Africa's barriers to trade included parallel imports, compulsory licensing, registration of generic forms of Taxol, and taking a leading role at the WHA. According to the USTR, "During the past year, South African representatives have led a faction of nations in the World Health Organization (WHO) in calling for a reduction in the level of protection provided for pharmaceuticals in TRIPS" (Consumer Project on Technology 1999). Thus, from the perspective of the USTR, the problem was not only the protection of patent rights in South Africa but also the position South Africa was taking in the international debate over TRIPS. Although it is broadly understood that the TRIPS agreement introduced a new set of minimum standards for the protection of intellectual property rights, there remained wide disagreement as to the meaning of the embedded exceptions to those rights, raising questions regarding the clarity of

TRIPS rules. More significantly, the broad language of the exceptions contained in TRIPS meant that the degree of legal uncertainty remained broad, allowing member states to assert very different interpretations.

In this context, the WHO began questioning the relationship between the new international trade regime and its own mandate to promote world health. In January 1998, just over a month after the adoption of the new South African law allowing parallel importation, the Executive Board of the WHA recommended the adoption of the "Revised Drug Strategy" (World Health Organization 1999). It called on member states to "ensure that public health interests are paramount in pharmaceutical and health policies" and "to explore and review their options under relevant international trade agreements, to safeguard access to essential drugs" (WHO 1999). In May 1998, when the WHA began discussing the recommendation at its meeting in Geneva, the proposal came under heated attack from the developed countries, including the United States, the European Union, and Japan. Supporting the proposals and leading the negotiations for the African countries was Dr. Olive Shisana, from the South African Ministry of Health. The WHA's actions called into question the legitimacy and coherence of the developed countries' interpretations of the TRIPS agreement. The WHA's support facilitated the push by South Africa and other developing countries, assisted by a network of transnational NGOs, for the WTO Doha Declaration on the TRIPS Agreement and Public Health of 2001, which recognized TRIPS "flexibilities."

C. *Domestic Resistance and Legal Change*

The domestic struggle over access to affordable medicines in South Africa did not end there. The South African government's victory in the case brought by the Pharmaceutical Manufacturers' Association, which withdrew its claims in 2001, together with the 2001 Doha Declaration, helped to counter transnational political and legal pressure on the government to prioritize intellectual property protection over public health concerns. The next phase of legal activity was initiated by the TAC and given its impetus by the consolidation of a new broad-based social movement including TAC branches and the People Living with AIDS organization, with support from the Trade Union movement and the Communist Party. It included two legal challenges that would further a right to health care. The first challenged the government to provide mothers and their newborn babies access to nevirapine, an antiretroviral that, when administered to both mother and child during birth and shortly thereafter, more than halved the rate of mother-to-child transmission of HIV. Second, the TAC brought a complaint before the Competition Commission alleging that a number of the major pharmaceutical corporations had colluded in maintaining the high price of particular medicines. The impact of these two initiatives was to alter dramatically the debate over access to antiretroviral treatment and to set the stage for a major reduction in the price of medicines. In other words, in these cases, South African courts were used both to force executive action and to reshape debates within the executive branch.

In the Mother-to-Child-Transmission (MTCT) case, the Constitutional Court essentially upheld a high court decision requiring the government to provide mothers and newborns access to nevirapine in public health facilities. Relying on the constitutional guarantee of a right to the progressive realization of access to health care services, the Constitutional Court argued that under the circumstances in which the cost of the drug and the provision of appropriate testing and counseling to mothers was less burdensome than the failure to provide nevirapine, the government had a constitutional duty to expand its program beyond the eighteen test sites the health authorities had already planned. In the second case, the TAC, pursuing its aim to lower drug prices and thus expand access to ARV treatment, launched a complaint with the newly constituted Competition Commission against two of the major pharmaceutical corporations active in South Africa – GlaxoSmithKline (GSK) and Boehringer Ingelheim. It accused them of engaging in excessive pricing of medicines. After the Commission found that the companies had colluded to fix prices, the companies reached an out-of-court settlement with the government. The settlement granted at least three generic pharmaceutical companies voluntary licenses of three major retrovirals, thus allowing more competition into the market and lowering the price of the drugs in the South African market (AIDS Law Project 2003). Despite these dramatic interventions and legal victories, the problem of access remains unsolved. For the majority of HIV-infected South Africans, even the reduced price of the drugs on the private market is unaffordable. Until the government manages to roll out the public sector program, most people in need of treatment will continue to be denied access.

The Doha Declaration, with its broad interpretation of the TRIPS agreement and its future implementation, amounted to a major shift in the rhetoric about the protection of intellectual property rights. Given the realities of pharmaceutical production and distribution, however, it did not go very far toward ensuring access to urgently needed HIV/AIDS-related medications. Despite acknowledging that many countries have "insufficient or no manufacturing capacities in the pharmaceutical sector" and thus cannot make effective use of compulsory licensing, the Declaration failed to accept the developing countries' interpretation that, in order to gain access to medicines, they have the right to grant a compulsory license to a producer in another country having manufacturing capacity. Instead, the Declaration instructed the TRIPS Council to find a solution to this issue and to report to the WTO General Council by the end of 2002. Without the capacity to produce under compulsory license or import generic equivalents of the necessary medications, the problem of access for the millions infected or suffering from life-threatening diseases in developing countries remains unresolved. It took the TRIPS Council a further twenty-one months, to late August 2003, to reach agreement on the problem of access to medicines for countries that do not have manufacturing capacity.

Heralded at first as the solution to the problem of lack of capacity, the pre-Cancun agreement has since been criticized for placing so many prerequisites on its implementation. It requires proof by a country that it does not have production capacity or access to affordable medicines and has an existing health emergency that will be unworkable. Already, while the Canadian government has changed Canadian law to make the export of medicines made under compulsory license possible, the international brand-name pharmaceutical industry has begun to raise questions about whether Canada is not precluded from supplying these medicines under the North American Free Trade Agreement (NAFTA). Even the Canadian government seems to be limiting its proposals to drugs designed to address only HIV/AIDS, malaria, and tuberculosis (TB), a restriction rejected by the developing countries and the pre-Cancun agreement.

Although it is clearly true that drug prices are not the only issue limiting access to essential medicines in developing countries, the cost of medicines remains a central concern. Unlike the broader structural problems of upgrading the health care system or monitoring patients, there just are no substitutes or alternatives to the provision of these particular drugs. To this extent, the cost of the medicines is in fact the "inelastic" part of the essential medicines equation. Yet even as innovative programs have been designed to facilitate access to health care (WHO 2003), the debate over drug costs has focused on collective purchasing strategies, philanthropic initiatives, and international assistance or aid rather than on the creation of a competitive market that would be the most effective way to reduce prices and increase supply. Nevertheless, drug prices have fallen dramatically from around $10,000 per patient per year in the late 1990s to around $99 today in some cases (Médecins Sans Frontieres [MSF] 2007). The actual cost of providing "free" drugs, even through many of the philanthropic schemes, remains slightly above the actual cost of large-scale generic production and distribution. The developed country governments insist that these medicines be purchased either from the brand-name firms or their licensed producers, in the case of the US President's Emergency Plan for Aids Relief (PEPFAR), or specifically marked and packaged to avoid their illegal reimportation and distribution in developed country markets. Even as prices have dropped and aid increased, the question has arisen to whether these developments will be able to assure a stable supply of these medicines. Given that no known cure exists, the stable and affordable supply of these medications is essential to the productive lives of millions of HIV-positive individuals around the world, particularly in developing countries.

To evaluate the stability of any policy or program to provide access to affordable essential medicines, it is important to briefly review the political pressures and sources of supply that have brought down the cost of these medicines over the past few years. First, it was the offer by Indian drug producer Cipla in March 2001 to provide the first-generation ARV drugs for $350 per patient per year to developing countries, a fraction of the going price in the developed country markets, which brought about the initial fall in prices. Brazil had already managed to reduce the price from $10,000 per patient to around $2,800 per patient within its own public health system, but this was based on the government-controlled industry's capacity to reverse engineer and manufacture the relevant drugs. Second, it was the response of the multinational drug companies to the accusations of activists and the bad publicity they received after they sued the South African government and named President Nelson Mandela as the first defendant, that led to offers by these companies to supply drugs to some developing countries at vastly reduced costs and, in some cases, at no cost for certain periods of time and for specified classes of poor patients. Third, the establishment of the Global Fund and later President George W. Bush's PEPFAR initiative provided a source of funding for anti-AIDS programs, including the provision of essential medicines in the public sector. Fourth, the entry of the Gates and Clinton Foundations as both funders and as a source of political coordination of efforts aimed at the procurement of cheaper drugs bolstered the long-standing efforts of NGOs, such as Doctors Without Borders, James Love's Consumer Project on Technology, the Canadian HIV/AIDS Legal Network, and the AIDS Law Project in South Africa as well as various AIDS-specific activist organizations such as ACT-UP in the United States and the South African-based TAC. Finally, the establishment in 2006 of UNITAID, initiated by the governments of Brazil, France, and Norway, promised a long-term source of funding through a type of Tobin tax on international airline ticket sales and an international organization committed to pooling demand and using the resulting bargaining power to obtain medicines at reduced cost in the international market.

D. *Legal Constraints and the Future of Affordable Medicine Supplies*

Although these different initiatives and strategies have very different protagonists and modes of operation, the underlying premise of all of them is the continued existence of an adequate supply of the required medicines at affordable prices. Already there have been a number of incidents in which the supply of ARVs has been interrupted, with obvious consequences for individual patients and possible drug resistance if patients are unable to maintain their treatment programs. In the case of the ARV ritonavir, for example, there were five occasions in 2004 when drug companies in South Africa were unable to supply the drug (Berger 2005) in either pediatric dozes or adult capsules, forcing patients to switch their medications and forcing the South African government to briefly halt the rollout of its public sector program for children. These incidents and concern over the cost of second-line drugs, as well as the WHO's new treatment guidelines that suggest the use of more expensive drugs (MSF 2007), all raise questions about the stability and sustainability of the supply chain of affordable drugs. To understand the magnitude of this problem, it is important to note two facts: first, under normal conditions, the cost of a patented drug drops by only 20 percent when the first generic enters the market at the end of the patent term; and second, it is only when there are three or more generic companies competing to supply a particular drug that the cost falls to anywhere between 70 and 90 percent below the original price of the patented drug (Pile 2005: 18).

Until 2005, Indian drug producers were able to produce "generic" versions of these medicines so long as they were able to come up with a process of production that had not been previously patented. As a result, Indian pharmaceutical companies have in recent years been producing approximately "one-fifth of the world's generic drugs" (Stokes 2005: 1146–50). Since January 2005, however, the implementation of the TRIPS agreement in India requiring the reintroduction of product patents into Indian law has created uncertainty about the ability these companies will have to produce "generic" versions of the next generation of ARVs (Kapczynski 2009). The danger is that the only way these companies will be able to enter the market to provide "generic" forms of any new drugs will be as licensed producers, whether under voluntary or compulsory licenses (Shadlen 2007). In South Africa, the brand-name companies have increasingly licensed local manufacturers to produce their products for the local and regional market. Most prominent of these companies is Aspen Pharmacare. Its main aim is to acquire patent-expired medicines from multinational drug firms, and it now controls 35 percent of South Africa's generic drug market (Pile 2005: 18). While the turn to local licensing may have been made in the face of growing international pressure and after settling the case against them before South Africa's Competition Commission, a number of the brand-name companies have now licensed Aspen to manufacture their products locally. Aspen, in turn, has succeeded in having its newly constructed oral solid dosage (OSD) plant in the Eastern Cape region of South Africa approved by both the "local regulator, the Medicines Control Council, [and] . . . the American Food & Drug Administration and the UK's Medical Health & Regulatory Authority" (Pile 2005: 19). The company was placed in a position not only to win the South African State Tender in 2004, producing R3,4bn in ARV drugs over three years, but also potentially to win large international aid contracts from the PEPFAR and the Global Fund (Pile 2005: 20).

In addition to questions of supply, the availability of medicines also depends on the regulatory regime that controls access to the market. All medicines in the South African market must be registered by the Medicines Control Council (MCC), a statutory body made up of up to twenty-four part-time appointees who are experts in pharmacology, pharmaceutical chemistry, pharmaceutics, and the clinical management of disease (both human and animal). The MCC is supported by a full-time secretariat located in the National Department of Health; while its members are not part of the civil service, it is "organized as a 'cluster'" known as the Medicines Regulatory Affairs (MRA) cluster (Hassim, Heywood, & Berger 2007: 420). The chief director of the MRA cluster is also the Registrar of Medicines, who is responsible for keeping a register of all medicines that may be legally sold in the country. The approximately 20,000 medicines registered are classified into nine categories – schedules 0–8 – which determine the extent of regulation to which each medicine is subject, including who may prescribe, who may sell, and who may purchase the particular medicine. Apart from new applications – which may take over two years to process – the MCC is considering making the approximately 18,000 additional complementary medicines, such as indigenous or traditional herbal remedies and modern dietary supplements, available in the market "under effective regulatory control" (Hassim et al. 2007: 424).

The MCC, created after the passage of the 1965 Medicines Act, remained initially unchanged in the new South Africa. However, it came under increasing pressure as both drug policy changed and the question of complementary medicines – from vitamin supplements to traditional herbal medicines – came to the fore. While the institution managed to survive the initial political reconstruction unchanged, the change in drug policy in 1996, as well as a direct confrontation with the Minister of Health over the refusal to allow clinical trials of virodene brought confrontation and the removal of the old leadership in 1998. Although Nathan Geffen holds this old leadership in high esteem and credits it with blocking the irresponsible and unauthorized, if not criminal, virodene clinical trials, his own legitimate focus on the prevention of quackery seems to have blinded him to some of the underlying tensions that might also explain the attempts to transform this institution at this time (Geffen 2010). On the one hand, it is true that the MCC had developed a good international reputation as a regulatory body and that its chairperson from 1981, Dr. Peter Folb, was an internationally recognized expert on drug safety. On the other hand, the registrar of medicines at the time, Johan Schlebusch, was clearly unenthusiastic about the reform agenda of the new government (CCMA 1999). Not only did he imply that the parallel importation of registered drugs would require the medicines to be tested for the same "standards of safety, quality and efficacy" as the registered versions, thus negating the cost savings of parallel importation, but his continued leadership of the MCC seemed to be marked by internal management conflict with various newly hired personnel who would have been historically excluded from holding posts at the MCC based on their race. The MCC also did not seem to grasp the concerns expressed about the problem of conflict of interest that many of the part-time reviewers used by the MCC inherently had, given that these same reviewers often served as consultants for the pharmaceutical industry.

Events came to a head in April 1998, when the top leader of the MCC were relieved of their posts based on the Report of the Medicines Regulatory Task Team, a review body appointed by the Minister of Health and chaired, on the advice of Dr. Folb, by Professor Graham Dukes, an Emeritus Professor of Drug Policy Studies at the University of Groningen in the Netherlands. While Nathan Geffen is convinced that the true cause of the change was the fact that the MCC had stood up to the Mbeki government and refused to sanction clinical trials of virodene, he fails to recognize that the subsequent head of the MCC, Dr. Helen Rees, also defied political pressure on this issue and, together with the newly appointed registrar, Precious Matsoso, refused to sanction clinical trials of virodene, a product that was supposed to be a cure for HIV/AIDS and had the support of President Mbeki's government (Australian Federation of AIDS Organization 2000).[6] Although Johan Schlebusch and Christel Brückner won their cases on the grounds of wrongful termination – since as public servants they were guaranteed their posts under the negotiated settlement – the resulting conflict within the MCC led to the resignation of many of the old guard, severely hampering the institution just as it was being thrust into the center of the conflict over the new medicines law.

At the same time, the MCC attempted to broaden its own jurisdiction by taking up the issue of complementary medicines and, in 2002, published an official Government Notice calling for the registration of these products. Thousands of applications flooded and overwhelmed the review process. At a briefing to the Parliamentary portfolio committee on health in 2008, the newly appointed Registrar for Medicines, Mandisa Hela, revealed that the backlog in the number of applications for registration that had been received but not completed each year had increased from 28 percent in 2003 to a colossal 98 percent in 2007. She explained that the number of evaluators and committee members had not changed since the 1960s and that the MCC continued to rely on part-timers (Thom 2010). Changes to the Medicines Act, including the legal framework for a completely new regulatory body to be named the South African Health Products Regulatory Authority (SAHPRA) and the introduction of regulations to separate the registration of complementary and alternative medicines from scientific medicines, led Stavros Nicolaou, Senior Executive of Aspen Pharmacare, to note that "the Department of Health has commenced a process aimed at clearing the Medicines Control Council backlog and improving approval timelines. Whilst these are early days, initial progress with the process is encouraging and we look forward to completion of the process." This sentiment is shared by Nathan Geffen, who concludes his account of the MCC with a more skeptical view of the process of transformation undergone by the institution. Nevertheless, he feels that, despite concerns he has over the bureaucratization implicit in the proposed new regulatory authority, the appointment of a new technical task team, headed by Precious Motsotso and including Jonathan Berger, Peter Folb, and Andy Gray, will once again bring the "proliferation of untested remedies . . . under control" (Geffen 2010: 187). Even though the proposed new regulatory authority is yet to be launched, the appointment of new members to the MCC, including Jonathan Berger, a lawyer for the Aids Law Project, TAC, and now Section 27, who has long campaigned for access to affordable medicines, gives some credence

[6] Geffen also fails to mention that it was Dr. Rees who, as head of the MCC, approved the importation of "generic" fluconazole by the Treatment Action Campaign and granted a section 21 exemption allowing the drug to be prescribed, despite the generic version not being formally registered. (See the letter of congratulations by the Australian Federation of AIDS Organization to Dr. Helen Rees sent in response to a request by the TAC for letters of thanks to be sent to Dr. Helen Rees as Chairperson of the MCC.)

to Geffen's optimism (Government Notice No. 180, Government Gazette 33006, 12 March 2010, 15).

6. CONCLUSION

While the South African state since 1990 has undergone a dramatic transformation from apartheid authoritarianism to a constitutional democracy, the specific nature of this transformation varies across different policy areas and institutions shaped by the interaction of both domestic political conditions and the wider transnational context that simultaneously constrain local alternatives and provide opportunities for different policy and political initiatives. Both trade and competition policy reform took place under similar global conditions, but the nature of the state transformations manifested by the particular interaction between transnational opportunities and constraints led to different emphases and outcomes. Although the initial pressures to reestablish the country's international trade relations led to an overenthusiastic embrace of the WTO agreements, in which the country failed to take advantage of purely legitimate opportunities, the later adoption and implementation of competition law was broadly shaped by the new emphasis on a market orientation. The specifics, however, reflect a more complex interaction. These interactions have included the traditional concerns of competition law, such as price setting and the improper use of market power, but have also included domestic concerns about addressing such legacies of apartheid as the historical exclusion of the black majority from the market and the racial structure of corporate ownership. Competition law and the institutions created to implement the new law represent a regular market-oriented reform required by the problem of market failure, but are also being used to address specific social and political goals that are designed to achieve a broader transformation of the South African economy and society.

Specific decisions and legal reforms, such as South Africa's adoption of the TRIPS agreement as part of its entry into the WTO, or the passage and implementation of a new competition law and the institutional developments that accompanied it within the context of the International Competition Network, create further constraints and opportunities for and within the state. Although the new government in South Africa saw trade liberalization as a necessary step to reenter the global economy after apartheid, it was soon confronted by the consequences of having agreed to the immediate and full implementation of the related TRIPS agreement. As the government adopted well-accepted global health policies designed to provide increased access to essential medicines, it faced direct opposition from the United States and other governments that felt that these options had now been foreclosed by the TRIPS agreement. At the same time, the growing HIV/AIDS pandemic in South Africa would, after the entry of antiretroviral treatments in 1996, add another dimension to the conflict. Now the ANC government was being pressured by a new local social movement – the TAC – which demanded that the government provide access to treatment for the approximately five million South Africans who were HIV-positive.

After the TAC won its Constitutional Court case requiring the government to begin providing an antiretroviral drug to expectant mothers and newborns to prevent mother-to-child transmission of HIV, it was only a matter of time before the government was pressed into rolling out a national treatment program. At the same time, the TAC was seeking ways to challenge the high costs of medicines and recognized that the newly emergent Competition Commission might provide a venue through which to challenge the drug companies. Although the new competition law and its related institutions were beginning to make significant progress in challenging the cartels that dominated the South African economy, the government's attempt to reduce medicine costs by adopting a new drug policy and making amendments to the Medicines Act faltered in the face of international opposition and the denialism that marked local political failure to address the country's horrendous HIV/AIDS pandemic. Instead, it would be the challenge from civil society – in the form of the TAC – that would be able to renew the debate over medicine costs, mobilizing both political pressure and the new competition law and institutions to challenge the dominance of the multinational drug companies in the South African market. The settlement of these claims, requiring the corporations to provide voluntary licenses to a number of generic drug producers in South Africa, provided the landscape for yet another transformation in the state, leading to shifts in policy and institutional capacities.

Instead of continuing its previous challenge to the effectiveness of these drugs and resisting public pressure to provide them in the public health system, the state now began to seek ways to encourage the emergence of a viable South African-based pharmaceutical industry. The perceived constraints of TRIPS have themselves been transformed into the opportunities of the Doha Declaration and the special provisions of US law that will not challenge the production of essential medicines in South Africa so long as they are to be sold in the domestic and regional market. Depending on how that region is defined, there is a chance that generic producers will be able to establish themselves and help to build, with adequate assistance from the state, a new industry in South Africa that will provide greater and more sustainable access to medicines in the region. At the same time, political pressures to expand access to ARVs within the budgetary constraints faced by the government and the limited number of local "generic" producers brought pressure on the government to seek cheaper drugs on the international market. Continuing pressures to address the national health crisis, as well as shifting political and economic environments, domestically and globally – including the international financial crisis – set the stage for further transformations of the state.

Political rejection of Thabo Mbeki's policies within the ANC, followed by the election of Jacob Zuma as president of South Africa, produced a restructuring of the cabinet and the creation of a planning commission within the presidency that is headed by Trevor Manuel, the former powerful Minister of Finance. An element of economic coordination that has been missing since the fall of apartheid has been created. These changes will once again transform the conditions within which different policies are conceived and implemented, as well as the relative authority and resources that different institutions within the state will be able to exercise. In this context, debates over competition policy, subsidies for the emerging pharmaceutical industry, and the transformation of the health care system will be carried out. The recalibration of existing opportunities and constraints will shape government decisions and lead to further shifts within the various legal regimes and institutions that are the foci of policy formulation and legal development in these various arenas. Understanding the repeated transformations of the state in this context by focusing simultaneously on the constitutive elements of each policy area, as well as the complex environment of "structured agency" within a transnational context that provides the space in which participants are able to achieve institutional and policy innovations, provides the opportunity to understand how the allocation of significant resources may be reconfigured both nationally and globally.

7

The Limits of Transnational Transformations of the State

Comparative Regulatory Regimes in the Delivery of Urban Water Services

Bronwen Morgan

The problem of scarce water resources has emerged as a global policy issue of significant prominence over the past five to ten years. This chapter explores a very specific dimension of the broader question of access to water; namely, the delivery of water services to ordinary citizens in urban contexts for domestic use. Just over one hundred million people worldwide still lack access to minimal amounts of safe drinking water, although the seventh Millennium Development Goal hopes to halve this number by 2015. Of course, the provision of access to domestic drinking water is intimately linked to the quantity and quality of water resources more broadly, which are under pressure – some would say in crisis (Davis 2006) – from (1) rapid urbanization in developing countries, (2) degraded infrastructure in developed countries, and (3) pollution in both settings. But the angle of analysis for present purposes is on the delivery of essential services and not on the larger ecological picture.

This is a different issue from the international law of shared water resources, which is an inherently "transnational" issue. The much narrower question of access to sufficient clean water for domestic human use in urban settings[1] has traditionally been an intensely local issue, embedded in local physical infrastructure, often the responsibility of local governments or, where no networks exist, of ordinary citizens. Yet, as this chapter will show, in recent decades, a significant transnational global water policy field has emerged that has an important bearing on the question of basic access to drinking water. I will argue nonetheless that the case of access to water also demonstrates the *limits* of any actual transformations wrought by the emergence of this field.

On the one hand, important institutional transformations in how the state is organized, and its functions, are undoubtedly shaped by transnational flows of money and ideas. Specifically, institutions that regulate essential services have emerged

[1] Given the focus on urban rather than rural contexts, the analysis largely excludes issues pertaining to water needed for subsistence food provision.

and spread widely since the 1990s (Jordana & Levi-Faur 2005), influenced both by international financial pressures (especially in relation to debt obligations) and by a relatively strong international mainstream consensus about the shape and purpose of regulatory agencies. I develop an account of this consensus that I call a "transactional" model of regulation. This consensus is embedded in strong transnational epistemic communities specializing in the technical aspects of regulation.

The chapter explores the dynamics of domestic (national-level) regulation of access to water issues in Chile, Bolivia, and Argentina in the late 1990s and early 2000s. The transnational policy context created a noticeable imitation effect in the introduction of regulatory agencies, particularly in Latin America, where the case studies explored here are all located. In each, control is in fact partially ceded to semi-independent regulatory institutions that strongly resemble the institutional recommendations of the transnational consensus, representing a change in the institutional architecture of the state. But an exploration of the implementation dynamics of these institutions, focused on a time in each of conflict and dispute, reveals significant national differences. In Bolivia, the role played by the regulator in each case is coherent with the transactional model, but it is politically marginalized; in Chile, a strongly transactional regulator maintains political salience; and, in Argentina, a more political model of regulation is erratically salient. The empirical work from which this chapter draws is from a larger project involving six qualitative comparative case studies of water services disputes carried out in Argentina, Bolivia, Chile, France, New Zealand, and South Africa and updated by desk research. The methodology included interviews with international actors and observations over two years of multistakeholder fora and trade and investment negotiations.[2]

These differences can be explained by integrating political dimensions at two levels, which the transactional model of regulation either sidesteps or demonizes. The first level is that of contingent events at the macro level: Thus, Bolivia experienced a social and political revolution of sorts over the period studied, whereas Argentina experienced an economic crisis and a divided state, and Chile remained in a stable, depoliticized, investment-friendly context. At a related, but more micro level, the political context in each country varies, particularly the strength of the social groups that contest the transactional model of regulation promoted by the dominant transnational epistemic community.

Importantly, not only do these two interact to limit the impact of a transnationally promoted transactional model of regulation, but they also catalyze feedback into the transnational regulatory space of policies related to water service delivery. This

[2] The larger project explored the relationship among the local, national, and transnational aspects of regulatory governance and grassroots advocacy and social activism in relation to urban water services policy. Detail and data relating to social activism on the cases studies in this chapter have been necessarily truncated. I am grateful to the UK Economic and Social Research Council for funding the research under the title "The Commodification of Water, Social Protest and Cosmopolitan Citizenship": RES-143–25-0031.

leads to reciprocal influences that will be discussed in the conclusion to this chapter, showing that transnational transformations are a product of local political dynamics and contexts, just as much as they are an effect of external influences on a state.

1. TRANSNATIONAL DIMENSIONS OF GLOBAL WATER SERVICE DELIVERY

Water service delivery is still deeply embedded in national domestic structures and institutions, especially from the formal perspective of legal rights and obligations in relation to access to basic drinking water. Moreover, public operators deliver 95 percent of networked water services.[3] However, large private corporations are increasingly involved in water services delivery, including on a cross-border basis (LeClerc & Raes 2001; Silva, Tynan, & Yilmaz 1998). An extraordinary 7,300 percent increase of private sector investment in water sanitation occurred between 1990 and 1997, in comparison with the levels from 1974 to 1990. After 1997, there was a marked withdrawal of multinational corporations from cross-border contracts, so that by 2005, private sector investment was half the 1997 peak, totaling 11 percent of all water and sanitation investments (Simpson 2005). Private sector investment has also shifted geographical focus; while Latin America took almost 50 percent of global private sector investment in water services in the 1990s, it has been replaced by East Asia as the major recipient in the 2000s (Kerf & Izaguirre 2007).

Reduced levels of multinational investment do not necessarily mean less interest by the private sector, and not only because of the increased interest in Asia. Rather, more local private sector firms are involved, and private sector actors in general are focusing on shorter term, less expensive projects (Marin & Izaguirre 2006).[4] The urban population served by the private sector in the developing world has continued to grow from 1990 onward, reaching 160 million in 2007 (Marin 2009). Moreover, the withdrawal of multinational corporations from long-term, cross-border concession contracts has not altered the enduring importance of commercialization of water service delivery, as recent reports emphasize, arguing that successful public utilities require the same structural reforms that private sector participation brings (Marin 2009). In short, pressures to restructure service provision – whether publicly or privately provided – along commercial lines persist. And these pressures are increasingly playing out in a transnational field of global water policy.

[3] In poorer countries, where networks are limited, small-scale private, independent operators (ranging from individual water vendors to low-technology neighborhood systems) have always dominated provision.

[4] This is exemplified by the fact that, although quantitative levels of overall investment have reduced sharply since the 1990s, nonetheless, 2005 was a record year for growth in new contracts: forty-one projects were concluded in 2005, the most since 1990.

This field of global water policy, in relation to urban water service delivery, refers to the regulation, provision, and policymaking environment of urban water services.[5] Narrowly understood, the regulatory framework for delivery of water services is carried out by domestic institutions. As the case studies presented in this chapter show, national and local regulatory dynamics are the most crucial aspects of water service delivery on the ground. However, despite the absence of any formal international institutions responsible for the regulation of water services, transnational influence in the provision and policymaking environment of urban water services is now substantial. On the whole, those influences have promoted what I describe in more detail below as a *transactional model of regulation*.

The key transnational actors and spaces in this development are international and regional financial institutions, multinational private water companies, international dispute resolution fora, and transnational "think tanks." The World Bank and, in the case studies presented in this chapter, the Inter-American Development Bank, funded the provision of water services during the 1990s and early 2000s on the assumption of a commercial model of delivery, and strongly encouraged consideration of direct involvement of the private sector. Although not all of the loans from international financial institutions necessarily came with formal conditionality, the provision of expertise, advice, and support strongly shaped national trajectories, as the case studies will illustrate.

Multinational water companies, in particular from the United Kingdom and France, grew substantially during the 1980s and started investing heavily in cross-border service provision during the 1990s. The transnational markets for water services delivery were led by British and French companies Suez (Ondeo), Vivendi (Veolia), and Thames, who are the three largest water service operators globally in absolute terms, as well as in terms of foreign investment. These companies entered into transnational contracts with national or local authorities that, in turn, often provided for international arbitration.

The shadow of an international arbitration forum was a powerful influence on national policy trajectories, particularly in Argentina and Bolivia. Its availability to foreign companies investing in water service provision depended on bilateral international treaties (BITs) between investor companies and host national government. BITs are an important feature of the transnational institutional landscape bearing on urban water service delivery, one that affects the influence of transnational companies in particular states. For example, France, whose water companies dominate

[5] I do not address the distinct issue of internationally shared water resources. See Conca (2006) for this. In Morgan (2007b), I argue that a policy regime I call "global water welfarism" is emerging around this narrower issue of urban water service delivery, operating in three dimensions: fiscal, administrative, and legitimation, all embedded in a tightly woven complex among poverty reduction strategy plans, Millennium Development Goals, and public-private partnership structures.

transnational provision, had concluded sixty-five BITs by 2003, and its water companies were involved in several specific disputes as complainant.[6]

Transnational private companies are also heavily involved in transnational initiatives that bear on the policymaking environment for urban water service delivery. The most important vehicle is the transnational think tank, the World Water Council.[7] The Council is legally a French-based nongovernmental organization (NGO), but in practice, it is composed of a curious amalgam of business-based NGOs and large corporations.[8] It is a site for debates over access to water and for the formulation of influential position papers on key issues, and it now prominently organizes the triannual World Water Forum. Each Forum generates principles and policy documents for guiding water governance. Although not a UN-sponsored event, each World Water Forum also hosts a formal intergovernmental Ministerial Meeting.

The complex of international and regional financial institutions, multinational private water companies, international dispute resolution fora, and transnational "think tanks" described above, obviously representing significantly divergent interests in the global water policy field, nonetheless express and disseminate a number of shared norms and priorities that have significant power and influence across that policy field. Three of the most important are, first, the principle of cost-recovery in the provision of water services to domestic end-users; second, the centrality of contractual and property rights to the organization of the delivery of water services (whether or not outright privatization occurs); and third (although adopted more recently than the other two [Bakker 2009]), the notion that independent regulation is the most appropriate means of supervising the implementation of the first two. The relative consistency of these normative priorities, as expressed in global policy fora such as the World Water Forum, underlies my characterization of the field of global water policy as one shaped importantly (and of course only partially) by an "epistemic community."

Of course, such norms are contested, and often intensely and even violently so, as the narratives articulated briefly in the case studies show, and as my wider work on the issue (Morgan 2011) discusses at length. For the purposes of this chapter, with more

6 Calculated from www.worldbank.org/icsid/cases. These numbers are likely to represent only a fraction of total claims against the countries examined in these case studies for two reasons: First, ICSID only publicizes a claim once it has been registered by the Secretary-General of ICSID, which can take some time, and, second, it does not take into account other fora for investor-state arbitration, such as the UNCITRAL and the International Chamber of Commerce, neither of which has an obligation to publish claims.

7 Other initiatives beyond the scope of this chapter are the Global Water Partnership (technical assistance), International Standards Organisation (voluntary management standards), and Aquafed (trade association).

8 Members include Suez, Severn Trent, Vivendi, Mitsubishi, Evian, Electricite de France, Japan Dam Engineering Centre, Mitsubishi Heavy Industries, PriceWaterhouse Coopers, and US Army Corps of Engineers.

of an emphasis on the transnational governance structure, it is also important to note the salience of the UN and intergovernmental initiatives, which are very important aspects of the transnational policy environment affecting urban water services delivery, and whose normative statements in the global water policy often emphasize conflicting values simultaneously, including ecological protection, participation, and economic efficiency (Dublin Statement, 1992; European Commission, 2004; UN, 1978, 2000, 2005). Furthermore, as Braithwaite and Drahos (2000) have argued, particular national interests often play a crucial role in shaping global business regulation trajectories, even where they generate transnational or even truly international policies and institutions, and typically the roles played by national interests undercut the coherence of transnational epistemic communities. In relation to urban water service delivery, France and, to a lesser extent, the United Kingdom, have provided the real energy behind the promotion of a transactional model of regulation. This is an interesting deviation from Braithwaite and Drahos' findings of the centrality of the United States to so much global business regulation. Urban water service delivery in the United States is intensely local and fragmented; there are more than 60,000 water service providers, the substantial majority of these are public in nature, and there are no private companies comparable to the size and scope of the French water multinationals. The prominence of France and the United Kingdom (and, in fact, Spain too) in the transnational water service delivery market is linked to their colonial histories. With historical ties that facilitate contact all the way down to localized administrative structures, France and the United Kingdom have been able to harness the significant growth of their nationally based companies to transnational flows of money and ideas.

Interestingly, even though France is often seen as the exemplar of the European "social model," with more enthusiasm than most for an *etatist* vision of *le service public*, in the specific domain of water services, the role of the French state has been regulatory since the late nineteenth century. France has achieved public service goals in water service delivery, not by state provision, but by regulation,[9] focused initially on substantive but increasingly on procedural aspects of long-term contracting out for private sector provision. During the 1990s, as already noted, the transnational investment portfolios of French water companies increased significantly. Over the same period, France has been actively involved in trying to secure progress in transnational regulatory structures for water services. French companies and organizations were founding members of a voluntary self-regulatory regime through the International Standards Organization (Morgan 2006c), and have lobbied vigorously

[9] Until 1982, this centered on model contracts for leases and concessions whose terms were centrally controlled, especially in relation to prices. The decentralization reforms of the 1980s in France led to a period of fairly unregulated contractual amendments, but the 1990s saw a return of political regulation, focused now on *procedural* issues, such as transparency of tendering.

to include water services in the General Agreement on Trade in Services (GATS) of the World Trade Organization (WTO).[10] French companies also chose Latin America as their primary destination for pursuing long-term water concessions in the 1990s, a setting where more than perhaps anywhere else in the developing world, the spread of independent regulatory agencies had taken root (Jordana & Levi-Faur 2005). Finally, French water companies have extensively used the dispute resolution facilities provided by venues, such as the International Centre for the Settlement of Investment Disputes (ICSID) in the World Bank (Morgan 2006c).

The United Kingdom, which hosts the fourth largest global water company (then known as Thames), has a fully privatized water industry regulated by an independent, highly technocratic regulatory agency (Ofwat). France, by contrast, has self-consciously chosen *not* to establish, at least in relation to water and waste services provision, an independent regulatory agency with a full panoply of enforcement and monitoring powers. Instead, after a decade of intense political debate,[11] France opted for a "water observatory" that only has information-sharing powers.[12] Although the degree of institutionalization of an independent regulatory agency is very different between France and the United Kingdom, both countries have moved over time to a model for providing water services that is more transactional than political (a difference elaborated below). Developing countries, whose urban water service policy frameworks are shaped by the transnational forces detailed here, have often adopted a hybrid approach that mixes French-style, long-term concession contracts with UK-style independent regulatory agencies.

As shall be seen, these transnational developments have been deeply politically contested in the countries studied. Moreover, the organized social groups that oppose transactional directions of, reform for, or water service provision have become increasingly embedded in a different web of transnational institutions and actors focused on a legalized conception of the human right to water. One could argue that the policy trajectories traced in this chapter, combined with organized social opposition at the national and local levels, have helped *constitute* emerging transnational articulations around the human right to water. But such an argument is beyond the scope of this chapter (see Morgan 2007e, 2011 for more detailed treatment).

[10] Although they form important lobbying targets, neither ISO standards nor GATS undertakings have so far affected the specific national and local trajectories discussed in the case studies of this chapter.

[11] In 1999, the report of the High Council on Public Services called for a slightly stronger form of national regulation: *Quelle régulation pour l'eau et les services publics*. Haut Conseil du Secteur Public, Paris 1999; available through http://www.ladocumentationfrancaise.fr/rapports-publics/004000299/ext.shtml. In 2001, Dominique Voynet of the Jospin government proposed the creation of a Haut Conseil des Services Publics de l'Eau et de l'Assainissement, which was to regulate the price, quality, and performance of water and wastewater services. This was again rejected, although regulation of water *resources* in the aquatic environment has become more formalized (with the 2007 creation of ONEMA, the French acronym for the National Office of Water and the Aquatic Environment). The framework for water *service provision* is still essentially supported self-regulation.

[12] See http://www.onema.fr/IMG/EV/EV/plus/Fiche-Observatoire.pdf.

2. POLITICAL AND TRANSACTIONAL REGULATION

Regulation is salient on *both* sides of the dichotomous conceptualization of "water as a human right" versus "water as a commodity" (Morgan 2005). Whether state or private provision is envisaged, regulation is crucial. These two models of regulation for urban water service provision (political and transactional) are nonetheless useful for understanding the empirical findings of the case studies in this chapter. The development of these two contrasting models is part of a larger process of neoliberal policymaking embedded in transnational settings (Conca 2006; Goldman 2005). Discussions of the "neoliberal shift" in policymaking (Peck & Tickell 2002) emphasize that, although earlier phases of state reform may have focused on "rolling back" the state, contemporary policy approaches are more inclined to stress "rolling out" the state; in other words, altering the shape and form of the state's involvement with economic activities in ways that both extend and flatten the state's reach, affecting both the boundary between the state and the market, and the institutional architecture of the state.

This trend is exemplified in the regulation of access to water. Regulatory frameworks, institutionalized at the national or local level rather than globally, are an increasingly important aspect of the overall structure of water service provision. These developments often (although not always) center on independent regulatory agencies. As will be explored in detail in Section 3, the specific trajectories of regulatory dynamics in different countries vary considerably. The variations can be ordered by using a lens of two "ideal type" images of regulation, each of which has a dystopic mirror image. These two images are of a political conception of regulation, on the one hand, and – perhaps more familiar – a transactional image, on the other hand.

A political conception of regulation draws from the French school of "regulationist theory," which has neo-Marxist roots, but is also compatible with a range of essentially Keynesian social welfare accounts of citizen-state relations (Klerck 1996). Here, different modes of regulation, one mode of which may be law, are envisioned as tools for balancing and ensuring a "relatively harmonious relationship" among production, consumption, and exchange in the accumulation process. Regulation, in this view, is importantly mediated by "*historically and spatially specific* institutional forms and norms of behaviour" (Klerck 1996: 111), making the contingencies of specific local contexts and the *quality of social relations* between producers and consumers highly salient to any analysis. In particular, the regulationist school pays specific attention to "the impact of *non-commodity forms of social relations* which may assist in balancing consumption and production cycles" (Klerck 1996: 111).

Transactional regulation is perhaps more familiar, in content if not in name. Embedded in Weberian notions of calculability, it involves the state moving away from earlier welfare economics notions of preemptively correcting market failures that might harm vulnerable consumers. The state focuses instead on a more Spartan role of facilitating transactional frameworks. Inside these transactional frameworks, those who implement delivery can and do address social issues, but within the purview of managerial discretion rather than as the implementation of a formal, even legal, obligation. The "transaction" is the relationship between government and private provider, not between vulnerable consumers and a provider (public or private). Thus, the quality of social relations between producers and consumers is not a direct concern for politics or law in this approach, but becomes part of market or commodity relations. Politics and law focus on the attempt to produce what one commentator vividly called "bureaucrats with an entrepreneurial kick"![13]

The difference between political and transactional regulation is partly a difference of ideology and substantive belief, focused on whether allocating resources should be tied to price or to political power. It is also a different approach to the *quality* of rules that structure the allocation of resources. In transactional regulation, stability is paramount and thus these rules should be "time-consistent"; in political regulation, rules structuring the allocation of resources are more fluid and responsive to the changing social contexts of different consumer groups. On the whole, transnational actors, such as multinational companies or international financial institutions, promote a transactional model, whereas most developing country national governments tend to prefer a political model. But as we shall see in Section 3, the full story is more complex, centering on different coalitions whose members include both national and international actors. A shift to transactional regulation privileges new kinds of expertise, bringing economists and management consultants to the fore, rather than engineers and local politicians, calling into question the role of different forms of expertise in governance. National elites include people with personal and educational ties to the institutions that have promoted transactional regulation.

It is important not to assume that the two necessarily fall on opposite sides of the political conflicts that typify access to water debates. Although the emphasis on regulation that has emerged in global water policy has taken root in a broadly neoliberal context, which became more salient after the fall of the Berlin Wall, that context has significant nonmarket social aspirations. These aspirations lead to an emphasis not only on the provision of stable property rights for investors, but also on complementary subsidy schemes and extensive "stakeholder" participation. Moreover, "political" regulation may not necessarily benefit the poor through redistribution, but may instead cement the position of local elites.

It is also helpful to insist on the dystopian potential of each ideal type. To acknowledge that both political and transactional regulation can take pathological forms is to recognize, in a somewhat stylized way, the plural standpoints that necessarily characterize any collectivity. The following pictorial representation (Figure 7.1), which is drawn from a World Bank paper on regulation in Latin American water services (Foster 2001), shows, I would argue, a dystopic version of political regulation that is "cured" by an "ideal type" of transactional regulation. The "reformed" model

[13] Alexander Somek, "On Delegation," (2003) 23 *Oxford Journal of Legal Studies* 703, p. 703.

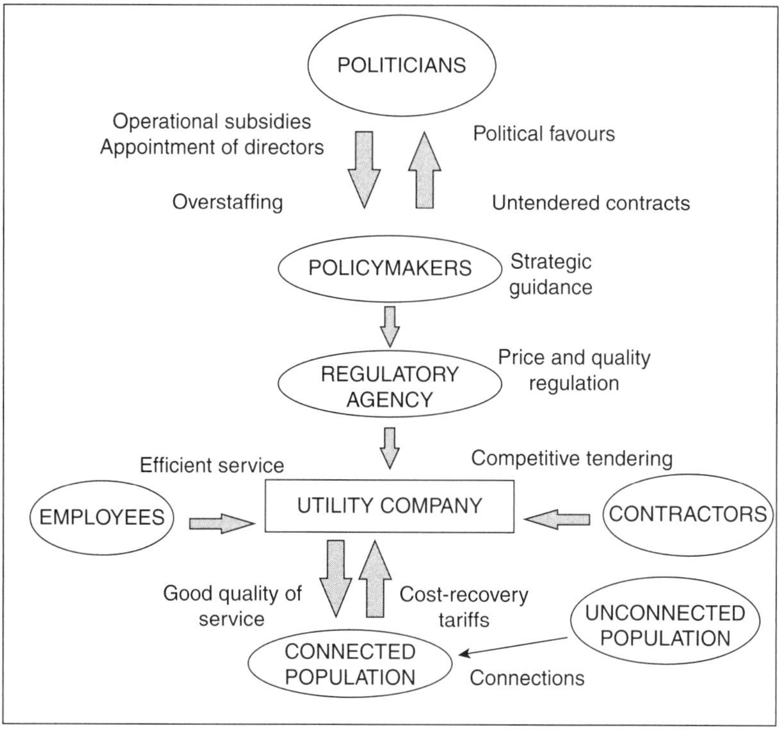

FIGURE 7.1. "Clientilist" model of water provision.

of regulation (an ideal type transactional view in my argument) seeks to eliminate "dole handouts and partisan loans." The vision is one of purifying "clientilism"; politicians become policymakers giving strategic guidance; the creation of a regulatory agency replaces political favors with a focus on technical decisions about quality and price, introduces competition, and improves cost recovery and labor efficiency; as a consequence, the unconnected are drawn into the circle of connection.

The trouble is, of course, that one person's "dole handouts and partisan loans" may be another person's legitimate redistributive politics. Similarly, one person's view that price and quality regulation applies independent expertise to issues formerly subject to arbitrary political discretion may be mirrored by others' opinion that this technocracy simply masks an inversely malign politics of regulatory capture. There are, in other words, "missing" politics in the reformed model that could equally be characterized *either* as features of political regulation's ideal type *or* as dystopic features of transactional regulation. Figure 7.2 shows how these "missing politics" recur in a reformed model, creating pressures that supporters of the political ideal type could argue require a legitimate response (e.g., creating processes of consumer involvement that balance regulatory capture by powerful contractors, providing

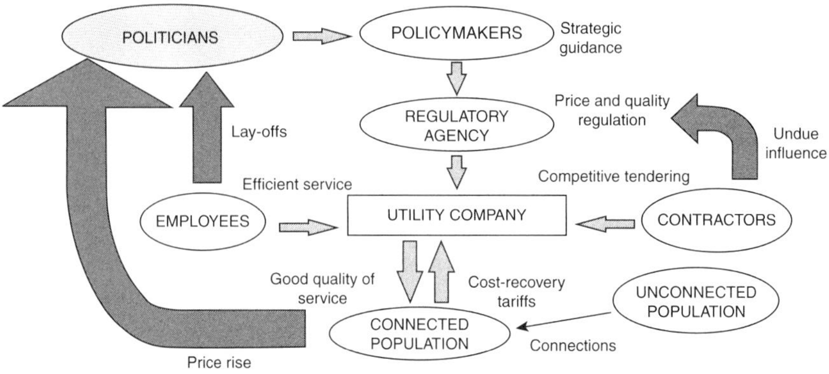

FIGURE 7.2. "Reformed" model of water provision. *Source:* Adapted from Vivien Foster, "Ten Years of Water Service Reform in Latin America: Towards an Anglo-French Model" (2005:8).

retraining and redeployment programs that respond to lay-offs, or providing subsidies to offset price rises).

Section 3 of this chapter will explore the ways in which these "missing politics" shape the regulatory dynamics that emerged in Chile, Argentina, and Bolivia around the delivery of water services. Although the initial presentation of the case studies suggests a clash between incompatible models of governance, exploring regulatory implementation in some detail reveals interesting feedback loops. These loops integrate *constructive* conflict into regulatory relationships. They integrate professional expertise with modulated political input in such a way that, over time, a regulatory culture that blends politics and expertise is institutionalized. Such a vision builds bridges between regulatory and citizen space (Morgan 2008), while still acknowledging the political character of regulation (Dubash 2005; Minogue & Carino 2006). I argue that such bridges depend more crucially on local and national institutions, particularly of dispute resolution, than on transnational ones. Productive feedback loops can nonetheless be absorbed and diffused by transnational processes over time.

3. COMPARATIVE REGULATORY DYNAMICS AND THE REVERBERATIONS OF "MISSING POLITICS"

This section explores the regulatory dynamics that emerged in relation to the delivery of water services in urban contexts in three Latin American case studies in Bolivia, Chile, and Argentina in the late 1990s and early 2000s. All three countries also experienced extensive foreign investment from the world's largest water multinationals during the 1990s. Of the four largest water services firms active in the transnational water services market, three are headquartered in France (Ondeo, Veolia, and Saur) and one in the United Kingdom (Thames Water). The two largest, Ondeo and Veolia, may be more commonly known as Suez and Vivendi.[14] Suez, Vivendi, and Thames all invested significantly in Chile, Bolivia, and Argentina during the 1990s.[15] The fieldwork on which the research is based was structured around major disputes involving transnational water companies, using Chile as a control case because it *lacked* a single major dispute. All three countries established regulatory agencies: Argentina at the provincial level, and Bolivia and Chile at the central government level. In Bolivia and Argentina, the disputes studied ended with the transnational investor terminating the concession and lodging a dispute in an international arbitration forum.

The three countries had shared experience of transnational investment in cross-border markets for the delivery of water services, and this generated a common pressure for transactional regulation, evidenced by some basic formal similarities in their common adoption of semi-independent regulatory agencies in the water sector. However, this adoption occurred under very different contextual conditions: Bolivia was experiencing developments that led eventually to a social and political revolution of sorts with the election of Evo Morales as president; Argentina experienced a serious economic crisis in 2000; and Chile continued to provide a stable, depoliticized, investment-friendly context during the period studied. These different macrocontexts, together with differences in the microcapacities of organized social groups opposed to transactional regulation, resulted in significant national variation in outcome.

Broadly, the outcomes are as follows. In Bolivia, transactional regulation was politically marginalized in favor of broad political mobilization around a participatory, developmental vision. In Chile, transactional regulation became relatively internalized and stable, ironically in the context of much more dilute transnational pressures as compared with the other two case studies. Argentina is a hybrid case: Transactional regulation failed, but in regulatory terms, no stable political alternative emerged, except as briefly catalyzed by synergy with the role of an ombudsman.

An explanatory account of this variation is summarized in tabular form. Table 7.1 suggests that exposure to international arbitration, together with either strong pressure from international financial institutions (Bolivia) or opportunistic populist use

[14] The two largest by some margin are Ondeo (previously Suez and before that Lyonnaise des Eaux), which serves 110 million people in more than 100 countries, and Veolia (previously Vivendi Environnement and before that Compagnie Generale des Eaux), which serves 96.5 million people in 90 countries: See Gleick et al., *The New Economy of Water* (2002) pp. 24–5. Thames Water serves 22 million people: see Yaron, *The Final Frontier* (2000).

[15] Suez bought the regional water company providing water to Santiago, Chile and secured long-term concessions in Buenos Aires, Santa Fe, and Cordoba, Argentina and La Paz, Bolivia. Thames bought initially one and eventually three regional water companies in the south of Chile. Vivendi had a stake in the Buenos Aires concession and also secured a long-term concession in the province of Tucuman, Argentina. Except for Suez in Chile, the companies have now disinvested in all these locations.

TABLE 7.1. *Operational comparison of national regulatory dynamics*

	Bolivia	Chile	Argentina
Catalyst for private sector participation (PSP)	Social goals and international pressure (IADB)	Economic goals and international incentives (WTO)	President Menem's reforms
Timing and level of government	Just before PSP Central	Nine years before PSP Central government	With PSP Provincial
Role and attributes of regulator	Basic technical expertise, inadequate legal structure, independent	Expert technocracy, low discretion, relatively independent	Low on expertise, played populist role
International arbitration?	Yes	No	Yes
Overall	Some formal technical capacity from a transactional perspective; politically marginalized	Formal and substantive transactional capacity; politically salient	Politicized; salient when catalyzed by ombudsman

IADB, Inter-American Development Bank; PSP, private sector participation; WTO, World Trade Organization.

of conditionality (Argentina) can result in rushed reforms that create agencies with inadequate expertise for their new role. This is particularly so where decentralization accompanies the introduction of a regulator (Argentina). By contrast, the Chilean case shows how domestic internalization of the transactional model over a long period, combined with retaining central control, results in a more politically salient, stable regulatory agency.

Table 7.2 broadens the lens to show where regulatory politics were focused, or refocused, and where agencies were marginalized. In each of the case studies, a distinct social imaginary animates local politics, understood in the sense of the set of values, institutions, laws, and symbols common to a particular society. In Bolivia, where a macrocontext of incipient revolution subsisted, conflict over regulatory frameworks for water persistently expanded what was at stake, encompassing broad issues of water resources going well beyond water service delivery, and implicating large, well-mobilized social groups from farmers to irrigators in mass direct action. A vision of a politically driven development state, which came to the fore in Bolivia over the period studied, was symbolized in particular by the creation of a public socially

TABLE 7.2. *Contextual comparison of national regulatory dynamics*

	Bolivia (transactional but marginalized)	Chile (transactional and politically salient)	Argentina (politicized but – erratically – salient)
Key focus of broad regulatory dynamics	Legislative framework for water resources broadly: irrigation, mining	Procurement policies, tariff-setting and accounting processes, mergers	Legislation mandating social tariffs
"Main action"	Popular politics and mass mobilization, legislative negotiations	Legalized power struggles between major interests; limited, ineffective party politics	Mix of party politics and popular action, and small claims lawsuits
Principal source of rich data	Deliberative and participatory drafting; social control of company	Regulator-company disputes within regulator and in court	Ombudsman-court-regulator sequence
Implicit social imaginary	Politically driven local development	Legalistic public interest	"Popcorn" incrementalism

controlled company to replace the transnational concessionaire in Cochabamba and the emergence of deliberative and participatory institutions for drafting legislation. Indeed, one can argue that the Bolivian state, by the end of the dispute, had shifted its frame of reference of legitimacy and accountability, symbolized by its withdrawal from the International Convention on the Settlement of International Disputes, and its reorientation toward the institutions and actors of the Bolivarian Alternative for the Peoples of Our America. Of course, this shift is only partly a product of the intersection of the transnational pressures in urban water service delivery with the specificity of a Bolivian political and social imaginary.[16] And, in substantive terms, the distributive consequences have yet to bear fruit for those lacking access to water; expansion of network access or lower prices have not yet resulted from the new operator structures or legislative schemes (Terhorst 2003).

[16] Conflicts over natural resources more broadly, particularly gas and minerals, also played an important role. But it is interesting to note that the current president, Evo Morales, was involved in protests around the Cochabamba dispute and that one of the leading water activists in the conflict over water services in La Paz, Abel Mamani, became the first Water Minister for Bolivia under Morales.

The Chilean case illustrates how a regulatory agency becomes institutionalized and stable absent major disputes in a relatively depoliticized, investment-friendly context, one animated by a social imaginary of legalistic public interest. The regulatory dynamics centered on legalized power struggles between the regulator and private companies rather than citizen disputes directly. Although by no means apolitical, they focused on aspects of water service delivery, such as tariff-setting and accounting processes, in relatively closed fora dominated by technical language and expertise. Other currents of "missing politics" were channeled into party politics and relatively weak consumer mobilization, but made little headway against the centralized executive power structures that dominate the Chilean state. The congruence of domestic Chilean regulatory dynamics with a transactional model of regulation does not, however, contrary to what one might expect, seem closely correlated with strong transnational influences, barring the catalyst effect of WTO rules. Rather, the case may demonstrate the depth of internalization of ideological flows, such as those diffused by the "Chicago boys" (economic technocrats holding powerful positions in government, many of whom were educated at the University of Chicago economics department [Valdes 1995]), as well as the persistence of local politics in the clientilistic version of neoliberalism articulated in Chile.

Finally, Argentina provides an example of hybrid trends, showing both how the transactional model, when implemented, emerged mainly as a dystopic form of political regulation, yet one that could occasionally interact synergistically and constructively with local dispute resolution processes involving an ombudsman. Unlike the Chilean case, party politics and popular action had more traction in Argentina, yet unlike the Bolivian case, they did not entirely marginalize day-to-day regulatory and political dynamics. Rather, in somewhat unpredictable "popcorn" fashion, bursts of popular energy were able to intersect with small claims lawsuits and party-political efforts to sustain legislative attempts to implement social tariffs. Thus, even though distributional issues, as in Bolivia, were not practically solved, questions of redistributive equity remained on the political agenda. The Argentinian narrative also shows how the legitimation framework shifted to a degree, particularly vis-à-vis the tension between local, small-scale dispute resolution (via the ombudsman) and remote supranational dispute resolution (via international arbitration). By the end of the dispute, the possibility emerged of wider participation of ordinary citizens in the transnational judicial process of international arbitration, a shift in the interpretative community of transnational economic governance to encompass local actors in developing countries.

In sum, domestic regulatory dynamics in urban water service delivery, even when powerfully shaped by transnational interests, institutions, and norms, provide an important counter to assumptions too often made that globalization involves the subjection of developing countries to "external" pressures to which they "respond." The most important reciprocal narrative, based on participatory visions of democracy, is rooted in events that unfolded in Bolivia.

A. *Water and Regulation in Bolivia*

Although Suez had a major contract in Bolivia's capital, La Paz, the field research on which this chapter draws focused on an earlier concession in Cochabamba held by a joint venture between Bechtel and International Water. The Cochabamba dispute has become an iconic reference point (in either positive or negative terms, depending on one's perspective) regarding international regulatory and political dynamics around struggles over access to water. The presence of "repeat players," such as Suez in La Paz, nonetheless importantly shaped the Bolivian government's response to conflict over water service delivery in Cochabamba.

In 1997, Bolivia decided to involve the international private sector in water provision in Cochabamba, in part motivated by a very ambitious vision of water resource development for this normally very arid region, involving not only the operation of urban water services but also the construction of a major dam (the Miscuni Dam). Although there was certainly pressure from the Inter-American Development Bank to contract out this work to the private sector, there was also an undoubted enthusiasm on the part of local political elites for securing the financial backing of a large multinational for this project. As a result of this local-international coalition, the key political dynamics likely to disrupt the process were those at the municipal level. These dynamics fitted badly with the timing and placement of the relevant regulatory agency. Bolivia had established a detailed legislative structure for utilities as a whole (gas, electricity, telecommunications, and water) in 1994, with a "super-regulator" (Sistema de Regulacion Sectorial [SIRESE]) overseeing a range of sectoral regulators.[17] This operated at the central government level and involved little consultation with municipal governments. The government originally planned to establish separate regulators for water *resources* and for water *services*, but the former ran into sufficient political opposition so that, by 1997, detailed regulations were adopted only for the creation of a regulatory agency for water *services*.

More problematically, the framework of legal duties for the water services regulator, the Superintendent of Basic Sanitation (SISAB), was substantially amended just one month *after* Cochabamba's water services were concessioned to Bechtel in September 1999. The 1999 *Ley de Servicios de Agua Potable y Alcantarillado Sanitario* (Law 2029), despite its title focusing on the provision of water and waste services, in fact empowered SISAB to regulate water *resources* more generally (agricultural, irrigation, industrial, mining, etc.) at least until a specific body was created for this purpose.[18] This gave SISAB highly controversial powers at the precise moment when

[17] 1994 Ley No. 1600, October 28, 1994 framework of all regulators (Sistema de Regulacion Sectorial [SIRESE]).

[18] Specifically, the very last provision of Law 2029 (dubbed a transitory article) provides that the concessions and authorizations for the usage of hydrological resources as well as their revocation will be granted by a regulator to be created under the Framework Regulatory System of Renewable Natural

its regulatory task expanded enormously with the entry of the transnational private sector into the Bolivian water services market.

Despite SISAB's possessing some formal technical capacity, it was politically marginalized. It was structured to emulate an idea of transactional regulation, but embedded in a broader context that supported political regulation at best, and from some quarters, a far more populist and participatory, politically driven vision of local development. It was located at the central government level, although water services had been delivered by public municipal-level entities. Although it was relatively independent from immediate political influence of any crude kind, and although its employees did possess basic technical expertise, it had an inadequate legal structure and only thirty-one staff. Its birth and administrative culture were also heavily shaped by international expertise and support, and the agency continues to be heavily dependent on this expertise for operating; international financial institutions staffed the initial unit that drafted the SIRESE framework and continue to support SISAB extensively with consultancies and even basic staff support.[19] The Inter-American Development Bank in 2002 actually became a member of ANESAPA, the Bolivian professional association of water companies, illustrating the deep interpenetration of the national and international sector in the Bolivian context.[20]

The regulatory role performed by SISAB in supervising international contracts took place in the shadow of Bolivia's commitment to systems of international arbitration for dispute resolution through various bilateral investment treaties (BITs). Here, in particular, the influence of international politics has been very powerful. For example, shortly after signing the concession, Bechtel relocated its corporate headquarters to the Netherlands, making it possible for Bechtel to take advantage of the protection afforded by the BIT between the Netherlands and Bolivia (there was no equivalent United States-Bolivia BIT). Evidence from Argentina discussed below suggests that ICSID-based dispute resolution undermines a political response to regulatory conflict, and may shore up a transactional response. However, in Bolivia, SISAB's position was not shored up, raising the question of why the regulator was so politically marginalized despite its technical capacity and strong international support.

The answer lies in the restricted ambit of what social groups perceived as SISAB's legitimate jurisdiction. The key focus of broad regulatory dynamics in the Bolivian case was the legislative framework for water resources, broadly speaking, provisions

Resources (SIRENARE). It adds, however, that once this regulator is created, such functions will be performed by SISAB.

19 Silvia Arzabe, Planning Support Officer for SISAB, interviewed by Carolina Fairstein, La Paz, April 27, 2004.

20 *Semapa: a un ano de la institucionalizacion*, Semapa annual report 2002–3. ANESAPA began as a public sector trade organization in 1982, expanded to allow private and cooperative companies as members in 1997, and, in 2002, expanded to include "national and international institutions, NGOs, or natural persons with legal relations with the water sector": p. 67.

affecting irrigation, mining, and so forth. This focus was far broader than the infrastructural issues that the SISAB regulatory framework addressed and, even though the government formally gave broader duties to SISAB in the 1999 amendments, the lack of perceived legitimacy for this action stymied its progress. These processes involved popular politics and mass mobilization, together with legislative negotiations, to create a new framework for governing water *resources* generally. SISAB had little chance of emerging as an important player in this context, appearing as an agency bravely trying to join a field of professional expertise with which few of the politically salient local players were familiar; the technical minutiae of regulatory politics with which it had competence did not resonate or engage with local political dynamics.

Two examples illustrate this tension. The first occurred during the dispute. In December 1999, SISAB held a public hearing on tariffs. They required those who attended to register and to bring identification; consequently, only fourteen people preregistered. The hearing was suspended when SISAB realized it was likely to catalyze a large social mobilization. This risk was much more salient in shaping the policy trajectory on tariffs than SISAB's attempts at transparency. The second example comes from the period after the Cochabamba municipal water company was remunicipalized. Since around 2002, SISAB has valiantly tried (with World Bank funding) to install a consumer education program, focused on training neighborhood board leaders, social groups, guilds, mothers' associations, and church groups in matters of "regulation, rights, obligations, complaints, and water care." However, at the same time, the groups most capable of derailing the larger policy agenda were involved in extensive deliberative, participatory drafting of the new water resources legislative framework,[21] and in instantiating "social control" of the municipal company (Terhorst 2003). In their view, this extensive consumer outreach program only reached issues at the margins of what mattered most to people, at a point in time that was too late for them to shape the more structural decisions that would determine the allocation of resources and power.[22] Co-management, not consultation, was the politically salient issue, and it was sidestepped by the design of SISAB's consumer awareness program.

In short, the regulatory agency was focused on a transactional approach to the "minor water cycle," whereas the most politically salient players placed the "major water cycle" at the center of a highly politicized and expressive politics of struggle. The implicit social imaginary driving the politics of the Bolivian case – a vision of

[21] This evolved from a civil society-based organization, Comité de Gestión Integral del Agua en Bolivia (CGIAB), in 1998, to an Interinstitutional Water Council (CONIAG), which had representatives from agriculture, sustainable development, economics, housing, and basic services from the government, as well as five civil society representatives from peasants, irrigators, indigenous people, private sector, and academia. By 2004, CONIAG had drafted and passed Law 2878 for the support of irrigators.

[22] Crespo Carlos Crespo Flores, Oxford Brookes University, "Superintendencias: Nuevos Superpoderes (Democracia y Regulación en Bolivia)," paper on file with author.

politically driven, locally rooted, holistic development – had little synergy with the independent regulatory agency modeled on the "best practice" recommendations of international financial institutions. Rather, a reinvigorated vision of participatory public management was the predominant vision, one aspired to replace the managed liberalization of global water welfarism. After the election of Evo Morales, whose success was deeply rooted in struggles over access to natural resources, the international arbitration action arising from the Cochabamba dispute was settled for the symbolic sum of two Bolivian pesos. Bolivia subsequently withdrew from the ICSID in a very public manner. What is emerging in Bolivia is not purely nationalist, but is embedded in moves on the international stage since Evo Morales became president,[23] some in alliance with Cuba and Venezuela.[24] These moves are arguably coalescing into a broader agenda, the Bolivarian Alternative for the Peoples of Our America (Gott & Bartoli 2005; Muhr 2008). These dynamic changes illustrate that important transnational political-ideological responses that address struggles over access to basic essentials – what I have called the "politics of necessity" (Morgan 2006c) – are rooted in developing world contexts just as much as they are emanating from the industrialized world.

B. *Water and Regulation in Chile*

Chile's regulatory institutions represent something much closer to the "ideal" transactional vision supported by international financial institutions and a strong epistemic community. A number of features make Chile's politics of water privatization unique. First, access to water in Chile is far more widespread than in other developing countries. In 1930, the Chilean central government made the provision of water and sewage services a developmental priority. Unusually high coverage has subsisted especially since the 1970s.[25] Second, the provision of water services is unusually centralized. Even a restructuring along regional lines in the 1970s followed technocratic lines, resulting in twelve centrally controlled regional public companies, rather than the decentralization of any authority to more local political levels of government. In the 1980s, the decentralization sweeping the rest of Latin America was rejected in Chile, influenced by the "Chicago boys," who argued that there was insufficient professional capacity at local government levels and that the private sector would provide more reliable expertise, leading to efficiency gains. Third, Chile is unusually urban – only 10 percent of the population lives in rural areas. And finally,

[23] For example, the withdrawal from the ICSID Convention, the appointment of one of the major El Alto water activists in La Paz to the post of Water Minister.

[24] For example, the dissenting Ministerial Declaration at the Fourth World Water Forum in Mexico in 2006, drafted by Bolivia and endorsed by Cuba and Venezuela.

[25] Coverage is 99.7 percent and 24 hours a day and sewage is 94 percent: Alexander Chechilnitzky, "AIDIS: 55 anos de fructifera labor," *La Revista de Aidis-Chile*, September 2003.

there is a relatively low level of civil society activism, particularly around issues of socioeconomic policy.[26]

Thus, rather than an urgent need for investment for basic access to water, the catalyst for the entry of the international private sector into Chile's water and sewage services sector was twofold in the 1980s: ideological neoliberalism, and the need to raise private financing to build waste treatment plants. Some argue that the United States-Chile free trade agreement created legal pressures to meet international standards in wastewater treatment in order to facilitate fruit exports. Yet it is not entirely clear if this was a post hoc justification for an otherwise ideological decision to involve the private sector. It does appear, however, that economic export-oriented goals were an important part of the motivation, which succeeded in almost doubling the percentage of wastewater treated between 1998 and 2005.[27]

Chile's water services have undergone three main reforms in the structure of provision: corporatization 1989–1998 (associated with efficiency gains), a brief period of privatization 1998–2001 (associated with raising capital to build waste treatment plants), and concessioning 2001–present (associated with a political backlash against privatization). The public water companies were restructured along "corporatized" lines in 1989, just before democracy returned to Chile,[28] and Aylwin's center-left government left this in place. Almost a decade later, after a stormy debate in 1998 under the center-left government of Eduardo Frei, legislation to allow privatization was passed, albeit with a ceiling on ownership.[29] This ceiling was quietly removed a few months later in a little-noticed tax bill.[30] Between 1998 and 2000, five of the thirteen regional companies were privatized.[31] The remaining eight were contracted out as long-term concessions, rather than being privatized outright.[32] Few seem to think that the difference between outright asset sales and long-term concession has any significant political or even practical implications. Indeed, despite the shift away from privatization toward the concession system, another little-noticed tax bill

[26] The causes of this are not clear; many interviewees attributed it to Chilean culture, but the lingering effects of Pinochet's dictatorship may be just as material: See Houtzager and Kurtz 2000 for an argument about the lingering effects of institutional and structural changes introduced by Pinochet on rural grass-roots mobilization. See also Foweraker 2001.

[27] Treated wastewater levels were 42 percent in 2003, but were on target to reach 81 percent by the end of 2005: Alexander Chechilnitzky, "AIDIS: 55 anos de fructifera labor," *La Revista de Aidis-Chile*, September 2003.

[28] The state industry development arm CORFO was relieved of service delivery obligations in water. Thirteen regional joint-stock companies were created: Ley 18.777 of January 17, 1989.

[29] General Law for Sanitation Services (Law 19,549, 1995 bill) of February 5, 1998.

[30] Article 5 of Ley 19,888 of July 14, 1998 (a general tax law) abolished any ceiling on the sale of shares in water companies.

[31] Emos (Santiago - Suez), Esval (Valparaiso, Region V - Anglian), Essbio (Concepion, Region VIII - Thames), Essel (Region VI – Thames), and Essal (Region VIII - Iberdrola).

[32] An internal review by then President Richard Lagos in the late 1990s, then Minister of Public Works (and later to be president in 2001), underpinned this policy shift.

in 2003 allowed four of the five companies originally privatized in the late 1990s to be sold entirely.[33] This narrative encapsulates Chilean regulatory dynamics in the water sector – an odd mix of polarized public political debate that fails to alter the direction of the policy trajectory, together with major decisions made in the interstices of technical and obscure legislation.

Water services in Chile are regulated by SISS (Superintendency of Sanitation Services).[34] SISS is a regulatory agency that replaced a government department in 1990 when corporatization took place. Consistent with transactional models of regulation, the key relationships were those between the regulator and the regional companies, rather than those with consumers. During the 1990s, these relationships (between SISS and the regional companies) were ones of negotiation and fairly cordial bargaining. The shift to privatization in 1998 inaugurated a more adversarial relationship between operators and regulator. In the wake of the rapid privatization of five of the thirteen companies, fines imposed by SISS increased by 69 percent between 2000 and 2001.[35] An analysis of SISS data on adjudicatory decisions by the regulator, together with judicial appeals (1995–2005; see Table 7.3), shows that the privatized companies are predominantly the subject of above-average fines, the highest fines, and the highest appeals against fines.[36] The legal actions were also, almost without exception, initiated by the regulator or the company, rather than by consumers, and they focused mainly on defining the limits of property rights as between regulator and operator (i.e., typical of transactional regulatory politics). Moreover, although SISS usually prevailed on appeal, and although at least some of these instances should have indirectly benefited consumers, the Chilean water sector lacks any legal device for indemnifying consumers.

Regulatory politics in Chilean water services are characteristic of broader macrocharacteristics of Chile's economy, which is heavily structured along market lines, yet markedly unfriendly to consumers:[37] a kind of openly clientilistic version of neoliberal reforms. Chilean water regulation exemplifies a specific ideal of transactional regulation in that the regulatory agency was established nine years

[33] A bill to "establish the funding needed to ensure the priority social objectives of the government," Ley 19888 of August 2003, Article 5. Emos, the Santiago company and the most politically sensitive, was not included.

[34] Chile's water *resources* are regulated by the general water department (DGA), a unit of the Ministry of Public Works that oversees a complex system of tradeable water rights established in 1981 (a system beyond the scope of this research).

[35] Morrison Foerseter, Quarterly Report on Water Industry Developments in Latin America – March 2002. The fines for 2001 were thirty-three, totaling US$1.07 million.

[36] One interesting exception to the general pattern is Essbio, the Thames-owned company, which attracted the highest fines, but did not feature in the high appeal statistics. This can be explained by the fact that Essbio attracted more political controversy than any other water company in Chile and may have considered the political costs of appealing greater than the likelihood of success.

[37] In 2005, the World Economic Forum gave Chile first place for macroeconomic handling in a global survey, but only 53rd place for consumer responsiveness: Eduardo Engel, "Consumidores: tres tareas pendientes," La Tercera, November 20, 2005.

TABLE 7.3. *Analysis of cases brought to Chilean water regulator SISS 1995–2005*

Company	No of fines	Total (%)	Appealed or not	Appealed (%)	Fines = or >300 UTM	Average fine
Aguas Andinas	3	2	3	100	0	200.0
Essar	5	3	0	0	0	9.0
Esmag	2	1	0	0	0	55.5
Essan	3	2	0	0	0	85.67
Essel	23	16	2	9	10	243.43
Essam	10	7	1	10	1	259.8
Essat	12	8	2	17	2	260.33
Essbio	23	16	5	22	8	488.91
Essco	7	5	2	29	2	137.14
Emmssa	3	2	1	33	0	48.67
Essal	13	9	6	46	3	217.15
Emssat	6	4	3	50	0	48.33
Emos	21	15	11	52	3	137.14
Esval	13	9	8	62	5	446.85
TOTAL	144	100	31%	33.10	23.61	202.92
Average fine	202.92					
Above average fines	Essbio, Esval, Essat, Essam, Essel, Emmssa				(descending order)	
Average appeal rate	31%				(descending order)	
Those with highest appeal rates	Esval, Emos, Essal				(descending order, all above 1,000 UTM)	
Highest rate of big fines	Essbio, Essel, Esval, Essal, Essat, Emos, Essam				(descending order)	
Highest fines per se	Essbio, Esval, Essam, Essat					
Big fines as % of total fines	Essbio + Esval + Essam + Essat = 10,968/total fines 36,487 = 30.06%					

Source: Compiled from analysis of Superintendency of Sanitation Services (SISS) records.

before full privatization as a way of disciplining the (then) newly corporatized water services companies. The key issues that attract regulatory activity are tariff-setting, accounting processes for investment obligations, procurement processes, and mergers. The regulatory agency does not engage with social issues, except indirectly through a complex subsidy scheme administered by the municipalities.

A brief description of how tariffs are set exemplifies the texture of Chilean regulatory politics in water. The tariff system is based on hypothetical models of a perfectly efficient company, rather than on trying to internalize the costs of existing inefficiencies. Both the regulator and the company produce estimates based on their own models, using complex formulae that are laid down by the legislative framework and public terms of reference for the models. Fifteen days of negotiation follow the production of estimates, and, if no consensus can be reached, an expert panel of three makes the final decision.[38]

Interestingly, international arbitration is not a powerful feature of the regulatory space in Chilean water politics. One interpretation of this result is that international investors respect the combination of the *formal independence and substantive expertise* of the regulator as sufficient to provide the political stability they need and seek. But an equally plausible reason for this comfort could be the *political support* enjoyed by international investors. The international private sector directly provides a majority of Chile's citizens with water services. The policy environment is sensitive to perceptions of "investment climate" held by these investors, and this undoubtedly shapes the regulatory dynamics.[39] Moreover, the separation between economic and social issues mentioned above in the domestic context is mirrored in relation to transnational links. Although *dispute settlement* does not strongly shape the Chilean regulatory environment in the water sector, Chile has extensive links to regional and global associations that *set standards*, such as AIDIS (the Spanish acronym for the Inter-American Association of Engineers). Santiago also hosts the Latin American branches of both the UN Economic and Social Commission and of Consumers International, embedding it in international networks of actors who develop the social and consumer dimensions of water policy.

Overall, the day-to-day regulatory dynamics are dominated by a legalized power struggle between major interests, irritated at the margins by party-political dynamics that are often limited in their effectiveness because of the strong centralization of executive power in the Chilean constitutional structure. This institutional structure creates less of a basis for constructive conflict in regulatory politics in Chile than

[38] One member is nominated by the relevant company, one by the regulator SISS, and the third agreed upon by both. Often the third member (typically a PhD-qualified economist) effectively decides the issue. The expert panel decisions have never been judicially reviewed, although heated technical debates regarding the parameters of the models have persisted and been clarified over time by legislative revision.

[39] Some interviewees made off-the-record comments regarding the subtle, but powerful (investor-friendly), influence of the Ministry of Economics over SISS.

might initially seem to be the case. Routinized technocracy coexists with, but is relatively unresponsive to, a politicized debate portrayed in black-and-white terms. In this context, there is little or no integration of professional expertise with modulated political input and feedback, and thus only very weak institutionalization of a regulatory culture that blends politics and expertise.

Arguably, an important "missing link" is the absence of space for the routinized incorporation of "everyday citizen" demands. In Bolivia, these demands were expressed through mass mobilization and direct action. At best, what exists in Chile is a highly individualized form of action within consumer law. In Argentina, as we shall see, lower levels of direct action coexist with administrative law-type procedures for vindicating the public interest. But in Chile there is a marked absence of such devices.[40] Even though interviewees evoke an implicit political climate of a legalistic conception of the public interest underpinning regulatory dynamics, there is little institutional support for actually making this a reality. The legal device of *recurso de proteccion* (effectively, the ability to obtain an injunction) does not facilitate collective consumer action: It is used mainly by the companies against the regulator (not least because it must be filed within fifteen days of the occurrence of any harm). In addition, it creates no *stare decisis* and relies on a dogmatic, slow, and nontransparent judicial process. There are no administrative courts where individuals can challenge abusive and illegal action. The most powerful oversight institution is the *Controloria*, which is an auditor and ensures the legality of executive decrees. The *Controloria* has facilitated an obsessive focus on legality and administrative probity, but in business-friendly ways. In short, the space for articulating claims of fairness, equity, or human rights is severely constricted.

Of course, there are still "missing politics" that drive the regulatory dynamics away from the transactional model. It is not that lay-offs, tariff rises, or undue contractor influence do not exist in Chile. Rather, they have not sparked the same kind of political mobilization as they have in, for example, Argentina. One interviewee from the Central Labour Union in Chile said – with some regret – that "in Argentina, when the lights go off, the people burn tires on the roadways and build barricades, while in Chile they simply go down to the supermarket and buy candles."[41] Direct action is remarkably muted, and public media coverage of water provision issues focuses overwhelmingly on making the country safe for foreign investors. This may be in part due to the extensive direct subsidy scheme for low-income water consumers that exists in Chile. This scheme, implemented by municipalities in ways that only

40 In 2004, consumer protection legislation was finally amended, after a six-year battle, to include a mild form of class action and some incentives to encourage collective consumer associations. However, even this reform (which itself is much criticized: Eduardo Engel, "Consumidores: tres tareas pendientes," La Tercera, November 20, 2005, noting that only three collective actions were lodged in the first year since the law was passed) does not include public services within its remit.

41 Miguel Soto, Central Workers' Union, interviewed by Bronwen Morgan and Carolina Fairstein, Santiago, January 27, 2004.

tangentially and marginally involve the regulatory agency, neutralize to some extent the political resonance of affordability issues. Despite this, there is certainly contestation. Some comes from individual legislators who take up the cause of constituency members.[42] Citizen groups have also mobilized from time to time, albeit weakly. But the tight connections between local elites and the mainstream transactional consensus on water service provision have given rise to managed liberalization and transactional regulation in Chile.

C. *Water and Regulation in Argentina*

In the early 1990s, President Menem's sweeping neoliberal reforms of the Argentine economy set the stage for multinational companies to enter into the Argentine water services sector. At the provincial level, these reforms were enacted more as a result of pressure from the federal government than from any locally relevant political dynamics, and this haunted the regulatory dynamics from the start. In Tucumán province, the troubled provincial state water company la Dirección Provincial de Obras Sanitarias (DIPOS) had been governed by fifteen different directors between 1981 (when it was first transferred to provincial control from the federal government) and 1996. Just over a year after the Tucumán government passed a legislative framework for privatization in March 1994, it awarded a thirty-year concession contract to Vivendi in May 1995.[43] At the same time, there were attempts to transform DIPOS into a regulator entitled ERSACT (Ente Regulador del Servicio de Agua y Cloadas de Tucumán). These attempts began in late 1994, and changes were formalized by November 1995, in the process downsizing the 1,800 employees of DIPOS to 900. The transformation was formal and superficial, arguably one in name only, as employees were given little additional training or preparation for this entirely new role of regulating rather than operating.[44]

In this messy fashion, DIPOS became ERSACT, now ostensibly an independent regulator with the job of monitoring concessionaire providers of water. ERSACT suffered from being a provincial regulator established more or less through central fiat, as well as one having no time to establish its new role before the international private sector began operating in the province. As a result, the regulator lacked substantial

[42] See motions filed by Chilean House of Representatives member Patricio Walker, of the Christian Democratic (DC), deputy Antonella Sciaraffia, and senate candidate Fernando Flores: *La Estrella de Iquique*, reported in Morrison and Foerster quarterly update.

[43] Formally speaking, the contract was with Vivendi's Argentine affiliate Aguas del Aconquija. The parent company was known as Compagnie Générale des Eaux (CGE) at the time of entering into the concession and, more recently, as Veolia, although still more popularly recognized as Vivendi, which will be the name used here. Although Aguas del Aconquija has a separate legal personality, it is controlled in substance by Vivendi.

[44] Daniel Arancibia, former president of the regulatory body ERSACT (Ente Regulador del Servicio de Agua y Cloadas de Tucuman) and director of the former state-run water company, interviewed by Carolina Fairstein, Tucuman, Argentina, July 1, 2004.

expertise, and played a populist role in the regulatory dynamics – one that was at times politically salient, although certainly not in the ideal-typical image of transactional regulation. The most interesting moment of ERSACT's political salience was when it coordinated with the ombudsman, as discussed below. Although there were definite limits to the constructive nature of these regulatory politics, the episode illustrates an interesting interaction of international, national, and local pressures within one regulatory space, one that shows both the necessity of taking into account consumer group perspectives, and the significant limits on state responsiveness created by transnational pressures.

The concession contract contained detailed provisions about the service that Vivendi would provide, the tariffs it would charge, and the investments it would make. After the agreement was entered into, disputes arose between Vivendi and Tucumán over various issues, including the method for measuring water consumption, the level of tariffs to customers, the timing and percentage of any increase in tariffs, the remedy for nonpayment of tariffs, Vivendi's right to pass through to customers certain taxes, and the quality of the water delivered. The disputes took multiple forms at the domestic level, but led ultimately to an arbitration claim lodged by Vivendi before the ICSID.[45]

The possibility of international arbitration under ICSID shaped the larger political context. The federal government undertook a diplomatic mission to resolve the dispute informally, sending former President Menem of Argentina to France to negotiate, pressuring provincial officials in Tucumán both publicly in the press and privately,[46] and helping prepare a new agreement between Vivendi and Tucumán Province through a Working Group of the Provincial Attorney General, a union representative, and the Chief Executive Officer (CEO) of Vivendi.[47] This created significant pressure on the local dispute resolution dynamics, however subtly. A key focus of the broader regulatory dynamics was the attempt to pass legislation that would have mandated "social tariffs" in order to temper the effects of tariff rises under the concession. A mix of party political moves, popular action on the streets, and small claims lawsuits kept pushing forward this focus. But, ultimately, it clashed with the transnational dimension, as we now illustrate.

In the summer of 1996, many thousands of users ceased paying their water bills in the wake of brown water and rising costs. The Tucumán ombudsman advised consumers who ceased payment to lodge an administrative dispute with the company alleging deficient rendering of services in respect of water quality and incorrectly

45 *Compañia de Aguas del Aconquija, S.A. & Compagnie Générale des Eaux* v. *Argentine Republic*, Award, ICSID Case No. ARB/97/3 (12 November 2000), 40 ILM 426; also available (with subseqent decisions on the same case) at http://www.worldbank.org/icsid/cases/awards.htm#award15. The case was originally filed on February 19, 1997, relying on a 1991 BIT between Argentina and France.

46 The Minister of Economy at the time, Fernandez, even threatened a federal-provincial lawsuit for the damage caused to Argentina's image in the eyes of foreign investors.

47 Interview with Maria Pedicone de Valles, Provincial Attorney-General of Tucuman, August 2004.

calculated tariffs.[48] Nonresponse to this dispute letter within fifteen days bounced the dispute to the regulator, ERSACT, who issued two resolutions discounting consumers' bills in two respects.[49] Although only about 10 percent of payment boycotters filed the appropriate paperwork, this still amounted to some thousands of people. Vivendi did not challenge the decrees of the ombudsman and regulator in local courts, but continued to voice its disagreement even while invoicing customers in accordance with the decrees, and then immediately filing suit against the boycotters to recover the unpaid charges once they had rescinded the contract. Before the ICSID claim was filed, however, the parties preferred to continue with political negotiations.

The ombudsman took two unprecedented steps in response to Vivendi's lawsuits against the boycotters, basing its strategy on the fact that the company was no longer the water provider by this time. First, the ombudsman tried to lodge a collective action lawsuit in the courts on behalf of the boycotters, but this was rejected in multiple consecutive fora by a series of different judges. Second, it offered individual legal assistance to consumers, having failed to secure such assistance from the local bar association.[50] It is difficult to substantiate directly the shadow effect of the international power dynamics, not least because of the delicate political nature of the conflict.[51] But a somewhat extraordinary sequence of judicial evasions in response to the ombudsman's claim resulted. In essence, "they passed the ball from one to the other and nobody wanted to receive us."[52] The local bar association was similarly reluctant to become involved, and there were vociferous – albeit disputed[53] – claims that the World Bank inserted a condition around that time on a large health and education loan that required conflicts with public service concessions to be eliminated or resolved. ERSACT was marginalized by the provincial government

48 This advice was supported by a series of resolutions issued by the ombudsman's office (No. 66 and No. 67 of 1996) that highlight the details of why the invoicing was incorrect, drawing also on a public auditors' report to the same effect (Tucuman Audit Office Report 015; on file with author).

49 Resolution No. 212 and No. 213, discounting the bills, first, by the amount of disputed taxes that Vivendi was passing through on the bill and, second, by the amount paid for water during the periods that turbid, chocolate-colored water was provided.

50 Maria Bossio, Ombudsman, interviewed by Carolina Fairstein, Tucuman, August 10, 2004.

51 This sensitivity is illustrated by the fact that a lawsuit filed by the provincial attorney-general against Vivendi for breach of contract was later withdrawn when a change of government occurred and has never been refiled, despite the promises of three consecutive attorney-generals to do so (interviews with Ombudsman Bossio fn 52; Maria Pedicone de Valls, Provincial Attorney-General of Tucuman, interviewed by Carolina Fairstein, Tucuman, August 11, 2004; Jose Domieu and Jorge Abdala, President and Vice-president of ADEUCOT consumer association, interviewed by Carolina Fairstein, Tucuman, August 22, 2004.

52 Pedicone de Valls interview. The courts were willing to hear many *individual* claims against nonpayers and issued sentences in relation to them, but the legislature intervened and passed a law suspending the enforcement of these sentences for six months. This law became another aspect of Vivendi's claim in the ICSID process

53 Interviewees gave conflicting reports but an August 13, 1998 report in the local newspaper *La Gaceta* quoted Governor Bussi as saying that US$55 million from the World Bank could not be disbursed until the federal government had taken over the concession, allowing Vivendi to leave.

who intervened in a receiverlike process, appointing an alternative auditor to oversee the concession on the grounds that the company felt persecuted by ERSACT.[54] Overall, there was a distinct sense that World Bank and ICSID processes constrained the domestic substantive and procedural possibilities, even if the precise mechanisms of intervention were disputed or indirect.

In terms of outcomes, the legacy of this intersection of national and transnational developments was ambiguous. The Tucumán water services were renationalized in 2004. Although the state company has struggled to improve water services, the forms of civil society involvement that were catalyzed initially by private sector involvement persisted into the renewed era of public service operation. Civil society continued to promote, after renationalization, many legislative proposals, particularly relating to tariff structures, disconnection, and the recovery of unpaid bills, both before and after the return of water services into public hands. In the short term, effects on participation opportunities in the narrower context of Tucumán were disappointing. No right to public hearings was obtained (although a precedent for this existed in electricity), and a promised consumer representative on ERSACT's Board of Directors never came to fruition. Yet substantive gains were made, including legislative prohibition of water cut-offs to those using less than the basic minimum and a "dispute letter," which boycotting consumers successfully used to stave off legal action by Vivendi for nonpayment, even after the ombudsman's legal action stalled.[55] Procedurally, a kind of "popcorn" incrementalism resulted, with the cumulative, but unintended, effects of opening up more space for responding to consumer concerns.

Beyond Tucumán, however, after a series of consumer group mobilizations in relation to different water services contracts across Argentina, several involving coalitions with international NGOs, a procedural victory of considerable significance emerged – the acceptance by ICSID tribunals of *amicus curiae* briefs from civil society organizations, even in the face of objections from the parties.[56] Interestingly, what we see in these two kinds of gains is an uneasy truce between political regulation at the local level, and a more transactional model, which is the subject of litigation before an international arbitration forum. Even though the ICSID process amendment is a victory for participation, it is a form of participation that still sidesteps democratically elected governments and does nothing to expand their policy space. Taken in conjunction with the recent award of US$105 million by ICSID to Vivendi

[54] Daniel Arancibia, former president of the regulatory body ERSACT (Ente Regulador del Servicio de Agua y Cloadas de Tucuman) and director of the former state-run water company, interviewed by Carolina Fairstein, Tucuman, Argentina, July 1, 2004.

[55] Interview with Jiminez Lascano, DUDAS consumers' association, interviewed by Carolina Fairstein, Tucuman, August 24, 2004.

[56] *Aguas Argentinas S.A., Suez Sociedad General de Aguas de Barcelona S.A., Vivendi Universal S.A. c. República Argentina.* Caso, ARB/03/19. See also more recently a similar order in a case involving the British water company Biwater in Tanzania: *Biwater v Tanzania*, Case No ARB/05/22, Procedural Order No. 5.

for compensation in this dispute, the opportunity to lodge a brief in ICSID hearings appears to be a marginal tweak to the overriding dominance of transactional regulation.

4. CONCLUSION

The three case studies discussed have shown how models of transactional regulation that circulate in the transnational policy field of urban water services regulation are brought to life at local and national levels. Three interrelated findings stand out. First, national variation in the type and salience of regulatory dynamics persists, despite the existence of transnationally rooted "models." Second, where deep political conflict persists, quasi-judicial institutions, especially at the local or national level, are better able to respond to the legitimacy challenges raised by disaffected consumers and citizens than are regulatory agencies, especially agencies modeled on a transactional approach. Third, there are possible feedback effects, where local and national trajectories influence transnational norm flows and the policies of transnational institutions. Together, these results primarily demonstrate the *limits* of transnational legal ordering of state change, and thus the ways in which an understanding of national and local dynamics is essential both to deepening an appreciation of transnational flows of legal norms and to containing the conflicts that are generated. The chapter concludes by summarizing these three findings.

First, the limits of transnational legal ordering: The case studies focused on similar organizational choices in three Latin American countries in the 1990s, each of which formally established semi-independent regulatory agencies to monitor the delivery of water services. These emerged in a context shaped by the influence of conditional lending by international financial institutions and of a strong mainstream transnational consensus on the desirability of transactional regulation. This consensus was embedded in a technocratic epistemic community whose members *included* national elites; in other words, national-international coalitions. No story of a "transnational" transformation of the state is ever purely a story of external molding. Nor is it, in these cases, a story of deep similarities beyond the initial limited degree of institutional isomorphism (Di Maggio & Powell 1991). Rather, national variations persisted, as demonstrated by divergent roles played by the regulator in each case – transactional but marginalized in Bolivia, transactional and politically salient in Chile, political and erratically salient in Argentina. The difference can partly be accounted for by the larger political context in each country: Chile's stability and foreign-investment-friendly approach, provincial-federal conflict in Argentina's divided state followed by an economic crisis, and Bolivia's political and social transformation toward the left. Differences among the configuration of organized social opposition in the three countries, their relative exposure to transnational pressures, and the timing and structure of their reforms also mattered.

While counterposing the Bolivian story with the Chilean story seems to contribute to a sense of polarized conflict *between* regulatory models, certain aspects of Argentina's story point toward the second finding: Where deep political conflict persists, quasi-judicial institutions, especially at the local or national level, are better able to respond to the legitimacy challenges raised by disaffected consumers and citizens than are regulatory agencies. Agencies, especially those modeled on a transactional approach, can rarely absorb conflict from direct protest. The technical and apolitical nature of regulatory discourse is often incommensurable with the value-driven nature of direct protest. In none of the case studies did a regulatory agency *by itself* generate politics that constructively accommodated citizen opposition. In the case of Bolivia, the agency was politically almost irrelevant. In Chile, "bureaucrats with an entrepreneurial kick" were constructive up to a point, but limited in their capacity to draw in the interests of ordinary citizens. In Argentina, the agency risked sliding into unproductive political clientilism, yet did have moments of productive synergy in its interactions with quasi-judicial fora, such as ombudsmen or small claims tribunals.

Such synergies at least routinize conflict, allowing winners and losers to emerge incrementally over time, rather than intensifying polarization in high-stakes rule-making decisions. In this way, quasi-judicial fora can, up to a point, absorb the "missing politics" in regulatory dynamics in constructive ways, as was arguably the case in Argentina. In both Chile and Bolivia, the *lack* of such fora could be seen as undermining the overall legitimacy of the water services policy arena. Here, the macropolitical context for each country is again salient, creating in Bolivia, but not in Chile, an outlet for discontent in mass mobilization and direct protest.

Bridges between regulators and citizens are more sturdily embedded in local and national institutions, particularly of dispute resolution, than in transnational ones. The type of legitimacy deficit that bedeviled the water services investment contracts explored in this chapter is one most intensely felt by local citizens, for whom an international investment arbitration forum *compounds*, rather than tempers, any felt injuries. Of course, transnational companies investing in long-term service contracts in developing countries feel the opposite – that local and national judicial and quasi-judicial fora lack the requisite legitimacy. In Argentina, widening participation rights in international investment arbitration was the response – an uneasy compromise, because this did not alter the distributive politics at the root of the conflict.

However, this development does illustrate the third finding – correlations between local and national trajectories and shifts in transnational flows of regulatory policy norms affecting transnational institutions. I stress "correlations" rather than "feedback effects" because the causality is not always clear. In the specific instance of the expansion of participation avenues in international arbitration, the role of the Argentine experience is unusually clear because this was the first case where NGO participation as *amicus curiae* had been permitted in ICSID. However, this shift was made in the context of broader campaigns of transnational coalitions of social movements, including in light of the Bolivian case, so that the chain of causality is linked not just to the Argentine conflict. The emergence of a transnational coalition of social movements around the issue of water (particularly focusing on the human rights dimension) is a significant recursive effect, one beyond the scope of this chapter.[57]

More broadly, the local support in Bolivia of a political model of regulation may well have implications for future refinement of an approach to global water governance based on participatory democracy. Bolivia's collaboration with Cuba, Nicaragua, and Venezuela on the "Bolivarian Alternative for the Peoples of Our America" supports the development of such an approach for social services in general, including health, education, and other essential infrastructure services.

Other changes in international institutions are indirectly related to the case studies covered here. These have emerged in the wake of repeated and widespread conflicts during the 1990s and early 2000s of the kind chronicled in the case studies. The World Bank has increasingly acknowledged that the "missing politics" identified in this chapter matter, and has responded by funding programs that target legislative institutions in developing countries. These initiatives are contentious and have been criticized for being primarily aimed at public relations, rather than providing a substantive response to the substantive issues, but they nonetheless reflect pressure on international financial institutions. The Inter-American Development Bank has increasingly supported exploration of the role that small-scale independent providers can play in providing water services, and such providers are much more likely to be locally embedded players. Finally, the heated debates on water service provision have, to some extent, moved beyond dichotomous discussions of "public vs. private," to focus increasingly on complex ranges of mixed public-private structures. For example, the German development aid institution Deutsche Gesellschaft für Internationale Zusammenarbeit (GIZ) now supports mixed public-private companies in Bolivia as a viable alternative in the wake of the failed private concessions. Also, the UN Secretary-General's Advisory Group on Water and Sanitation worked with UN-Habitat to focus on supporting public water service providers, mainly through North-South utility partnerships that will provide technical assistance.[58]

This chapter has shown that domestic regulatory politics in relation to social struggles have a transnational dimension. Transnational is neither national nor international, external nor internal; rather, it is a hybrid character embedded in coalitions of local, national, and international actors. Importantly, such coalitions are not restricted to those who support the transactional approach to regulation in the context of global governance. From the currents of conflict over access to water, we also find transnational flows of regulatory policy norms reflecting the

[57] See footnote 12.

[58] See the Global Water Operators' Partnership Alliance: http://www.unhabitat.org/categories.asp?catid=568, as well as www.unsgab.org.

political regulatory alternative, most strongly in Bolivia. These constitute new forms of the transnational, within the contours of particular states and beyond. These forms are emblematic of potential trajectories of transnational regulatory politics in areas beyond water, most obviously affecting other public utilities such as gas and electricity, as well as health and education. The regulatory issue of access to basic drinking water, in sum, provides a case study suggesting that debates over whether it is possible to integrate social policy effectively into global governance are necessarily also debates over domestic regulatory dynamics and how they are shaped by local social and political imaginaries.

8

Conclusion

The Study of Transnational Legal Ordering

Gregory Shaffer

Positivist international law scholars tend to narrow their focus on traditional concepts of international law and, thus, are skeptical of referring to transnational law, transnational legal ordering, and transnational legal process. Yet, focusing on the construction and migration of transnational legal norms through transnational legal processes is critical for the analysis of both how international law itself is constituted and has effects, and how national law and institutions are shaped. This book has evaluated how transnational legal norms and processes *interact* with domestic contexts. In the sociolegal tradition, it heeds close attention to the variable adoption and adaptation of transnational legal norms in particular fields and the factors that explain this variation. The case studies in this book focus their inquiry on distinct regulatory fields (as opposed to separate levels of governance) to assess how the transnational and national interpenetrate. In this way, they illustrate the factors that lead to variation in the location, type, extent, and timing of change spurred by transnational legal processes. Their combination of methods, regulatory areas, and countries helps us create a map for studying how transnational legal ordering works and the limits that it confronts.

The studies do not reify transnational legal ordering, but show how transnational legal norms provide tools for particular actors to advance their aims. Each study examines the role of public and private actors, mechanisms, and attributes of power involved in a particular legal context in different countries. Through a comparative approach, the studies explain variation in countries' responses. Transnationally promoted legal change sometimes catches and sometimes does not, and the studies explain why in light of the stakes arising from the import of transnational legal norms.

This book has set forth a framework for evaluating how transnational legal ordering works, and the implications of such ordering for national law and institutions. We conclude by highlighting six points that the application of this framework illustrates. First, we need to clarify what we mean by transnational law, legal process, and legal orders, in contradistinction to international law and global law. Chapter 1 distinguished *two conceptions* of transnational law, the first being Transnational Law Applying to Transnational Situations (suggesting a particular body of law), and the second being *Transnational Legal Ordering* (a methodology for assessing the transnational construction and flow of legal norms and their implications for state change). The empirical case studies in Chapters 3–7 illustrate and apply this second conception.

Second, we need to more carefully specify the *dimensions* of transnational-induced change within states, because state change is differentiated. Chapter 2 identified five dimensions: (1) change in substantive law and practice; (2) change in the boundary of the state, the market, and other forms of social ordering; (3) change in the institutional architecture of the state; (4) change in professional expertise and expertise's role in governance; and (5) change in associational patterns, which are institutionalized through transnational accountability mechanisms with their accompanying normative frames. By viewing transnationally induced legal change in terms of differentiated dimensions of state change, we gain a richer understanding of how transnational legal ordering operates and the dimensions of change at stake within the nation-state.

Third, we must identify and evaluate the *factors that explain variation in the impact* of transnational legal processes. The second part of Chapter 2 organized these factors into three clusters: (1) the nature of the transnational legal process; (2) its relation to the receiving state; and (3) the particular political, institutional, and cultural context of the receiving state. Where transnational legal norms are clear, coherent, and perceived to be legitimate, they are best positioned to bear influence. Asymmetries of power between the transnational legal order and the receiving state create opportunities for the use of coercive mechanisms, but the effectiveness of these mechanisms may be limited at the implementation stage. Intermediaries are critical for conveying and adapting transnational legal norms to local settings. Crucially, the impact of transnational legal ordering depends on the fit of a transnational legal norm with domestic demand in light of domestic contests for power, institutional capacities and path dependencies, and the extent of change at stake. Where the trajectory of change within a state is synchronous with the transnational legal norm, or where powerful domestic actors wish to harness it as leverage in domestic struggles, then transnational legal processes are more likely to be transformative. Where domestic demand is lacking, change will more likely be thwarted or be purely symbolic. Because domestic institutions and configurations of power mediate the reception of transnational legal norms, the transnational legal norm is often appropriated, adapted, hybridized, and used in distinct and unanticipated ways.

Fourth, the book illustrates the *heterogeneous nature* of transnational legal processes. The term "transnational legal process" is misleading to the extent that it suggests that transnational legal process involves a one-way conveyance of coherent transnational legal norms until they become internalized and embedded within countries, resulting in "compliance." Rather, often multiple transnational actors, institutions, and processes are in competition with each other to convey different legal norms and prescriptions. This competition affects the relative coherence, clarity, and perceived legitimacy of transnational legal orders. In this way, it affects the development of normative consensus regarding a transnational legal order, and, ultimately, the impact of such legal order within states. This is not to say that transnational legal ordering does not matter. To the contrary! It rather means that we need to study both the conditions under which it matters and the variation such ordering takes.

Fifth, studies need to address the *multidirectional nature* of transnational legal processes. Theorizing transnational law in terms of being adopted, adapted, or resisted within national contexts constitutes only part of transnational legal processes. Those focusing only on transnational law's reception fail to capture how national dynamics can generate new politics that affect the transnational legal norm in question. These responses include not only responses of states that are strong and proximate to international institutions, but also those of states that are weak, distant, and peripheral. Assessments of transnational legal ordering should address the dynamic processes pursuant to which the national reception of transnational legal initiatives interacts with the transnational production of legal norms.

Sixth and finally, changes of national law and institutions *cannot be reduced to international realpolitik*. Law plays a mediating role, together with configurations of power. Changes are often initiated, negotiated, and implemented by the agents, practitioners, and institutions of law – government lawyers, legal departments of international organizations, judges, private lawyers, corporate legal officers, legal academics, and lawyers for nongovernmental organizations. This complex of legal actors is neither uniform in its legal views nor united in a policy agenda, and it operates in the shadow of configurations of national and global power structures.[1] These actors nonetheless form an important part of the politics of transnational lawmaking and transnational legal norm conveyance. Moreover, national institutions and legal norms are resilient. When transnational legal processes lead to legal and institutional change, they do so in context-specific ways involving the intermediation of transnational legal processes with domestic institutions, political struggles, and cultural norms. This book's empirical studies provide grounding for understanding these processes and their impacts.

Although this book's analytic framework and empirical case studies are not prescriptive, their implications for the advancement of any normative goal are critical. What is at stake is the effectiveness of transnational legal processes and legal orders, on the one hand, and the degrees of freedom that states and nonstate constituencies retain to determine their futures, on the other. Whether one is an advocate of international or transnational law in promoting state change in a particular domain, or

[1] Cf. Dezalay & Garth 2010; and Halliday, Karpik, & Feeley 2007.

a resister of such international and transnational pressures and influences, understanding the broader institutional and social implications of transnationally induced legal change, and the factors that promote or impede it, is critical. That is what is at stake in transnational legal ordering, whether the substantive field entails human rights law, public regulatory law, or private business law.

This book is not normative in its approach, but its framing implicitly reflects two normative concerns. First, understanding the processes of international and transnational law's production, which often has a structural tilt in favor of certain states and nonstate actors, is important for understanding their relative effectiveness (or ineffectiveness) at the implementation stage. In this way, the project draws attention to the role of the legitimacy of transnational legal orders. Second, it is important that international and transnational law scholars give greater attention to the implications of transnational legal process in non-US and non-European states in light of their particular contexts. In the process, they can provide greater voice to the perceptions and priorities of constituencies in those locations.

The study of transnational legal process and state change beckons for further analysis and, thus, calls for systematic research agendas. The costs of engaging in this research are relatively high, but so are the payoffs. How do transnational legal orders maximize their authority? When is transnationally induced legal change primarily symbolic, and when does it have practical effects? When are particular national institutions, such as courts and legislatures, empowered or disempowered? What are the critical factors and conditions? What spurs the reassessment and development of transnational legal norms over time? By focusing on the dynamic interaction of transnational legal norms and national law and institutions in particular regulatory fields, the studies in this book provide the basis for a richer understanding of transnational legal ordering and state change, its opportunities, its limits, and its implications.

References

Abbott, Kenneth W., and Duncan Snidal. 2000. Hard and Soft Law in International Governance. *International Organization* 54:421–56.

Abouharb, Rodwan D., and David L. Cingranelli. 2006. The Human Rights Effects of World Bank Structural Adjustment, 1981–2000. *International Studies Quarterly* 50:233–62.

Achen, Christopher H. 2000. Why Lagged Dependent Variables Can Suppress the Explanatory Power of Other Independent Variables. *Political Methodology Working Paper*.

African National Congress. 1994a. A *National Health Plan for South Africa: Prepared by the ANC With Technical Support of WHO and UNICEF*.

______. 1994b. *The Reconstruction and Development Programme: A Policy Framework*. Johannesburg: South Africa.

African National Congress NEC Subcommittee. 2009. National Health Insurance Policy proposal, 22 June 2009.

African National Congress National General Council. 2010. Additional Discussion Documents, Section 1: National Health Insurance.

Ahdieh, Robert. 2006. Dialectical Regulation. *Connecticut Law Review* 38:861–965.

AIDS Law Project and Treatment Action Campaign. 2003. The Price of Life: Hazel Tau and Others versus GlaxoSmithKline and Boehringer Ingelheim. A Report on the Excessive Pricing Complaint to South Africa's Competition Commission.

Alford, William P. 1997. *To Steal a Book Is an Elegant Offense: Intellectual Property Law in Chinese Civilization*. Stanford, CA: Stanford University Press.

Alldridge, Peter. 2008. Money Laundering and Globalization. *Journal of Law and Society* 35:437–63.

Aman, Alfred C. Jr. 2004. *The Democracy Deficit: Taming Globalization through Law Reform*. New York: New York University Press.

Andreas, Peter, and Ethan Nadelmann. 2006. *Policing the Globe: Criminalization and Crime Control in International Relations*. New York: Oxford University Press.

Asian Development Bank (ADB). 1996. *Final Report, State Enterprise Insolvency Reform*. Manila: Asian Development Bank.

______. 1999. *Law and Development at the Asian Development Bank*. Manila: Asian Development Bank.

______. 2000. Report on Insolvency Law Reforms in the Asian and Pacific Region. *Law and Policy Reform Bulletin* I:10–86.

Australian Federation of AIDS Organization. 2000. Letter of cogratulations to Dr Helen Rees, Chairperson of the MCC, 12 December 2000.
Avelino, George, David S. Brown, and Wendy Hunter. 2005. The Effects of Capital Mobility, Trade Openness, and Democracy on Social Spending in Latin America, 1980–1999. *American Journal of Political Science* 49 (3):625–41.
Ayres, Ian, and John Braithwaite. 1992. *Responsive Regulation*. New York: Oxford University Press.
Babb, Sarah. 2005. The Social Consequences of Structural Adjustment: Recent Evidence and Current Debates. *Annual Review of Sociology* 31:199–222.
BACENJUD. 2005. *Manual Básico*.
Bachrach, Peter, and Morton Baratz. 1962. Two Faces of Power. *American Political Science Review* 56:947–952.
Bakker, Karen. 2009. Regulation of Water and Sanitation Services: Insights from The Water Dialogues, www.waterdialogues.org/thematic.htm.
Baltagi, Badi. 1995. Editor's Introduction: Panel Data. *Journal of Econometrics* 68:1–4.
Bappenas. 1998. *Law Reform in Indonesia: Diagnostic Assessment of Legal Development in Indonesia*. Edited by Ali Budiardjo, Nugroho, and Reksodiputro. Jakarta: Cyberconsult.
Barnett, Michael, and Raymond Duvall. 2005. Power in Global Governance. In *Power in Global Governance*, edited bys. Michael Barnett and Raymond Duvall. New York: Cambridge University Press.
Barrett, Deborah, and Amy Ong Tsui. 1999. 'Policy as Symbolic Statement: International Response to National Population Policies.' *Social Forces* 78:213–34.
Benavot, Aaron, and Julia Resnick. 2006. Lessons from the Past: A Comparative Socio-Historical Analysis of Primary and Secondary Education. In *Educating All Children: A Global Agenda*, edited by Joel E. Cohen, David E. Bloom, and Martin B. Malin, 123–229. Cambridge, MA: American Academy of Arts and Sciences.
Benavot, Aaron, and Phyllis Riddle. 1988. The Expansion of Primary Education, 1870–1940: Trends and Issues. *Sociology of Education* 61 (3):191–210.
Berger, Jonathan, 2005. AIDS Law Project, letter to Angelo Kondes, CEO Abbot Labs, South Africa re shortages of Ritonavir, February 14, 2005.
Berkovitch, Nitza. 1999. *From Motherhood to Citizenship*. Baltimore: Johns Hopkins University Press.
Berkowitz, Daniel, Katharina Pistor, and Jean-Francois Richard. 2003. Economic Development, Legality, and the Transplant Effect. *European Economic Review* 47:165–195.
Berman, Paul Schiff. 2007. Global Legal Pluralism. *Southern California Law Review* 80:1155–1238.
Blazejewski, Kenneth. 2008. The FATF and Its Institutional Partners: Improving the Effectiveness and Accountability of Transgovernmental Networks. *Temple International and Comparative Law Journal* 22:1–62.
Block-Lieb, Susan, and Terence C. Halliday. 2006. Legitimation and Global-Normmaking, http://papers.ssrn.com/sol3/papers.cfm?abstract_id=952492.
Block-Lieb, Susan, and Terence C. Halliday. 2007a. Harmonization and Modernization in UNCITRAL's Global Legislative Guide on Insolvency Law. *Texas International Law Journal* 42:481–514.
———. 2007b. Incrementalisms in Global Lawmaking. *Brooklyn Journal of International Law* XXXII:851–903.
Bobbitt, Philip. 2002. *The Shield of Achilles: War, Peace, and the Course of History*. New York: Alfred A. Knopf.

Bodansky, Daniel. 1999. The Legitimacy of International Governance: A Coming Challenge for International Environmental Law. *American Journal of International Law* 93:596–624.

Boli, John, and George Thomas, eds. 1999. *Constructing World Culture: International Nongovernmental Organizations since 1875*. Stanford, CA: Stanford University Press.

Booz Allen, and Hamilton. 1997. Revitalizing the Korean Economy towards the 21st Century. Seoul, Korea.

Boyle, Elizabeth Heger, and Minzee Kim. 2009. International Human Rights, Neoliberal Economic Reforms, and Child Well-Being. *Law and Society Review* 43 (3):455–90.

Boyle, Elizabeth Heger, and John W. Meyer. 1998. Modern Law as a Secularized and Global Model. *Soziale Welt* 49:275–94.

Boyle, Elizabeth Heger, Trina Smith, and Katja Guenther. 2006. The Rise of the Child as an Individual in Global Society. In *Youth, Globalization, and the Law*, edited by Sudhir A. Venkatesh and Ronald Kassimir, 255–83. Stanford, CA: Stanford University Press.

Braithwaite, John. 1993. Following the Money Trail to What Destination? An Introduction to the Symposium. *Alabama Law Review* 44:657–68.

______. 2002. Rules and Principles: A Theory of Legal Certainty. *Australian Journal of Legal Philosophy*. 27:47–82.

______. 2005. Methods of Power for Development: Weapons of the Weak, Weapons of the Strong. *Michigan Journal of International Law* 26:297–330.

Braithwaite, John, and Peter Drahos. 2000. *Global Business Regulation*. New York: Cambridge University Press.

Braithwaite, John, and Philip Petit. 1990. *Not Just Deserts: A Republican Theory of Criminal Justice*. Oxford: Oxford University Press.

Brazilian Parliament. 2004. Foreign Affairs and National Defense Commission. Request no. 25/2004. Available at www.camara.gov.br/proposicoesWeb/fichadetramitacao?idProposicao=250378 (accessed June 25, 2012).

______. 1998. Law no. 9613, March 3, 1998 (Brazil, Money Laundering Act).

Brewster, Rachel. 2003. Domestic Origins of International Agreements. *Virginia Journal of International Law* 44(2):1–42.

Brummer, Chris. 2011. How International Financial Law Works (and How It Doesn't). *Georgetown Law Journal* 99:257–327.

Burley, Anne-Marie Slaughter. 1993. International Law and International Relations Theory: A Dual Agenda. *American Journal of International Law* 87:205–39.

Business Insights. 2010. The South African Pharmaceutical Market Outlook to 2014: Policy Environment, Market Structure, Competitive Landscape, Growth Opportunities. Available at http://www.google.com/url?sa=t&rct=j&q=&esrc=s&source=web&cd=4&ved=0CDMQFjAD&url=http%3A%2F%2Fwww.research-store.com%2Ftechnologynetworks%2FDownload%2FToc%2F%3FproductId%3DDF1C2BF8-FCBD-408D-9FA8-936887FB9D46&ei=tCJGUNWZJIbKrAf7xIH4Dg&usg=AFQjCNEmP-uOh2AbXjPv_APvFNbIxl6tiw (accessed September 4, 2012).

Büthe, Timothy, and Walter Mattli. 2011. *The New Global Rulers: The Privatization of Regulation in the World Economy*. Princeton, NJ: Princeton University Press.

Buxbaum, Hannah L. 2006. Transnational Regulatory Litigation. *Virginia Journal of International Law* 46:251–317.

Calliess, Gralf Peter, and Peer Zumbansen. 2010. *Rough Consensus and Running Code: A Theory of Transnational Law-Making*. Oxford: Hart.

Campbell, John L. 2004. *Institutional Change and Globalization*. Princeton, NJ: Princeton University Press.

Cao, Siyuan. 1998a. The Storm over Bankruptcy (I). *Chinese Law and Government* 31(1):3–90.

______. 1998b. The Storm over Bankruptcy (II). *Chinese Law and Government* 31(2):11–96.

Carruthers, Bruce G., Sarah L. Babb, and Terence C. Halliday. 2001. Institutionalizing Markets, or the Market for Institutions? Central Banks, Bankruptcy Law and the Globalization of Financial Markets. In *The Rise of Neoliberalism and Institutional Analysis*, edited by John Campbell, and Ove Pedersen, 94–126. Princeton, NJ: Princeton University Press.

Carruthers, Bruce, and Terence C. Halliday. 1998. *Rescuing Business: The Making of Corporate Bankruptcy Law in England and the United States*. Oxford: Oxford University Press.

______. 2006. Negotiating Globalization: Global Scripts and Intermediation in the Construction of Asian Insolvency Regimes. *Law and Social Inquiry* 31:521–84.

______. 2007. Law, Economy and Globalization: How Modern International Financial Institutions Embraced Adam Smith and Accidently Discovered Max Weber. In *The Spirit of Global Capitalism*, edited by Richard Swedberg and Victor Nee, 128–51. Stanford, CA: Stanford University Press.

______. Forthcoming. Law, Economy and Globalization: How Modern International Financial Institutions Embraced Adam Smith and Accidently Discovered Max Weber. in *The Spirit of Global Capitalism*, edited by Richard Swedberg and Victor Nee. Stanford, CA: Stanford University Press.

Caruso, Daniela. 2006. Private Law and State – Making in the Age of Globalization. *New York University Journal of International Law and Politics* 39:1–74.

Chabbott, Colette. 1999. Defining Development: The Making of the International Development Field, 1945–1990. In *Constructing World Culture: International Nongovernmental Organizations Since 1875*, edited by John Boli and George Thomas, 222–48. Stanford, CA: Stanford University Press.

Chase-Dunn, Christopher, and Thomas Hall. 1997. *Rise and Demise: Comparing World Systems*. Boulder, CO: Westview Press.

Chng, N. 2007. Civil Society and Water Services Provision in the Philippines. Discussion Paper prepared for Wateraid, on file with author.

Clemens, Michael. 2004. The Long Walk to School: International Education Goals in Historical Perspective. *Working Papers* 37, Center for Global Development.

Clift, Jenny. 2002. *The UNCITRAL Model Law on Cross-Border Insolvency* – An Answer to Insolvency Issues in the Framework of International Trade and of International Projects. *UCL/Siena Symposium on International Insolvency*. Louvain-la-Neuve, Belgium.

COAF – Conselho de Controle de Atividades Financeiras. 2008. *Relatorio de Atividades*.

Commission for Conciliation, Mediation and Arbitration (CCMA). 1999. *Commission for Conciliation, Mediation and Arbitration Award in the case of Public Servants Association of South Africa (on behalf of J. Schlebusch & C. Brückner) vs. the Department of Health*, Case No.GA51345, Commissioner J. Hiemstra, awarded on November 26, 1999.

Conca, K. 2006. *Governing Water: Contentious Transnational Politics and Global Institution Building*. Cambridge, MA: MIT Press.

Consumer Project on Technology. 1999. Appendix B: Time-Line of Disputes Over Compulsory Licensing and Parallel Importation in South Africa, August 5, 1999, http://www.cptech.org/ip/health/sa/sa-timeline.txt (accessed June 28, 2012).

Cornia, Giovanni Andrea. 1987. Adjustment at the Household Level: Potentials and Limitations of Survival Strategies. In *Adjustment with a Human Face*, edited by Giovani Andrea Cornia, Richard Jolly, and Frances Stewart, 90–104. New York: UNICEF/Oxford: Clarendon Press.

Costa, Carlos. 2008. Entrevista com Antonio Gustavo Rodrigues: Uma Visão Mais Pragmática do Direito Penal. *Revista Getulio* 11:36–40.

Cotterrell, Roger. 1992. *The Sociology of Law: An Introduction*, 2nd ed. Austin, TX: Butterworths.
Cox, Robert W. 1994. Global Restructuring: Making Sense of the Changing International Political Economy. In *Political Economy and the Changing Global Order*, edited by Richard Stubbs and Geoffrey R. D. Underhill. New York: St. Martin's Press.
Cumings, Bruce. 1997. *Korea's Place in the Sun: A Modern History*. New York: Norton.
Dahl, Robert. 1957. The Concept of Power. *Behavioral Science* 2:201–15.
______. 1968. Power. In *International Encyclopedia of the Social Sciences*, ed. David Sills. New York: Macmillan.
Davis, Kevin E., Benedict Kingsbury, and Sally Engle Merry. 2012. Indicators as a Technology of Global Governance. *Law and Society Review* 46(1):71–104.
Davis, M. 2006. *Planet of Slums*. London: Verso.
De Beer, Cedric. 1984. *The South African Disease: Apartheid, Health and Health Services*. Johannesburg: South African Research Service.
Deeb, M. T. 1998a. Founding Affidavit by M.T. Deeb, 18 February 1998, High Court of South Africa, Pretoria, South Africa.
______. 1998b. Supplementary Affidavit by M. T. Deeb, 23 July 1998, High Court of South Africa. Pretoria, South Africa.
Department of Health. 1996. National Drug Policy for South Africa, January 1996.
______. 1997. *White Paper for the Transformation of the Health System in South Africa*. Pretoria, South Africa: Government Press.
Delmas Marty, Mireille. 2004a. *Le Flou du Droit*. Paris: Presses Universitaires de France.
______. 2004b. *Les Forces Imaginante du Droit. Le Relatif et l'Universel* [Imaginative forces of law: the relative and the universal]. Paris: Seuil.
______. 2006. *Les Forces Imaginante du Droit. Le Pluralisme Ordonné* [Imaginative force of law: the organized pluralism]. Paris: Seuil.
De Soysa, Indra, and John R. Oneal. 1999. Boon or Bane? Reassessing the Productivity of Foreign Direct Investment. *American Sociological Review* 64 (5):766–82.
Dezalay, Yves, and Bryant Garth. 2002a. Introduction. In *Global Prescriptions: The Production, Exportation and Importation of a New Legal Orthodoxy*, edited by Yves Dezalay and Bryant Garth. Ann Arbor, MI: University of Michigan Press.
______. 2002b. *The Internationalization of Palace Wars: Lawyers, Economists, and the Contest to Transform Latin American States*. Chicago: University of Chicago Press.
______. 2010. *Asian Legal Revivals: Lawyers in the Shadow of Empire*. Chicago: University of Chicago Press.
Dibadj, Reza. 2008. Panglossian Transnationalism. *Stanford Journal of International Law* 44:253–99.
Digeser, Peter. 1992. The Fourth Face of Power. *The Journal of Politics* 54:977–1007.
Di Maggio, Paul J., and Walter W. Powell. 1991. *The New Institutionalism in Organizational Analysis*. Chicago: Chicago University Press.
Dublin Statement on Water and Sustainable Development. 1992. International Conference on Water and Environment.
Djelic, Marie-Laure, and Kerstin Sahlin-Andersson. 2006. *Transnational Governance: Institutional Dynamics of Regulation*, edited by Marie-Laure Djelic and Kerstin Sahlin-Andersson. Cambridge, UK: Cambridge University Press.
Doob, Anthony, and Cheryl Webster. 2003. Sentence Severity and Crime: Accepting the Null Hypothesis. *Crime and Justice* 30:143–95.
Doyle, Todd. 2002. Cleaning Up Anti-Money Laundering Strategies: Current FATF Tactics Needlessly Violate International Law. *Houston Journal of International Law* 24:279–313.

Drahos, Peter. 2008. 'Trust Me': Patent Offices in Developing Countries. *American Journal of Law and Medicine* 34:151–74.
———. 2009. Cooperation, Trust and Risk in the World's Major Patent Offices. *Science and Public Policy* 36:641–47.
———. 2010. *The Global Governance of Knowledge: Patent Offices and Their Clients*. New York: Cambridge University Press.
Drahos, Peter, and John Braithwaite. 2002. *Information Feudalism: Who Owns the Knowledge Economy?* New York: The New Press.
Dubash, N. 2005. Regulation as an Arena for Social Policy. Conference paper delivered for Arusha Conference, *New Frontiers for Social Policy*, December 2005.
Duraisamy, P., Estelle James, Julia Lane, and Jee-Peng Tan. 1997. Is There a Quantity-Quality Tradeoff as Enrollments Increase? Evidence from Tamil Nadu, India. *Policy Research Working Paper Series* 1768, World Bank.
Easterly, William 2007. *The White Man's Burden: Why the West's Efforts to Aid the Rest Have Done So Much Ill and So Little Good*. New York: Penquin.
Egmont Group. 2004. *Statement of Purpose*. 2010. *Annual Report*, 2009–2010.
Elkins, Zackary, Tom Ginsburg, and Beth Simmons. 2012. Constitutional Convergence in Human Rights: The Reciprocal Relationship of Human Rights Treaties and National Constitutions. In *Implementing Commitments: The Domestic Effects of Human Rights Treaty Ratification*, edited by Ryan Goodman and Beth Simmons, New York: Oxford
ENCCLA. 2010. *Plan of Action*.
Erwin, Alec. 1999. Interview published in *Global Dialogue*, Vol. 4(1). Johannesburg, South Africa: Institute for Global Dialogue.
Esty, Dan. 2006. Good Governance at the Supranational Scale: Globalizing Administrative Law. *Yale Law Journal* 115:1490–562.
European Bank for Reconstruction and Development (EBRD). 1999. Transition Report 1999: Ten Years of Transition. London: EBRD.
European Commission. 2004. EU Water Facility.
Evans, J., and A. Himelfarb. 2000. *Criminology: A Canadian Perspective*. Toronto, ON: Harcourt Brace.
Evans, Ruth. 2002. Poverty, HIV, and Barriers to Education: Street Children's Experiences in Tanzania. *Gender and Development* 10 (3):51.
Fausto, Boris, and Fernando Devoto. 2004. *Brasil e Argentina: Um Ensaio de História Comparada* [Brazil and Argentina: an essay of comparative history]. São Paulo: Editora 34.
FATF - Financial Action Task Force. 1990. *Annual Report*.
———. 2000. *Annual Report*.
———. 2003. Forty Recommendations.
———. 2004a. *Annual Report*.
———. 2004b. *Methodology for Assessing Compliance with the FATF 40 Recommendations and the FATF 8 Special Recommendations*.
———. 2009. *Annual Report*.
———. 2010. *Annual Report*.
Feldman, Yuval, and Dorion Teichman. 2009. Are all Legal Probabilities Created Equal? *New York University Law Review* 84: 980–1022.
Fernando, Jude L. 2001. Children's Rights: Beyond the Impasse. *The Annals of the American Academy of Political and Social Science* 575 (1):8.
Financial Action Task Force (FATF) and GAFISUD. 2004. *Informe de evaluacion mutual sobre lavado de activos y financiamento del terrorismo. Brasil*. (Evaluation report on money laundering and terrorism financing. Brazil.)

Fischer-Lescano, Andreas, and Gunther Teubner. 2004. Regime-Collisions: The Vain Search for Legal Unity in the Fragmentation of Global Law. *Michigan Journal of International Law* 25:999–1046.

Flaschen, Evan D. and Ronald J. Silverman. 1994. Maxwell Communication Corporation plc: The Importance of Comity and Co-operation in Resolving International Insolvencies. In pp. 41–57 in *Current Issues in Cross-Border Insolvency and Reorganisations*, edited by E. Bruce Leonard and Christopher W. Besant, 41–57. London: Graham and Trotman.

———. 1998. Cross-Border Insolvency Cooperation Protocols. *Texas International Law Journal* 33:587–613.

Fletcher, Ian. 1997. The European Union Convention on Insolvency Proceedings: An Overview and Comment, with U.S. Interest in Mind. *Brooklyn Journal of International Law* 23:25–55.

Foster, V. 2001. Ten Years of Water Service Reform in Latin America: Towards an Anglo-French Model., Water Supply and Sanitation Sector Board Discussion Paper 3, available at www.worldbank.org/watsan.

Foucault, Michel. 1984. *Legitimacy and the State*. New York: New York University Press.

Fourcade-Gourinchas, Marion, and Sarah Babb. 2002. The Rebirth of the Liberal Creed: Paths to Neoliberalism in Four Countries. *American Journal of Sociology* 108(3):533–79.

Foweraker, J. Grassroots Movements, Political Activism and Social Developments in Latin America: A Critical Comparison of Chile and Brazil. *Journal of Latin American Studies* 33(4) (2001):839–65.

Franck, Thomas. 1990. *The Power of Legitimacy among Nations*. New York: Oxford University Press.

Friedman, Lawrence M. 1996. Borders: On the Emerging Sociology of Transnational Law. *Stanford Journal of International Law* 32:65–90.

Friedman, Lawrence M. 1997. The Concept of Legal Culture: A Reply. In *Comparing Legal Cultures*, edited by David Nelken, 33–39. Dartmouth, NH: Dartmouth Publishing.

Friedmann, Wolfgang. 1964. *The Changing Structure of International Law*. New York: Columbia University Press.

G-22. 1998a. *Report of the Working Group on International Financial Crises*. Washington, DC: World Bank.

———. 1998b. Summary of Reports on the International Financial Architecture. Washington, DC: G22.

Garth, Bryant, and Yves Dezalay. 2010. Marketing and Selling Transnational 'Judges' and Global 'Experts': Building the Credibility of (Quasi) Judicial Regulation. *Socio-Economic Review* 8:113–30.

Gathii, James Thuo. 2010. *The Financial Action Taskforce and Global Administrative Law*. Legal Studies Research Paper Series, 10. Albany, NY: Albany Law School.

Geffen, Nathan. 2010. *Debunking Delusions: The Inside Story of the Treatment Action Campaign*. Auckland Park, South Africa: Jacana Media.

General Accounting Office (GAO). 1996. *Money Laundering: A Framework for Understanding U.S. Efforts Overseas*. Washington, DC: General Accounting Office

Gertler, Paul, and Paul Glewwe. 1992. The Willingness to Pay for Education for Daughters in Contrast to Sons: Evidence from Rural Peru. *World Bank Economic Review* 6:171–88.

Gevisser, Mark. 2007. *Thabo Mbeki: A Dream Deferred*. Cape Town, South Africa: Jonathan Ball Publishers.

Ginsburg, Thomas, and Gregory Shaffer. 2010. How Does International Law Work?: What Empirical Research Shows. In *Oxford Handbook of Empirical Legal Studies*, edited by Peter Cane and Herbert Kritzer. Oxford: Oxford University Press.

Gleick, Peter, Gary Wolff, Elizabeth L. Chalecki, and Rachel Reyes. 2002. *The New Economy of Water*. Oakland, CA: Pacific Institute for Studies in Development, Environment, and Security.

Glenn, H. Patrick. 2003. A Transnational Concept of Law. In *The Oxford Handbook of Legal Studies*, edited by Peter Cane and Mark Tushnet. Oxford: Oxford University Press.

Goldman, Michael. 2005. *Imperial Nature: The World Bank and Struggles for Social Justice in the Age of Globalization*. New Haven, CT and London: Yale University Press.

Goodman, Ryan, and Derek Jinks. 2012. *Socializing States: Promoting Human Rights through International Law*. Oxford: Oxford University Press.

———. 2004. How to Influence States: Socialization and International Human Rights Law. *Duke Law Journal* 54:1217–46.

Gott, Richard, and Georges Bartoli. 2005. *Hugo Chavez: the Bolivarian Revolution in Venezuela*. London: Verso.

Govender, Pregs. 2007. *Love and Courage: A Story of Insubordination*. Auckland Park, SA: Jacana Media.

Grattet, Ryken, Valerie Jenness, and Theodore R. Curry. 1998. The Homogenization and Differentiation of Hate Crime Law in the United States, 1978 to 1995. *American Sociological Review* 63:286–307.

Grootaert, Christiaan, and Ravi Kanbur. 1995. Child Labor: an Economic Perspective. *International Labour Review*, 134:187–203.

Grossman, Joel B., and Mary H. Grossman. 1971. *Law and Change in Modern America*. Eds. Joel B. Grossman and Mary H. Grossman. Pacific Palisades, CA: Goodyear Publishing Co.

Gruber, Lloyd. 2000. *Ruling the World: Power Politics and the Rise of Supranational Institutions*. Princeton, NJ: Princeton University Press.

Guehenno, Jean-Marie. 1995. *The End of the Nation-State*. Minneapolis: University of Minnesota Press.

Guizzini, Stefano. 2000. A Reconstruction of Constructivism in International Relations. *European Journal of International Relations* 6:147–82.

Hafner-Burton, Emilie M., and Kiyoteru Tsutsui. 2005. Human Rights in a Globalizing World: The Paradox of Empty Promises. *American Journal of Sociology* 110(5):1373.

Halaby, Charles N. 2004. Panel Models in Sociological Research: Theory into Practice. *Annual Review of Sociology* 30:507–44.

Hall, Peter. 1993. Policy Paradigms, Social Learning and the State. *Comparative Politics* 25:275–96.

Halliday, Terence C. 2007. Architects of the State: International Organizations and the Reconstruction of States in the Global South. Paper presented at the Annual Meetings of the Law and Society Association, July 2007, in Berlin, Germany.

———. 2009. Recursivity of Global Lawmaking: A Sociolegal Agenda. *Annual Review of Law and Social Science* 5:263–90.

———. 2010. Legal Yardsticks: International Financial Institutions as Legal Diagnosticians and Remedial Agents. In *Indicators as a Technology of Global Governance*. Institute for International Law and Justice New York University School of Law.

Halliday, Terence C., Susan Block-Lieb, and Bruce G. Carruthers. 2009. Rhetorical Legitimation: Global Scripts as Strategic Devices of International Organizations. *European Socio-Economic Review* 2009:1–36.

Halliday, Terence C., and Bruce Carruthers. 1996. The Moral Regulation of Markets: Professions, Privatization and the English Insolvency Act 1986. *Accounting, Organizations and Society* 21:371–413.

______. 1998. Making the Courts Safe for the Powerful: The Politics of Lawyers, Judges, and Bankers in the 1978 Rehabilitation of United States Bankruptcy Courts. In *Lawyers and the Rise of Western Political Liberalism: Legal Professions and the Constitution of Modern Politics*, edited by Terence C. Halliday and Lucien Karpik, 265–304. Oxford: Oxford University Press.

______. 2004a. Epistemological Conflicts and Institutional Impediments: The Rocky Road to Corporate Bankruptcy Reforms in Korea. In *Legal Reform in Korea*, edited by Tom Ginsburg, 114–33. London: RoutledgeCurzon Press.

______. 2004b. Institutional Lessons from Insolvency Reforms in East Asia. *Forum on Asian Insolvency Law Reform (FAIR), Insolvency and Risk Management in Asia*. Delhi, India: World Bank and Asian Development Bank.

______. 2007. The Recursivity of Law: Global Norm Making and National Lawmaking in the Globalization of Corporate Insolvency Regimes. *American Journal of Sociology* 112:1135–1202.

______. 2007. Foiling the Financial Hegemons: Limits to the Globalisation of Corporate Insolvency Regimes in Indonesia, Korea and China. In *Globabalisation and Resistance: Law Reform in Asia since the Crisis*, edited by Christoph Anton and Volkmar Gessner, 255–301. Oxford: Hart Publishing.

______. 2009. *Bankrupt: Global Lawmaking and Systematic Financial Crisis*. Stanford, CA: Stanford University Press.

Halliday, Terence C., and Pavel Osinsky. 2006. Globalization of Law. *Annual Review of Sociology* 32:447–70.

Halliday, Terence C., Lucien Karpik, and Malcolm M. Feeley. 2007. The Legal Complex in Struggles for Political Liberalism. In *Fighting for Political Freedom: Comparative Studies of the Legal Complex and Political Change*, edited by Terence C. Halliday, Lucien Karpik, and Malcolm M. Feeley. Oxford: Hart Publishing.

Halliday, Terence C., and Gregory Shaffer. 2012. Transnational Legal Orders (working paper).

Hansard. 1998. Debates of the National Assembly, Parliament, South Africa, vol. 19, September 9, 6835.

Harding, Christopher. 2006. Business Collusion as a Criminological Phenomenon: Exploring the Global Criminalisation of Cartels. *Critical Criminology* 14:181–205.

Harrigan, Jane, and Paul Mosley. 1991. Evaluating the Impact of World Bank Structural Adjustment Lending: 1980–87. *The Journal of Development Studies* 27(3):63–94.

Harrison, David. 2009. An Overview of Health and Health Care in South Africa 1994–2010: Priorities, Progress and Prospects for New Gains: A Discussion Document Commissioned by the Henry J. Kaiser Family Foundation* to Help Inform the National Health Leaders' Retreat Muldersdrift, January 24–26 2010.http://www.bhfglobal.com/files/bhf/overview1994-2010.pdf.

Hassim, Adile, Mark Heywood, and Jonathan Berger, eds. 2007. *Health & Democracy: A Guide to Human Rights, Health Law and Policy in Post-Apartheid South Africa*. Cape Town: SiberInk.

Hathaway, Oona A. 2005. Between Power and Principle: An Integrated Theory of International Law. *University of Chicago Law Review* 72:469–536.

Held, David. 2004. *Global Covenant: The Social Democratic Alternative to the Washington Consensus*. Cambridge, UK: Polity Press.

Held, David, et al. 1999. *Global Transformations: Politics, Economics and Culture*. Stanford, CA: Stanford University Press.

Helfer, Lawrence. 2004. Regime Shifting: The TRIPS Agreement and New Dynamics of Intellectual Property Lawmaking. *Yale Journal of International Law* 29:1–83.

Hepple, Bob. 2005. *Labour Laws and Global Trade*. Oxford; Portland, OR: Hart Publishing.
Heywood, Mark. 2005. The Achilles Heel? The Impact of HIV/AIDS on Democracy in South Africa. In *HIV/AIDS in South Africa*, edited by Abdool S. S. Karin and Q. Abdool Karim. Cambridge, UK: Cambridge University Press.
Hironaka, Ann, and Evan Schofer. 2002. Decoupling in the Environmental Arena: The Case of the Environmental Impact Assessment. In *Organizations, Policy, and the Natural Environment: Institutional and Strategic Perspectives*, edited by Andrew Hoffman and Marc Ventresca, 214–231. Stanford, CA: Stanford University Press.
Hirsch, Alan. 2005. *Season of Hope: Economic Reform under Mandela and Mbeki*. Scottsville, South Africa: University of KwaZulu-Natal Press.
Houtzager, Peter. 2005. The Movement of the Landless (MST), Juridical Field, and Legal Change in Brazil. In *Law and Globalization from Below: Towards a Cosmopolitan Legality*, edited by Boaventura Santos and Cesar Rodríguez-Garavito. New York: Cambridge University Press.
Houtzager, Peter, and Marcus J. Kurtz. 2000. The Institutional Roots of Popular Mobilization: State Transformation and Rural Politics in Brazil and Chile, 1960–95. *Comparative Studies in Society and History* 42(2):394–424.
Huber, Evelyne, and John D. Stephens. 2001. *Development and Crisis of the Welfare State: Parties and Policies in Global Markets*. Chicago: The University of Chicago Press.
Hulsse, Rainer, and Dieter Kerwer. 2007. Global Standards in Action: Insights from Anti-Money Laundering Regulation. *Organization* 14:625–42.
Hurd, Ian. 2007. *After Anarchy*. Princeton, NJ: Princeton University Press.
———. 2008. Theories and Tests of International Authority. In *The UN Security Council and the Politics of International Authority*, edited by Bruce Cronin and Ian Hurd. New York: Routledge.
International Labour Organization. 1973. Minimum Age Convention.
———. 1999. Worst Forms of Child Labour Convention.
International Law Commission. 2006. Fragmentation of International Law: Difficulties Arising from the Diversification and Expansion of International Law.: UN Doc. A/CN.4/L.682 (finalized by Martti Koskenniemi). Helsinki: University of Helsinki.
International Monetary Fund (IMF). 1999. *Orderly and Effective Insolvency Procedures: Key Issues*. Washington DC: International Monetary Fund.
———. Various years. *Government Finance Statistics Yearbook*. Washington, DC: International Monetary Fund.
Iskander, Magdi, Gerald Meyerman, Dale F. Gray, and Sean Hagan. 1999. Corporate Restructuring and Governance in East Asia. *Finance and Development* 36:42–45.
Jenness, Valerie, and Ryken Grattet. 2001. *Making Hate a Crime: From Social Movement to Law Enforcement*. New York: Cambridge University Press.
Jessup, Philip. 1956. *Transnational Law*. New Haven, CT: Yale University Press.
Jones, Phillip W. 2007. *World Bank Financing of Education: Lending, Learning, and Development*, Second edition. New York and London: Routledge.
Jones, Phillip W. with David Coleman. 2005. *The United Nations and Education*. New York, NY: RoutledgeFalmer.
Jordana, Jancint and David Levi-Faur. 2005. The Diffusion of Regulatory Capitalism in Latin America: Sectoral and National Channels in the Making of a New Order. *Annals of the American Academy of Political and Social Science* 598:102–24.
Jorge, Guillermo. 2010. Politicas de Control del Lavado de Dinero. In *Drogas y Prohibición. Una Vieja Guerra, un Nuevo Debate* [Policies of control of money laundering. Drugs and Prohibitions: An old war, a new debate], edited by Juan Gabriel Tokatlian. Buenos Aires: Libros del Zorzal.

Kapczynski, Amy. 2009. Harmonization and Its Discontents: A Case Study of TRIPS Implementation in India's Pharmaceutical Sector. *California Law Review* 97:1571.

Kapczynski, Amy, and Jonathan M. Berger. 2009. The Story of the TAC Case: The Potential and Limits of Socio-Economic Rights Litigation in South Africa. In *Human Rights Advocacy Stories*, edited by Deena R. Hurwitz, Margaret L. Satterthwaite, and Douglas B. Ford. New York: Foundation Press.

Kattan, Raja Bentaouet, and Nicholas Burnett. 2004. User Fees in Primary Education. *World Bank Report*.

Kaufman, Robert R., and Alex Segura-Ubiergo. 2001. Globalization, Domestic Politics, and Social Spending in Latin America: A Time-Series Cross-Section Analysis, 1973–97. *World Politics* 53:553–87.

Kaul, Inge, Pedro Conceicao, Katell le Goulven, and Ronald U. Mendoza. 2003. Why Do Global Public Goods Matter Today. In *Providing Global Public Goods: Managing Globalization*, edited by Inge Kaul, Pedro Conceicao, Katell le Goulven, and Ronald U. Mendoza. Oxford, UK: Oxford University Press/UNDP.

Keck, Margaret, and Kathryn Sikkink. 1998. *Activists beyond Borders*. Ithaca, NY: Cornell University Press.

Kelemen, R. Daniel. 2004. Globalization, Federalism, and Regulation. In *Dynamics of Regulatory Change*, edited by David Vogel and Robert A. Kagan. Berkeley: University of California Press.

Kennedy, David. 2005. Challenging Expert Rule: The Politics of Global Governance. *Sydney Law Review* 26:5.

Kennedy, Peter. 1998. *A Guide to Econometrics*, fourth ed. Cambridge, MA: The MIT Press.

Keohane, Robert, and Joseph Nye. 2003. Global Governance and Democratic Accountability. In *Taming Globalization: Frontiers of Governance*, edited by David Held and Mathias Koenig-Archibuigui.

Kerf, Michel, and Izaguirre, Ada K. 2007. *Revival of Private Participation in Developing Country Infrastructure: A Look at Recent Trends and Policy Implications*, Washington, DC: World Bank http://info.worldbank.org/etools/docs/library/240081/Revival%20of%20private%20participation%20in%20developing%20country%20infrastructure.pdf accessed June 25, 2012.

Kgara, Sidney, and Sheila Barsel. 2010. IPAP and the Need for a State-owned Pharmaceutical Company. *African Communist*: Special Issue: Towards a New Growth Path, Issue No. 180, 2nd and 3rd Quarter 2010.

Killick, Tony. 1996. Principals, Agents and the Limitations of BWI Conditionality. *World Economy* 19(2):211.

Kingsbury, Benedict. 2009. The Concept of 'Law' in Global Administrative Law. *European Journal of International Law* 20:23–57.

Kingsbury, Benedict, Nico Krisch, and Richard Stewart. 2005. The Emergence of Global Administrative Law. *Law and Contemporary Problems* 68:15–61.

Klerck, G. 1996. Regulation Theory: Towards a synthesis in development studies. In *Reconstruction, Development, and People*, edited by Jan Coetzee and Johann Graaff. Johannesburg, South Africa: International Thomson Publishing.

Klug, Heinz. 2000. *Constituting Democracy: Law, Globalism, and South Africa's Political Reconstruction*. New York: Cambridge University Press.

______. 2002. Hybrid(ity) Rules: Creating Local Law in a Globalized World. In *Global Prescriptions: The Production, Exportation and Importation of a New Legal Orthodoxy*, edited by Yves Dezalay and Bryant Garth. Ann Arbor, MI: University of Michigan Press.

———. 2005. Campaigning for Life: Building a New Transnational Solidarity in the Face of HIV/AIDS and TRIPS. In *Law and Globalization from Below: Towards a Cosmopolitan Legality*, edited by Boaventura de Sousa Santos and Cesar A Rodreguez. Cambridge, UK: Cambridge University Press.
———. 2008. Law, Politics and Access to Medicines in Developing Countries. *Politics and Society* 36:207–45.
———. 2010a. Risking Health: HIV/AIDS and the Problem of Access to Essential Medicines. In *Disaster and the Politics of Intervention*, edited by Andrew Lakoff. New York: Columbia University Press and Social Science Research Council.
———. 2010b. *The Constitution of South Africa: A Contextual Analysis*. Cambridge, UK: Hart Publishing.
Koh, Harold Hongju. 2006. Why Transnational Law Matters. *Penn State International Law Review* 24:745–53.
———. 2004. International Law as Part of Our Law. *American Journal of International Law* 98:43–57.
———. 1998. The 1998 Frankel Lecture: Bringing International Law Home. *Houston Law Review* 35:623–81.
———. 1997. Why Do Nations Obey International Law. *Yale Law Journal* 106:2599–2659.
Koslowski, Rey and Friedrich Kratochwil. 1994. Understanding Change in International Politics: The Soviet Empire's Demise and the International System. *International Organization* 48:215–47.
Kwamboka, Evelyn. 2011. High Court Enjoins UN in Case Against Generic ARVs Ban. *The Standard*, Nairobi, Kenya, January 17, 2011.
Lafer, Celso, and Celso La Peña. 1973. *Argentina e Brasil no Contexto das elações Internacionais* [Argentina and Brazil in the context of international relations]. São Paulo: Duas Cidades.
Lane, Timothy, Atish Ghosh, Javier Hamann, Steven Phillips, Marianne Schulze-Ghattas, and Tsidi Tsikata. 1999. *IMF-Supported Programs in Indonesia, Korea, and Thailand: A Preliminary Assessment*. Washington, DC: International Monetary Fund.
La Porta, Rafael, Florencio Lopez-de-Silanes, Andre Schleifer, and Robert W. Vishny. 1997. Legal Determinants of External Finance. *Journal of Finance* 52:1131–50.
LeClerc, Guy, and Thierry Raes. 2001. *Water: A World Financial Issue*. PriceWaterhouse-Coopers, Sustainable Development Series.
Lee, Kuk-Woon. 2007. Corporate Lawyers in Korea: An Analysis of the 'Big 4' Law Firms in Seoul. In *Korea and Japan: Judicial System in Transformation in the Globalizing World*, edited by Dai-Kwon Choi. Seoul: Seoul National University Press.
Legh, Robert. 2002. A History of South African Competition Law. In *Competition Law*, edited by Martin Brassey. Cape Town: Juta.
Leibfried, Stephan, and Michael Zürn. 2005. *Transformations of the State?* New York: Cambridge University Press.
Levi, Michael. 2002. Money Laundering and Its Regulation. *Annals of the American Academy of Political and Social Science* 582:181–94.
Levi, Michael, and William Gilmore. 2002. Terrorist Finance, Money Laundering and the Rise and Rise of Mutual Evaluation: A New Paradigm for Crime Control? *European Journal of Law Reform* 4:337–64.
Levi, Michael, and Peter Reuter. 2006. Money Laundering. *Crime and Justice* 4:289–375.
Levit, Janet Koven. 2008. Bottom-Up Lawmaking Through a Pluralist Lens: The ICC Banking Commission and the Transnational Regulation of Letters of Credit. *Emory Law Journal* 57:1147–1226.

Levi-Faur, David. 2005. The Global Diffusion of Regulatory Capitalism. *Annals of the American Academy of Political and Social Science* 598:12–32.

Liu, Sida, and Terence C. Halliday. 2009. Recursivity in Legal Change: Lawyers and Reforms of China's Criminal Procedure Law. *Law and Social Inquiry* 34:911–50.

Liu, Dongxiao, and Elizabeth Heger Boyle. 2001. Making the Case: The Women's Convention and Equal Employment Opportunity in Japan. *International Journal of Comparative Sociology* 42(4):389–404.

Loya, Thomas, and John Boli. 1999. Standardization in the World Polity. In *Constructing World Culture: International Nongovernmental Organizations since 1875*, edited by John Boli and George Thomas. Stanford, CA: Stanford University Press.

Lukes, Stephen. 1974. *Power: A Radical View*. New York: Macmillan.

Lumman, Niklas. 1982. *The Differentiation of Society*. New York: Columbia University Press.

Machado, Maira. 2011. Modern Penal Rationality Left Behind: A Call for Innovative Thinking and Practice in Criminal Law. In *The Law of the Future and the Future of Law*, edited by Sam Muller, Stravos Zouridis, Morly Frishman, and Laura Kistemaker, 683–93. Oslo: Torkel Opsahl Academic EPublisher.

Machado, Maira, and Guillermo Jorge. 2009. Los Regimenes Contra el avado de Activos en el Contexto del Derecho Administrativo Global. In *El Nuevo Derecho Administrativo Global en America Latina* [Money laundering regimes in the context of global administrative law. The new global administrative law in Latin America], edited by Benedict Kingsbury, and Richard Stewart. Buenos Aires: Ediciones Rap.

Mahdavi, Saeid. 2004. Shifts in the Composition of Government Spending in Response to External Debt Burden. *World Development* 32(7):1139–57.

Mail and Guardian. 2008. Cartel Country. *Mail and Guardian*, June 13, 2008.

Makene, Fortunata Songora. 2007. Tanzanian Responses to Contradictory Requirements in International Law on Issues Relating to Children and Elders. PhD dissertation, Department of Sociology, University of Minnesota, Minneapolis, MN.

Mako, William P. 2001. Corporate Restructuring in East Asia: Promoting Best Practices. *Finance & Development* 38:2–5.

______. 2002a. Corporate and Financial Sector Restructuring: Links and Necessary Conditions. In *Second Annual International Seminar on Policy Challenges for the Financial Sector in the Context of Globalization*. Washington, DC.

______. 2002b. Corporate Restructuring and Reform: Lessons from Korea. In *Korean Crisis and Recovery*, edited by David T. Coe and Se-Jik Kim, 203–28. Washington, DC: International Monetary Fund/Korea Institute for International Economy Policy.

______. 2003. Uses and Limitations of Out-of-Court Workouts: Lessons from East Asia. *Global Forum on Insolvency Risk Management*. Washington, DC.

Malanczuk, Peter. 1997. *Akehurst's Modern Introduction to International Law*, revised Seventh edition. London: Routledge.

Maloney, Christopher, and Nick Segal. 2007. Genesis: The Growth Potential of the Pharmaceuticals Sector in South Africa, May 29, 2007. http://www.imsa.org.za/download/imsa_and_pharmaceutical_industry_profile/GENESIS%20Pharmaceuticals%20Report%20070529%20(2).pdf, accessed June 25, 2012.

Marais, Hein. 2001. *South Africa: Limits to Change*. Cape Town: University of Cape Town Press (quoting Nelson Mandela).

______. 2002. The Logic of Expediency: Post-Apartheid Shifts in Macroeconomic Policy. In *Thabo Mbeki's World: The Politics and Ideology of the South African President*, edited by Sean Jacobs and Richard Calland. Scotsville. South Africa: University of Natal Press.

Marin, Philippe. 2009. *Public-Private Partnerships for Urban Water Utilities: A Review of Experiences in Developing Countries*. Washington, DC: World Bank

Marin, Philippe, and Izaguirre, Ada K. 2006. *Private Participation in Water: Toward a New Generation of Projects?* Washington, DC: World Bank.

Marshall, Monty G., and Keith Jaggers. 2002. *Polity IV Dataset*. College Park, MD: University of Maryland, Center for International Development and Conflict Management.

Marteau, Juan Felix. 2008. No Hay Castigo Para el Lavado de Dinero [There's no punishment for money laundering in Argentina.] *La Nacion* (Buenos Aires), October 02, 2008.

———. 2010. Lavado de Dinero: Estandardizacion y Criminalizacion. Notas para una Politica Criminal Contra el Criminen Financiero en la Argentina Globalizada [Money laundering: standardization and criminalization: Remarks for a criminal policy against financial crime in Argentina.] *Enfoques Contabilidad y Auditoria* 7:102–25.

Mattei, Ugo, and Laura Nader. 2008. *Plunder: When the Rule of Law Is Illegal*. Malden, MA: Blackwell.

McClintock, Brent. 1999. The Multinational Corporation and Social Justice: Experiments in Supranational Governance. *Review of Social Economy* 57:507–22.

McIntyre, Di, and Alex Van den Heever. 2007. Social or National Health Insurance. *South African Health Review* 71–88.

McLeod, Heather. 2009. National Health Insurance Background Brief: NHI in South Africa: 1940–2008 (Innovative Medicines South Africa, 2009). http://www.imsa.org.za/national-health-insurance/imsa-nhi-policy-briefs/

Mead, George Herbert. 1934. *Mind, Self, and Society from the Standpoint of a Social Behaviorist*, edited by Charles W. Morris. Chicago: University of Chicago Press.

Medecins Sans Frontieres. 2007. *Campaign for Access to Essential Medicines, Untangling the Web of Price Reductions: A Pricing Guide for the Purchase of ARVs for Developing Countries*, Tenth edition.

———. 2011. Don't Swallow This Pill, January 20, 2011.

Meidinger, Errol. 2009. Private Import Safety Regulation and Transnational New Governance. http://papers.*ssrn.com/sol3/papers.cfm?abstract_id=1416758*. Retrieved 05/24/10.

MER of Argentina. 2010. Mutual Evaluation Report of Argentina. FATF and GAFISUD.

MER of Brazil. 2010. Mutual Evaluation Report of Brazil. FATF and GAFISUD.

Merry, Sally Engle. 2006. *Human Rights and Gender Violence: Translating International Law into Local Justice*. Chicago: University of Chicago Press.

———. 2006. Transnational Human Rights and Local Activism: Mapping the Middle. *American Anthropologist* 108:38–51.

———. 1990. *Getting Justice and Getting Even: Legal Consciousness Among Working-Class Americans*. Chicago: University of Chicago Press.

Meyer, John W. 1980. The World Polity and the Authority of the Nation-State. In *Studies of the Modern World System*, edited by Albert Bergesen, 109–37. New York: Academic Press.

———. 2007. Globalization. *International Journal of Comparative Sociology* 48(4): 261–73.

Meyer, John, John Boli, George Thomas, and Frank Ramirez. 1997a. World Society and the Nation-State. *American Journal of Sociology* 103:144–81.

Meyer, John W., Ann Hironaka, Evan Schofer, and Nancy Tuma. 1997b. The Structuring of a World Environmental Regime, 1870–1990. *International Organization* 51:623–51.

Meyerman, Gerald E. 2000. The London Approach and Corporate Debt Restructuring in East Asia. In *Conference on Emerging Markets in the New Financial System: Managing Financial and Corporate Stress*. Upper Saddle River, NJ: Prentice Hall.

Mhone, Guy, and Omano Edigheji eds. 2003. *Governance in the New South Africa: The Challenges of Globalization*. Cape Town: University of Cape Town Press.

Ministry of Finance and Economy, Korea (MOFE). 2001. Law for Promotion of Corporate Restructuring. Seoul, South Korea: Government of Korea.

______. 2002. *Corporate Promotion Restructuring Act*. Seoul, South Korea: Government of Korea.

Minogue, Martin, and Ledivina Carino, eds. 2006. *Regulatory Governance in Developing Countries*. Manchester: Edward Elgar Press.

Moodaliyar, Kasturi, and Trudi Hartzenberg. 2006. Report on the Fifth Annual Conference of the International Competition Network. http://www.internationalcompetitionnetwork.org (accessed September 4, 2011).

Mooney, Gavin H., and Diane E., McIntyre. 2008. South Africa: A 21st Century Apartheid in Health and Health Care? *The Medical Journal of Australia* 189(11/12):637–40.

Moore, Sally, Falk. 1974. Law and Social Change: The Semi-Autonomous Social Field as an Appropriate Subject of Study. *Law and Society Review* 7:719–46.

Morgan, Bronwen. 2004a. The Regulatory Face of the Human Right to Water. *Journal of Water Law* 15:179–87.

______. 2004b. Water: Frontier Markets and Cosmopolitan Activism. *Soundings: A Journal of Politics and Culture*. 27: 10–24.

______. 2005. Social Protest against Privatization of Water: Forging Cosmopolitan Citizenship? In *Sustainable Justice: Reconciling International Economic, Environmental and Social Law*, edited by Marie-Clair Cordonier Seggier and Justice Weeramantry. Leiden, The Netherlands: Martinus Nijhoff Publishers.

______. 2006a. Emerging Global Water Welfarism: Access to Water, Unruly Consumers and Transnational Governance. In *Consumer Cultures, Global Perspectives*, edited by Frank Trentmann and John Brewer. Oxford: Berg Press.

______. 2006b. Turning Off the Tap, Urban Water Service Delivery and the Social Construction of Global Administrative Law. *European Journal of International Law* 17(1):215–46.

______. 2006c. The North-South Politics of Necessity: Regulating for Basic Rights Between National and International Levels. Special Issue: *Journal of Consumer Policy on The Politics of Necessity* 29(4):465–87.

______. 2007a. Consuming without Paying: Stealing or Campaigning? The Civic Implications of Civil Disobedience around Access to Water. In *Citizenship and Consumption*, edited by Kate Soper and Frank Trentmann. Basingstoke: Palgrave MacMillan.

______. 2007b. Local Politics and the Regulation of Global Water Suppliers in South Africa. In: *Making Global Self-Regulation Effective in Developing Countries*, Chapter 10, edited by Dana Brown, and Ngaire Woods. Oxford: Oxford University Press.

______. 2007c. Reflections on Governance in the International Context. In *Governance and Consumption: Agency and Resistance*, edited by Mark Bevir and Frank Trentmann. Basingstoke, UK: Palgrave MacMillan.

______. 2007d. Global Business, Local Constraints: The Case of Water in South Africa. In *Making Global Self-Regulation Effective in Developing Countries*, Chapter 10, edited by Dana Brown and Ngaire Woods. Oxford: Oxford University Press.

______ (ed.). 2007e. *The Intersection of Rights and Regulation: New Directions in Socio-Legal Scholarship*. Aldershot, UK: Ashgate Press.

______. 2008. Building Bridges Between Regulatory and Citizen Space: Civil Society Contributions to Water Service Delivery Frameworks in Cross-National Perspective. *Law, Social Justice & Global Development Journal* (1):1–16.

______. 2011. *Water on Tap: Rights and Regulation in the Transnational Governance of Urban Water Services*. Cambridge, UK: Cambridge University Press.

Morgan, Bronwen, and Frank Trentmann. 2006. The Politics of Necessity. Special Issue: *Journal of Consumer Policy on The Politics of Necessity* 29:4.

Mosley, Paul, Jane Harrigan, and John Toye. 1991. *Aid and Power: The World Bank and Policy-Based Lending*. London: Routledge.

Mugarura, Norman. 2011. The Global Anti-Money Laundering Court as a Judicial and Institutional Imperative. *Journal of Money Laundering Control* 14:60–78.

Muhr, Thomas. 2008. Venezuela: Global Counter-Hegemony, Geographies of Regional Development, and Higher Education for All. Ph.D. Dissertation, University of Bristol, December 2008.

Muncie, John. 2001. Official Crime Statistics. In *Sage Dictionary of Criminology*, edited by Eugene McLaughlin and John Muncie. London: Sage.

Mundy, Karen. 1998. Educational Multilateralism and World (Dis)order. *Comparative Education Review* 42(4):448–78.

Mundy, Karen, and Lynn Murphy. 2001. Transnational Advocacy, Global Civil Society? Emerging Evidence from the Field of Education. *Comparative Education Review* 45(1):85–126.

______. 2006. Education for All and the New Development Compact. In *Education and Social Justice*, edited by J. Zajda, S. Majhanovich, and V. Rust, 13–38. The Netherlands: Springer.

Mutangadura, Gladys B., Judith R. Blau, and Vicki L. Lamb. 2002. External Debt and Secondary Education in Sub-Saharan Africa: A Dynamic Analysis. *The Journal of African Policy Studies* 8(1):1–15.

Naldelmann, Ethan A. 1993. *Cops across Borders: The Internationalization of U.S. Criminal Law Enforcement*. University Park, PA: The Pennsylvania State University Press.

Nam, Il Chong, and Soogeun Oh. 2000. *Bankruptcy of Large Firms and Exit Mechanisms in Korea*. Seoul: Korean Development Institute.

Nattrass, Nicoli. 2007. *Mortal Combat: AIDS Denialism and the Struggle for Antiretrovirals in South Africa*. Scottsville, SA: University of KwaZulu- Natal Press.

Nelken, David, and Johannes Feest. 2001. *Adapting Legal Cultures, 2001*, edited by David Nelken and Johannes Feest. Oxford: Hart.

Nonet, Philippe, and Philip Selznick. 1978. *Law and Society in Transition, Toward Responsive Law* (new edition with preface by Robert Kagan 2001). New Brunswick, NJ: Transaction Publishers.

North, Douglass C. 1990. *Institutions, Institutional Change and Economic Performance*. Cambridge: Cambridge University Press.

O'Brien, Peter. 1998. The Normalization of the International Market for Pharmaceuticals: Future Impacts in Emerging Markets. In *Medicines and the New Economic Environment*, edited by Felix Lobo and German Velasquez. Madrid, Spain: WHO, University Carlos III, Civitas.

OECD. 2004. *Education at a Glance: OECD Indicators 2004*, pp. 233–40. Paris.

OECD. 2008. Asian Insolvency Systems: Closing the Implementation Gap. Paris: OECD Publishing.

Ogbu, Osita M., and Mark Gallagher. 1991. On Public Expenditures and Delivery of Education in Sub-Saharan Africa. *Comprehensive Educational Review* 35:295–318.

Oh, Soogeun. 1999. *An Institutional Perspective on Financial Reform in Korea*. Seoul: Korea Development Bank Report.

______. 2001. Bankruptcy Division and Commissioner. In *Insolvency Reform in Asia: An Assessment of the Recent Developments and the Role of the Judiciary*. Bali, Indonesia.

______. 2002. *Will Corporate Restructuring Promotion Act Really Promote Corporate Restructuring?* Hong Kong: Hong Kong University Faculty of Law.

———. 2003. Insolvency Law Reform of Korea: A Continuing Learning Process. In *Forum on Insolvency Risk Management*. Washington, DC.

———. 2005. Changes in Insolvency Practice, Restructuring of Ailing Firms and Risk Management after the Economic Crisis: The Korea Case. In *International Workshop on Reform of Corporate Governance: Corporate Rehabilitations in East Asia and its Lesson for China*. Beijing, China.

Oh, Soogeun, and Terence C. Halliday. 2009. Rehabilitating Korea's Corporate Insolvency Regime, 1992–2007. In *Pushing Back against Globalisation*, edited by John Gillespie and Randall Peerenboom, 13–38. London: RoutledgeCurzon.

———. Forthcoming. Rehabilitating Korea's Corporate Insolvency Regime, 1992–2007. In *Pushing Back against Globalisation*, edited by John Gillespie and Randall Peerenboom. London: RoutledgeCurzon.

Ohmae, Kenichi. 1990. *The Borderless World: Power and Strategy in the Inter-linked Economy*. New York: Harper Business.

———. 1995. *The End of the Nation-State: The Rise of Regional Economies*. New York: Free Press.

Ostrom, Charles. 1990. *Time Series Analysis: Regression Techniques*, Second edition. Newbury Park, CA: Sage.

Ottaway, Marina. 1993. *South Africa: The Struggle for a New Order*. Washington, DC: Brookings.

Palley, Thomas I. 2002. A New Development Paradigm: Domestic Demand-led Growth. *Foreign Policy in Focus* 1–8.

Passas, Nikos. 2009. Combating Terrorist Financing: General Report of the Cleveland Preparatory Colloquium. *Case Western Reserve Journal of International Law* 41:243–62.

Paxton, Pamela, Melanie M. Hughes, and Jennifer Green. 2006. The International Women's Movement and Women's Political Representation, 1893–2003. *American Sociological Review* 71(6):898–920.

Peck, J., and A. Tickell. 2002. Neoliberalizing Space. *Antipode* 34(3):380–404.

Peerenboom, Randall. 2002. *China's Long March toward Rule of Law*. New York: Cambridge University Press.

———. 2006. What Have We Learned about Law and Development? Describing, Predicting, and Assessing Legal Reforms in China. *Michigan Journal of International Law* 27:823–71.

Peng, Xiaohua. 1987. Characteristics of China's First Bankruptcy Law. *Harvard International Law Journal* 28:373–84.

Petryna, Adriana, and Arthur Kleinman. 2006. The Pharmaceutical Nexus. In *Global Pharmaceuticals: Ethics, Markets, Practices*, edited by Adriana Petryna, Andrew Lakoff, and Arthur Kleinman. Durham, NC and London, UK: Duke University Press.

Picciotto, Sol. 1996. Networks in International Economic Integration: Fragmented States and the Dilemmas of Neo-Liberalism. *Northwestern Journal of International Law and Business* 17:1014.

Pieth, Mark, and Gemma Aiolfi. 2003. The Private Sector Becomes Active: The Wolfsberg Process. *Journal of Financial Crime* 10:359–65.

Pile, Jacqui. 2005. Aspen Pharamcare: Clinical Coup. *Financial Mai* 182(3), July 15, 2005.

Pincus, Jonathan, and Rizal Ramli. 1998. Indonesia: From Showcase to Basket Case. *Cambridge Journal of Economics* 22:723–34.

Pires, Alvaro. 2001. La Rationalité Pénale Moderne, La Société du Risque et la Juridicisation de l'Opinion Publique [Modern penal rationality, risk society and the public opinion]. *Sociologie et Société* 33:179–204.

———. 2008. La Formation de la Rationalité Pénale Moderne au XVIIIe Siècle. In *Histoire des Savoirs sur le Crime et la Peine* [The modern penal rationality at the eighteenth century.

History of crime and punishment] vol. 2, edited by Christian Debuyst, Françoise Digneffe, Jean-Michel Labadie, and Alvaro Pires. Brussels: Larcier.
Pistor, Katharina, Yoram Keinan, Jan Kleinhesiterkamp, and Mark D. West. 2002. Evolution of Corporate Law and the Transplant Effect: Lessons from Six Countries. *World Bank Research Observer* 18(1):89–112.
Pistor, Katharina, and Philip Wellons. 1999. *The Role of Law and Legal Institutions in Asian Economic Development, 1960–1995*. New York: Oxford University Press.
Rajagopal, Balakrishnan. 2003. *International Law from Below: Development, Social Movements and Third World Resistance*. New York: Cambridge University Press.
Raustiala, Kal, and David G. Victor. 2004. The Regime Complex for Plant Genetic Resources. *International Organization* 58:277–309.
Resnik, Judith. 2006. Law's Migration: American Exceptionalism, Silent Dialogues, and Federalism's Multiple Ports of Entry. *Yale Law Journal* 115:1564–1670.
______. 2008. Law as Affiliation: 'Foreign Law,' Democratic Federalism, and the Sovereigntism of the Nation-State. *International Journal of Constitutional Law* 6:33–66.
Resnik, Judith, Joshua Civin, and Joseph Frueh. 2008. Ratifying Kyoto at the Local Level: Sovereigntism, Federalism, and Translocal Organizations of Government Actors (TOGAs). *Arizona Law Reviews* 50:709–786.
Rhodes, R.A.W. 1996. The New Governance: Governing without Government. *Political Studies* 44:652–67.
Richardson, James L. 2001. *Contending Liberalisms in World Politics: Ideology and Power*. Boulder, CO: Lynne Rienner Publishers.
Robinson, William I. 2001. Social Theory and Globalization: The Rise of a Transnational State. *Theory and Society* 30:157–200.
Rogowski, Ronald. 1989. *Commerce and Coalitions: How Trade Affects Domestic Political Alignments*. Princeton, NJ: Princeton University Press.
Rudra, Nita, and Stephan Haggard. 2005. Globalization, Democracy, and Effective Welfare Spending in the Developing World. *Comparative Political Studies* 38(9):1015–49.
Ruggie, John Gerard. 2003. Taking Embedded Liberalism Global: The Corporate Connection. In *Taming Globalization: Frontiers of Governance*, edited by David Held and Mathias Koenig-Archibugi. Cambridge, UK: Polity Press.
Sachs, Albie. 2009. *The Strange Alchemy of Life and Law*. Oxford, UK: Oxford University Press.
Sadasivam, Bharati. 1997. The Impact of Structural Adjustment on Women: A Governance and Human Rights Agenda. *Human Rights Quarterly* 19:630–65.
Salacuse, Jeswald W. 2000. From Developing Countries to Emerging Markets: The Legal Challenges of Economic Change. *International and Comparative Law Journal* 2:277–95.
Salama, Pierre. 2009. Argentina, Brasil e México Diante da Crise Internacional [Argentina, Brazil and Mexico facing the international crisis]. *Estudos Avançados* 23:27–48.
Sanders, David, and Mickey Chopra. 2006. Key Challenges to Achieving Health for All in an Inequitable Society: The Case of South Africa. *American Journal of Public Health* 96(1):73–8.
Sandholtz, Wayne, and Alec Stone Sweet. 2004. Law, Politics, and International Governance. In *The Politics of International Law*, edited by Christian Reus-Smit. New York: Cambridge University Press.
Santos, Boaventura de Sousa. 2000. Law and Democracy: (Mis)trusting the Global Reform of Courts. In *Globalizing Institutions: Case Studies in Regulation and Innovation*, edited by Jane Jenson and Boaventura De Sousa Santos, 252–81. Aldershot; Burlington: Ashgate.

———. 2003. *Toward a New Legal Common Sense*, Second edition. London: Butterworths LexisNexis.

Santos, Boaventura de Sousa, and Cesar A Rodriguez, eds. 2005. *Law and Globalization from Below: Towards a Cosmopolitan Legality*. Cambridge, UK: Cambridge University Press.

Sassen, Saskia. 1996. *Losing Control? Sovereignty in an Age of Globalization*. New York: Columbia University Press.

———. 2006. *Territory, Authority, Rights: From Medieval to Global Assemblages*. Princeton, NJ: Princeton University Press.

———. 2007. *A Sociology of Globalization*. New York: WW Norton.

Saul, John S. 2002. Cry For The Beloved Country: The Post-Apartheid Denouement. In *Thabo Mbeki's World: The Politics and Ideology of the South African President*, edited by Sean Jacobs and Richard Calland. Scotsville, South Africa: University of Natal Press.

Schafer, Mark J. 1999. International Nongovernmental Organizations and Third World Education in 1990: A Cross-National Study. *Sociology of Education* 72:69–88.

Scharpf, Fritz W. 1999. *Governing in Europe: Effective and Democratic?* New York: Oxford University Press.

Scheppele, Kim. 2011. Global Security Law and the Challenge to Constitutionalism after 9/11. *Public Law* 353–377.

Schmitthoff, Clive. 1961. International Business Law: A New Law Merchant. *Current Law and Social Problems* 2:129.

Scott, Craig. 2009. Transnational Law as Proto-Concept: Three Conceptions. *German Law Journal* 10:859–76.

Scott, Craig, and Robert Wai. 2004. Transnational Governance of Corporate Conduct Through the Migration of Human Rights Norms: The Potential Contribution of Transnational Private Litigation. In *Transnational Governance and Constitutionalism*, edited by Christian Joerges, Inger-Johanne Sand, and Gunther Teubner, 287–319.

Scott, Joanne. 2003. European Regulation of GMOs and the WTO. *Columbia Journal of European Law* 9:213–39.

———. 2009. From Brussels with Love: The Transatlantic Travels of European Law and the Chemistry of Regulatory Attraction. *American Journal of Comparative Law* 57:897–942.

Section 27 and TAC. 2010. Section 27 and TAC Applaud Successful ARV Medicine Tender – But Call for Continued Actions to Drive Price of Essential Medicines Down Further, December 15, 2010. Available at: http://www.section27.org.za/wpcontent/uploads/2010/12/ARV_2010_Ten der.pdf

Sell, Susan, 2003. *Private Power, Public Law: The Globalization of Intellectual Property Rights*. Cambridge, UK: Cambridge University Press

Sen, Amartya. 1999. *Developments as Freedom*. New York: Anchor Books.

Shadlen, Kenneth. 2007. The Political Economy of AIDS Treatment: Intellectual Property and the Transformation of Generic Supply. *International Studies Quarterly* 51(3):559–81.

Shaffer, Gregory. 2000. Globalization and Social Protection: The Impact of EU and International Rules in the Ratcheting Up of U.S. Privacy Standards. *Yale Journal of International Law* 25:1–88.

———. 2009. How Business Shapes Law: A Socio-Legal Framework. *Connecticut Law Review* 42:147–83.

———. 2012. Transnational Legal Process and State Change: Opportunities and Constraints. *Law and Social Inquiry* 3:1.

Shaffer, Gregory, and Thomas Ginsburg. 2012. The Empirical Turn in International Legal Scholarship. *The American Journal of International Law* 106(1):1–46.

Shaffer, Gregory, and Nathaniel Nesbitt. 2011. Criminalizing Cartels: A Global Trend. *Sedona Conference Journal* 12:313–36.

Shaffer, Gregory, and Mark A. Pollack. 2010. Hard vs. Soft Law: Alternatives, Complements and Antagonists in International Governance. *Minnesota Law Review* 94:706–99.

Shaffer, Gregory, Michelle Ratton-Sanchez, and Barbara Rosenberg. 2008. The Trials of Winning at the WTO: What Lies Behind Brazil's Success. *Cornell International Law Journal* 41:383–501.

Sharman, J. C. 2008. Power and Discourse in Policy Diffusion: Anti-Money Laundering in Developing States. *International Studies Association* 52:635–56.

Sikkink, Kathryn. 2011. *The Justice Cascade: How Human Rights Prosecutions Are Changing World Politics*. New York: WW Norton.

Silva, Gisele, Nicola Tynan, and Yesim Yilmaz. 1998. Private Participation in the Water and Sewerage Sector—Recent Trends. *Public Policy for the Private Sector* 147:1.

Simmel, Georg. 1994. Bridge and Door. *Theory, Culture & Society* 11:5–10.

Simmons, Beth. 2009. *Mobilizing for Human Rights: International Law in Domestic Politics*. Cambridge: Cambridge University Press.

Simmons, Beth, Frank Dobbin, and Geoffrey Garrett. 2008. *The Global Diffusion of Markets and Democracy*. Cambridge: Cambridge University Press.

Simpson, Robin. 2006. Universal Access in the Water and Sanitation Sector. In *Liberalisation and Universal Access to Basic Services* 97–134. Paris: OECD.

Slaughter, Anne-Marie. 2000. A Liberal Theory of International Law. *American Society of International Law Proceedings* 94:240–53.

———. 2003. Global Government Networks, Global Information Agencies, and Disaggregated Democracy. *Michigan Journal of International Law* 24:1041–75.

———. 2004. *A New World Order*. Princeton, NJ: Princeton University Press.

Smith, Jackie, Charles Chatfield, and Ron Pagnucco. 1997. *Transnational Social Movements and Global Politics: Solidarity Beyond the State*. Syracuse, NY: Syracuse University Press.

Smith, Jackie. 1995. Transnational Political Processes and the Human Rights Movement. *Research on Social Movements, Conflict, and Change* 18:185–220.

Snyder, Francis. 2002. Governing Globalisation. In *Transnational Legal Processes: Globalisation and Power Disparities*, edited by Michael Likovsky. London: Butterworths.

Sorensen, Georg. 2004. *The Transformation of the State: Beyond the Myth of Retreat*. New York: Palgrave Macmillan.

South Africa. 1997. Medicines and Related Substances Control Amendment Act 90 of 1997, December 12, 1997.

———. 1986. Government Notice 801, Government Gazette No. 10211, May 2, 1986.

Spar, Debora L. 1998. The Spotlight on the Bottom Line: How Multinationals Export Human Rights. *Foreign Affairs* 77(2):7–12.

Stanley, David T., and Marjorie Girth. 1971. *Bankruptcy: Problem, Process, Reform*. Washington, DC: Brookings Institution.

Steiner, Henry J., Detlev F. Vagts, and Harold Hongju Koh. 1994.*Transnational Legal Problems*, Fourth edition. Westbury, NY: Foundation Press.

Stessens, Guy. 2000. *Money Laundering: A New International Law Enforcement Model*. New York: Cambridge University Press.

Stokes, Bruce. 2005. Pachyderm Pharma. *National Journal*, April 16, 2005.

Strange, Susan. 1996. *The Retreat of the State: The Diffusion of Power in the World Economy*. New York: Cambridge University Press.

Suchman, Mark. 1995. Managing Legitimacy: Strategic and Institutional Approaches. *Academy of Management Review* 20:571–610.

t'Hoen, Ellen. 2009. *The Global Politics of Pharmaceutical Monopoly Power: Drug Patents, Access, Innovation and the Application of the WTO DOHA Declaration on TRIPS and Public Health*. Diemen, the Netherlands: AMB Publishers.

Talitman, Dorit, Alon Tal, and Shmuel Brenner. 2003. The Devil is in the Details: Increasing International Law's Influence on Domestic Environmental Performance – The Case of Israel and the Mediterranean Sea. *New York University Environmental Law Journal* 11:414–78.

Tang, Jun, and Lishan Ai. 2010. Combating Money Laundering in Transition Countries: The Inherent Limitations and Practical Issues. *Journal of Money Laundering Control* 13:215–25.

Terhorst, P. 2003. *Public-Popular Organisations: The Case of Cochabamba, Bolivia*. Master of Science thesis, Loughborough University, September 2003. On file with author.

Teubner, Gunther. 1996. Global Bukowina: Legal Pluralism in the World Society. In *Global Law without a State*, edited by Gunther Teubner. Aldershot: Dartmouth Gower.

———. 1998. Legal Irritants: Good Faith in British Law or How Unifying Law Ends Up in New Divergences. *Modern Law Review* 61:11–32.

Teubner, Gunther, and Zenon Bankowski. 1993. *Law as an Autopoietic System*. Oxford: Blackwell.

Thom, Anso. 2010. Change at the MCC—Too Little, Too Late? Available at: http://www.health–e.org.za/news/article.php?uid=20032808.

Tilak, Jandhyala. 1992. Education and Structural Adjustment. *Prospects* 22(4):407–22.

Tilly, Charles. 1992. *Coercion, Capital and European States: AD 990–1992*, Revised edition. Cambridge, MA: Blackwell.

Tomaševski, Katarina. 2003. *Education Denied: Costs and Remedies*. London: Zed Books.

———. 2005. Not Education for All, Only for Those Who Can Pay: The World Bank's Model for Financing Primary Education. *Law, Social Justice and Global Development* (1):1–19.

———. 2006. *The State of the Right to Education Worldwide: Free or Fee-2006 Global Report*. Copenhagen, Denmark.

Tonry, Michael. 2008. Learning from the Limitations of Deterrence Research. *Crime and Justice* 37:279–311.

Tsutsui, Kiyoteru, and Christine Min Wotipka. 2004. Global Civil Society and the International Human Rights Movement: Citizen Participation in Human Rights International Nongovernmental Organizations. *Social Forces* 83 (2):587–620.

Twining, William. 2005. Social Science and the Diffusion of Law. *Journal of Law and Society* 32(2):203–40.

Twining, William. 2009. *General Jurisprudence: Understanding Law from a Global Perspective*. Cambridge: Cambridge University Press.

Tyler, Tom R. 1990. *Why People Obey the Law*. New Haven, CT: Yale University Press.

UNESCO. 2003. *Bulletin of the UNESCO Education Sector*. No. 5, April-June. Paris.

Union of International Associations. Various years. *Yearbook of International Organizations*. Munich: Saur.

United Nations. 1959. Declaration of the Rights of the Child.

———. 1966. International Covenant on Economic, Social and Cultural Rights.

———. 1988. United Nations Convention against Illicit Traffic in Narcotic Drugs and Psychotropic Substances.

———. 1989. Convention on the Rights of the Child.

———. 1999. International Convention for the Suppression of Financing of Terrorism.

———. 2000a. United Nations Convention against Transnational Organized Crime.

———. 2000b. Optional Protocol to the Convention on the Rights of the Child on the Sale of Children, Child Prostitution and Child Pornography.

———. 2000c. Optional Protocol to the Convention on the Rights of the Child on the Involvement of Children in Armed Conflict.

———. 2002. *Guiding Principles for Partnerships for Sustainable Development ('type 2 outcomes') to be Elaborated by Interested Parties in the Context of the World Summit on Sustainable Development* (*WSSD*), 7 June 2002 (elaborating on GA Res. 56/226 (28 February 2002).

United Nations Commission on International Trade Law (UNCITRAL). 2004. *UNCITRAL Legislative Guide on Insolvency*. New York: United Nations.

United Nations Taskforce on Water and Sanitation. 2005. Final Report January.

US Bankruptcy Commission. 1973. Report of the Commission on the Bankruptcy Laws of the United States. Washington, DC: US Government Printing Office.

Valdes, Juan Gabriel. 1995. *Pinochet's Economists: The Chicago School of Economics in Chile*. Cambridge: Cambridge University Press

Van Duyne, Petrus, Marc Groenhuijsen, and A.A.P. Schudelaro. 2005. Balancing Financial Threats and Legal Interests in Money Laundering Policy. *Crime, Law and Social Change* 43:117–47.

Van Rensburg, H.C.J. 2004. HCI, National Health Systems: Structure, Types and Dynamics. In *Health and Health Care in South Africa*, edited by H.C.J. van Rensburg. Pretoria, South Africa: Van Schaik Publishers.

Van Rensburg, H.C.J., and A.J. Pelser. 2004. The Transformation of the South African Health System. In *Health and Health Care in South Africa*, edited by H.C.J. van Rensburg. Pretoria, South Africa: Van Schaik Publishers.

Vavrus, Frances. 2005. Adjusting Inequality: Education and Structural Adjustment Policies in Tanzania. *Harvard Education Review* 75(2):174–201.

Vogel, David, and Robert A. Kagan. 2004. *Dynamics of Regulatory Change: How Globalization Affects National Regulatory Policies*, edited by David Vogel and Robert A. Kagan. Berkeley: University of California Press.

von Benda-Beckmann, Franz, and Keebet von Benda-Beckmann. 2006. The Dynamics of Change and Continuity in Plural Legal Orders. *Journal of Legal Pluralism and Unofficial Law* 53–54:1–44.

Wai, Robert. 2008. The Interlegality of Transnational Private Law. *Law and Contemporary Problems* 71:107–127.

———. 2005. Transnational Private Law and Private Ordering in a Contested Global Society. *Harvard International Law Journal* 46:471–86.

Walker, Monica. 1983. Some Problems in Interpreting Statistics Relating to Crime. *Journal of the Royal Statistical Society* 146:281–93.

Wallerstein, Emmanuel. 2004. *World Systems Analysis: An Introduction*. Durham, NC: Duke University Press.

Waters, Melissa. 2005. Mediating Norms and Identity: The Role of Transnational Judicial Dialogue in Creating and Enforcing International Law. *Georgetown Law Journal* 93:487–574.

Watson, Alan. 1974. *Legal Transplants: An Approach to Comparative Law*. Charlottesville: University Press of Virginia.

Weber, Max. 1978. *Economy and Society*. Edited by Guenther Roth and Claus Wittich. Berkeley: University of California Press.

Wechsler, William. 2001. Follow the Money. *Foreign Affairs* 80:40–57.

Wessel, Jared. 2007. The Financial Action Task Force: A Study in Balancing Sovereignty with Equality in Global Administrative Law. *Widener Law Review* 13:169–98.

Westbrook, Jay Lawrence. 2000. A Global Solution to Multinational Default. *Michigan Law Review* 98:2276–2328.

Wilke, Marie. 2008. Emerging Informal Network Structures in Global Governance: Inside the Anti-Money Laundering Regime. *Nordic Journal of International Law* 77:509–31.

Whitman, James Q. 2009. Western Legal Imperialism: Thinking about the Deep Historical Roots. *Theoretical Inquiries in Law* 10:305–32.

Woo-Cumings, Meredith. 1999. The State, Democracy, and the Reform of the Corporate Sector in Korea. In *The Politics of the Asian Economic Crisis*, edited by T.J. Pempel. Ithaca, NY: Cornell University Press.

Woo, Jung-En [Meredith Woo-Cumings]. 1991. *Race to the Swift: State and Finance in Korean Industrialization*. New York: Columbia University Press.

World Bank. 1987. *Education Policies for Sub-Saharan Africa: Adjustment, Revitalization, and Expansion*. Washington, DC: World Bank.

———. 1994. *Adjustment in Africa: Reforms, Results and the Road Ahead*. New York: Oxford University Press.

———. 1999. *Principles and Guidelines for Effective Insolvency and Creditor Rights Systems*. Washington, DC: World Bank.

———. 2000. *World Development Report 2000/2001: Attacking Poverty*. World Bank, Oxford University Press.

———. 2001a. *Principles and Guidelines for Effective Insolvency and Creditor Rights Systems*. Washington, DC: World Bank.

———. 2001b. Several Targets in the Current Drafting of Bankruptcy Law. In *Symposium on Reforming the Bankruptcy Law*. Beijing, China.

———. 2002a. Achieving Universal Primary Education in Uganda: The Big Bang Approach. *Human Development Network Education Notes*, April.

———. 2002b. *World Development Report 2002: Building Institutions for Markets*. Oxford: Oxford University Press.

———. 2005. *Principles and Guidelines for Effective Insolvency and Creditor Rights Systems (Revised)*. Washington, DC: World Bank.

———. 2006. *World Development Indicators*. Washington, DC: World Bank.

World Bank/UNCITRAL. 2005. *Creditors Rights and Insolvency Standard*. Washington DC: World Bank.

World Health Organization. 1999. Revised Drug Strategy, World Health Assembly Resolution WHA 52.19, May 24, 1999, available at http://keionline.org/sites/default/files/WHA52.19_e19_revised_drug_strategy.pdf (accessed June 28, 2012).

———. September 22, 2003. World Health Organization Says Failure to Deliver AIDS Medicines Is a Global Health Emergency: Global AIDS Treatment Emergency Requires Urgent Response – No More Business as Usual. News release.

Woodward, David, and Richard D. Smith. 2003. Global Public Goods and Health: Concepts and Issues. In *Global Public Goods For Health: Health Economic and Public Health Perspectives*, edited by Richard Smith, Robert Beaglehole, David Woodward, and Nick Drager. Oxford, UK: Oxford University Press.

Yaron, Gil. 2000. The Final Frontier: A Working Paper on the Big 10 Global Water Corporations and the Privatization and Corporatization of the World's Last Public Resource. Available at http://www.iatp.org/files/Final_Frontier_A_Working_Paper_on_the_Big_10_G.htm (accessed September 4, 2012).

Zack-Williams, Alfred. 2000. Social Consequences of Structural Adjustment. In *Structural Adjustment: Theory, Practice, and Impacts*, edited by Giles Mohan, Ed Brown, Bob Milward, and Alfred Zack-Williams, 59–74. London: Routledge.

Zheng, Henry R. 1986. Bankruptcy Law of the People's Republic of China: Principle, Procedure and Practice. *Vanderbilt Journal of Transnational Law* 19:683–732.

Zheng, Yongnian. 2006. Explaining the Sources of de facto Federalism in Reform China: Intergovernmental Decentralization, Globalization, and Central-Local Relations. *Japanese Journal of Political Science* 7:101–126.

Zumbansen, Peer. 2010. Transnational Legal Pluralism. *Transnational Legal Theory* 1(2):141–89.

Zürn, Michael. 2004. Global Governance and Legitimacy Problems. *Government & Opposition* 39:260–87.

Index

Books in the Series (*continued from p. iii*)

The Colonies of Law: Colonialism, Zionism and Law in Early Mandate Palestine Ronen Shamir

Law and Nature David Delaney

Social Citizenship and Workfare in the United States and Western Europe: The Paradox of Inclusion Joel F. Handler

Law, Anthropology and the Constitution of the Social: Making Persons and Things Edited by Alain Pottage and Martha Mundy

Judicial Review and Bureaucratic Impact: International and Interdisciplinary Perspectives Edited by Marc Hertogh and Simon Halliday

Immigrants at the Margins: Law, Race, and Exclusion in Southern Europe Kitty Calavita

Lawyers and Regulation: The Politics of the Administrative Process Patrick Schmidt

Law and Globalization from Below: Toward a Cosmopolitan Legality Edited by Boaventura de Sousa Santos and Cesar A. Rodriguez-Garavito

Public Accountability: Designs, Dilemmas and Experiences Edited by Michael W. Dowdle

Law, Violence and Sovereignty among West Bank Palestinians Tobias Kelly

Legal Reform and Administrative Detention Powers in China Sarah Biddulph

The Practice of Human Rights: Tracking Law Between the Global and the Local Edited by Mark Goodale and Sally Engle Merry

Judges Beyond Politics in Democracy and Dictatorship: Lessons from Chile Lisa Hilbink

Paths to International Justice: Social and Legal Perspectives Edited by Marie-Bénédicte Dembour and Tobias Kelly

Law and Society in Vietnam: The Transition from Socialism in Comparative Perspective Mark Sidel

Constitutionalizing Economic Globalization: Investment Rules and Democracy's Promise David Schneiderman

The New World Trade Organization Knowledge Agreements. 2nd Edition Christopher Arup

Justice and Reconciliation in Post-Apartheid South Africa Edited by François du Bois and Antje du Bois-Pedain

Militarization and Violence against Women in Conflict Zones in the Middle East: A Palestinian Case-Study Nadera Shalhoub-Kevorkian

Child Pornography and Sexual Grooming: Legal and Societal Responses Suzanne Ost

Darfur and the Crime of Genocide John Hagan and Wenona Rymond-Richmond

Fictions of Justice: The International Criminal Court and the Challenge of Legal Pluralism in Sub-Saharan Africa Kamari Maxine Clarke

Conducting Law and Society Research: Reflections on Methods and Practices Simon Halliday and Patrick Schmidt

Planted Flags: Trees, Land, and Law in Israel/Palestine Irus Braverman

Culture under Cross-Examination: International Justice and the Special Court for Sierra Leone Tim Kelsall

Cultures of Legality: Judicialization and Political Activism in Latin America Javier Couso, Alexandra Huneeus, and Rachel Sieder

Courting Democracy in Bosnia and Herzegovina: The Hague Tribunal's Impact in a Postwar State Lara J. Nettelfield

The Gacaca Courts and Post-Genocide Justice and Reconciliation in Rwanda: Justice without Lawyers Phil Clark

Law, Society, and History: Themes in the Legal Sociology and Legal History of Lawrence M. Friedman Robert W. Gordon and Morton J. Horwitz

After Abu Ghraib: Exploring Human Rights in America and the Middle East Shadi Mokhtari

Adjudication in Religious Family Laws: Cultural Accommodation, Legal Pluralism, and Gender Equality in India Gopika Solanki

Water on Tap: Rights and Regulation in the Transnational Governance of Urban Water Services Bronwen Morgan

Elements of Moral Cognition: Rawls' Linguistic Analogy and the Cognitive Science of Moral and Legal Judgment John Mikhail

A Sociology of Constitutions: Constitutions and State Legitimacy in Historical-Sociological Perspective Chris Thornhill

Mitigation and Aggravation at Sentencing Edited by Julian Roberts

Institutional Inequality and the Mobilization of the Family and Medical Leave Act: Rights on Leave Catherine R. Albiston

Authoritarian Rule of Law: Legislation, Discourse and Legitimacy in Singapore Jothie Rajah

Law and Development and the Global Discourses of Legal Transfers Edited by John Gillespie and Pip Nicholson

Ethnographic Forays into Law's Transformations Edited by Julia Eckert, Zerrin Özlem Biner, Brian Donahoe, and Christian Strümpell

Transnational Legal Ordering and State Change Edited by Gregory Shaffer